PROGRAMMING LANGUAGE STANDARDISATION

THE ELLIS HORWOOD SERIES IN COMPUTERS AND THEIR APPLICATIONS

Series Editor: BRIAN MEEK
Computer Unit, Queen Elizabeth College, University of London

The series aims to provide up-to-date and readable texts on the theory and practice of computing, with particular though not exclusive emphasis on computer applications. Preference is given in planning the series to new or developing areas, or to new approaches in established areas.

The books will usually be at the level of introductory or advanced undergraduate courses. In most cases they will be suitable as course texts, with their use in industrial and commercial fields always kept in mind. Together they will provide a valuable nucleus for a computing science library.

Published and in active publication

THE DARTMOUTH TIME SHARING SYSTEM
G. M. BULL, The Hatfield Polytechnic

THE MICROCHIP AS AN APPROPRIATE TECHNOLOGY
Dr. A. BURNS, The Computing Laboratory, Bradford University

INTERACTIVE COMPUTER GRAPHICS IN SCIENCE TEACHING
Edited by J. McKENZIE, University College, London, L. ELTON, University of Surrey, R. LEWIS, Chelsea College, London.

INTRODUCTORY ALGOL 68 PROGRAMMING
D. F. BRAILSFORD and A. N. WALKER, University of Nottingham.

GUIDE TO GOOD PROGRAMMING PRACTICE
Edited by B. L. MEEK, Queen Elizabeth College, London and P. HEATH, Plymouth Polytechnic.

DYNAMIC REGRESSION: Theory and Algorithms
L. J. SLATER, Department of Applied Engineering, Cambridge University and H. M. PESARAN, Trinity College, Cambridge.

CLUSTER ANALYSIS ALGORITHMS: For Data Reduction and Classification of Objects
H. SPÄTH, Professor of Mathematics, Oldenburg University.

FOUNDATIONS OF PROGRAMMING WITH PASCAL
LAWRIE MOORE, Birkbeck College, London.

RECURSIVE FUNCTIONS IN COMPUTER SCIENCE
R. PETER, formerly Eotvos Lorand University of Budapest.

SOFTWARE ENGINEERING
K. GEWALD, G. HAAKE and W. PFADLER, Siemens AG, Munich

PROGRAMMING LANGUAGE STANDARDISATION
Edited by B. L. MEEK, Queen Elizabeth College, London and I. D. HILL, Clinical Research Centre, Harrow.

FUNDAMENTALS OF COMPUTER LOGIC
D. HUTCHISON, University of Strathclyde.

SYSTEMS ANALYSIS AND DESIGN FOR COMPUTER APPLICATION
D. MILLINGTON, University of Strathclyde.

ADA: A PROGRAMMER'S CONVERSION COURSE
M. J. STRATFORD-COLLINS, U.S.A.

PROGRAMMING LANGUAGE STANDARDISATION

Editors:

I. D. HILL, D.Sc.
Clinical Research Centre
Harrow, London

and

B. L. MEEK, M.Sc.
Director, Computer Unit
Queen Elizabeth College
University of London

ELLIS HORWOOD LIMITED
Publishers · Chichester

Halsted Press: a division of
JOHN WILEY & SONS
New York · Chichester · Brisbane · Toronto

First published in 1980 by

ELLIS HORWOOD LIMITED

Market Cross House, Cooper Street, Chichester, West Sussex, PO19 1EB, England

The publisher's colophon is reproduced from James Gillison's drawing of the ancient Market Cross, Chichester.

Distributors:

Australia, New Zealand, South-east Asia:
Jacaranda-Wiley Ltd., Jacaranda Press,
JOHN WILEY & SONS INC.,
G.P.O. Box 859, Brisbane, Queensland 40001, Australia

Canada:
JOHN WILEY & SONS CANADA LIMITED
22 Worcester Road, Rexdale, Ontario, Canada.

Europe, Africa:
JOHN WILEY & SONS LIMITED
Baffins Lane, Chichester, West Sussex, England.

North and South America and the rest of the world:
Halsted Press: a division of
JOHN WILEY & SONS
605 Third Avenue, New York, N.Y. 10016, U.S.A.

British Library Cataloguing in Publication Data
Programming language standardisation. –
(Ellis Horwood series in computers and their applications).
1. Programming languages (Electronic computers)
I. Hill, Ian David, b. 1926
II. Meek, Brian Lawrence
001.6'424   QA76.7   80–41092
ISBN 0–85312–188–5 (Ellis Horwood Ltd., Publishers)
ISBN 0–470–27077–2 (Halsted Press)

Typeset in Press Roman by Ellis Horwood Ltd.
Printed in Great Britain by R. J. Acford Ltd., Chichester

Table of Contents

Chapter 6 — BASIC by Dr. Gordon M. Bull

Chapter 7 — PASCAL by Anthony M. Addyman

Chapter 12 – METALANGUAGES by Roger S. Scowen

Chapter 13 – FLOWCHARTS AND DECISION TABLES
by Dr. Roger G. Johnson

**Chapter 14 – OTHER POTENTIAL PROGRAMMING LANGUAGE
STANDARDS** by Brian L. Meek

Preface

Let standard authors thus, like trophies borne,
Appear more glorious as more hacked and torn.

Alexander Pope

The principal aim of this book is to dispel some of the confusion and misunderstanding which surrounds the subject of programming language standardisation. Most programmers are aware that language standards exist, at least for Cobol and Fortran, but many are not very clear about what the existence of a standard means for them, or even whether particular features of their own implementation are standard or not; and relatively few could with confidence explain how language standards come about. We felt that there was a need for a book which would explain what the whole business is about — what has been achieved, how it has been achieved, what might be achieved in future, and the purpose of the whole exercise.

The book is in two parts. Part 1 describes the current situation in the programming language standards field — 'current' here meaning 'as at 1st January 1980'. Chapters are provided on each of the main languages in the standards arena at that time, and in some areas closely related to programming languages. The main criterion for inclusion has been whether a topic falls within the remit of the international (ISO) committee responsible for programming languages, and the emphasis throughout is on international standardisation, rather than simply national.

In contrast to Part 1, which is simply descriptive, Part 2 takes the form of a discussion of what programming language standards could be like, or should be like, rather than what they are like. Whereas the aim of Part 1 is to inform, the aim of Part 2 is to stimulate thought and discussion. We hope that one side-effect will be to prompt people to consider what standards might be able to do for them, rather than just take them for granted (or ignore them as irrelevant).

David Hill was principal editor of Part 1 and Brian Meek was principal editor of Part 2. However, each has offered editorial comment to the other and we accept joint editorial responsibility for the whole book. Opinions expressed in the chapters of Part 1 or in the contributions to Part 2 are those of the contributors concerned and should not be attributed to the organisations which employ them, which are named only for purposes of identification of the individuals. They also, as will be readily apparent from Part 2, do not necessarily coincide with the views of the editors — who themselves do not agree on every issue!

Within the book we have met our own standardising difficulties — not the least being the spelling of 'standardise' or 'standardize'. We have used the *s* spelling, but allowed the International Organization for Standardization to keep the *z*s in its own name. For the names of programming languages etc. we have tried to settle on lower case lettering (Fortran, Cobol rather than FORTRAN, COBOL) where pronounced as a word, upper case (APL not Apl) where pronounced as the names of the letters that spell the name, but we are aware that complete consistency has eluded us, and we have retained the usage of the original text where direct quotations are made.

In the context of international standardisation, we have persuaded our various authors to refer to the ISO character set rather than ASCII — the rather-better-known name of its American version. The two are virtually identical.

Parts of Chapter 2 are reprinted by permission from an article entitled 'Fortran 77' in Communications of ACM (1978), **21**, 806–820. These parts are copyright 1978, Association for Computing Machinery, Inc.

We should like to thank all the contributors, both for their work and for their co-operation in editorial amendments, some of which (especially in Part 2) were considerable. Peter Wells of the British Standards Institution read the first draft of Chapter 1 and put us right on several points of procedure. Thanks are also due to the following, who supplied information for Appendix B: Marvin Bass (U.S.A.), Ingemar Dahlstrand (Sweden), François Genuys (France), Paul ten Hagen (Netherlands), Jag Humar (Canada), L. Lauri (ECMA), Arthur Sale (Australia), Gerhard Schmitt (Austria), and E. Tokunaga (Japan). Miss Gim Tan of the Computer Unit, Queen Elizabeth College, dealt with a great deal of correspondence and other necessary secretarial work. The editing was done mainly with the aid of the text processing facilities on the Modular One computer at Queen Elizabeth College and the AES Plus word processor at the Clinical Research Centre, Chapters 2-14 all being typed on the latter machine by Mrs. Margaret Runnicles and Mrs. Maureen Moriarty.

We are grateful to David Beech and Michael Marcotty for allowing us to transfer the Alexander Pope quotation from their PL/I chapter to grace the book as a whole.

I. D. Hill

B. L. Meek

April 1980

Part 1:

The standardisation scene

CHAPTER 1

The standardisation process

1.1 INTRODUCTION

Standardisation, as a general idea, is easy enough to understand. If something is standardised, we know what to expect when we encounter it. If it is a physical object, and we have met objects of the same kind before, we know how to use it and how it will work. If it is a technique or procedure, we know what to do. If it is terminology, we know what it means and can use it with less fear of being misunderstood. We all know the problems that can arise when we come across an object or a procedure or an expression which is non-standard, or (which is sometimes worse) is almost standard but not quite.

Some standardisation — where it takes the form of 'standard practice' — comes about informally. It may be that there is only one known way to do something, which everyone follows; or that there is only one way which is obviously best, or one from a set of alternatives which has become standard through habit or tradition. It may be that a market leader, in the commercial field, adopts some method which other companies feel constrained to follow, or a major purchaser (typically a government department with a large budget) specifies some requirement which anyone who hopes for a contract will have to meet. Such informal standards come about naturally and are also easy to understand. However, in other cases standardisation can be achieved only by conscious effort on the part of those concerned. Over the years the industrial world has developed formal means of official standardisation by which such conscious effort can be channelled and co-ordinated. It is formal standardisation, in this sense, as applied to programming languages, with which this book is concerned.

It is quite clear that, while most people can understand how informal standards come about, very many have only a vague idea of how formal standards are developed and agreed. The bodies involved are many and various, and their procedures are complicated and confusing to the uninitiated. The object here is to explain the bodies and the procedures involved in the particular case of programming languages, and then in the rest of Part 1 to describe the state of standardisation in the area at the time of writing (the beginning of the 1980s). Part 2, which is necessarily more speculative, discusses the prospects for the future, and the directions in which programming language standardisation might be developed.

1.2 THE OFFICIAL STANDARDS BODIES

Description of the standardisation scene, in any context, must begin with the national and international bodies which have official (that is, government-recognised) responsibilities for standards activities. Most of the industrialised nations have their own national standards bodies, usually partly or wholly government-funded. Examples are the American National Standards Institute (ANSI) in the United States, the British Standards Institution (BSI) in the United Kingdom, the Deutches Institut für Normung e.V. (DIN) in the German Federal Republic, the Association Française de Normalisation (AFNOR) in France, and so on. Bodies such as these will be referred to so frequently in the book that their abbreviations will be used throughout. A degree of 'alphabet soup' (indeed, alphanumeric soup) is unavoidable, unfortunately. This is one of the reasons why the standards business can seem so confusing. It is hoped that this book will at least make the alphanumeric soup into clear soup as far as programming languages are concerned, but to help the reader as he works his way through, guides to the main standards bodies concerned with programming languages, and a glossary of abbreviations, are provided as appendices.

In addition to these national bodies there is the International Organization for Standardization (ISO). ISO develops standards at an international level, and helps to co-ordinate standards activities in its various national member bodies where (as in programming languages) such co-ordination is desirable. Countries are represented on ISO through their national standards bodies.

The ISO is governed by a Council which lays down the procedures whereby international (ISO) standards are determined. The rules cover such matters as the format of standards, the publication of draft standards for public comment, minimum times to be allowed for such comment, procedures for dealing with the comments received, voting rules for deciding whether a draft standard is to be adopted, rules governing the revision of standards, and so on. We shall see later what are the main stages that have to be gone through for a programming language to become an ISO standard, and the procedures which have to be followed at each stage. The whole business of 'processing' a potential standard is time-consuming and often seems very unwieldy, but is designed to ensure that, as nearly as possible, by the time the ISO standard appears there can be little doubt that it is widely accepted. The criteria for deciding on a standard are not purely technical; ISO has to take into account other factors, such as economics and the governmental policies of the various nations, as presented to it. Therefore an ISO standard represents what is acceptable generally, on technical and other grounds, rather than necessarily the ultimate in technical excellence.

It should be emphasised that this acceptance refers to opinion among the people particularly concerned with the matter in question, in the relevant countries, rather than among the general population. Thus, for example, the International Standard way of writing the date in numerical form, such as 1980-05-01 (to mean 1st May 1980) is accepted in places where it really matters to have international understanding. More traditional methods would not have been acceptable, since 1/5/1980 means 1st May in some countries, but 5th January in others. It seems likely, however, that the metaphorical 'man in the street' does not even know that the standard way exists, and would not accept it if he did.

The actual technical work of ISO is organised by Technical Committees (TCs) each of which is responsible for a specified area. The relevant Technical Committee for programming languages is TC 97, which is responsible for the whole field of data processing. This is such a wide area that responsibility for particular parts is delegated to Sub-Committees. Sub-Committee SC 5 of TC 97 is wholly concerned with programming languages. Again, there are so many actual or potential standard programming languages that yet another level in the hierarchy – that of the Working Group – becomes necessary if active detailed work on a new or revised standard has to be done. Thus Working Group WG 4 of SC 5 is responsible for Pascal. Since other Sub-Committees may have WG 4s and other Technical Committees may have SC 5s, and since other standards bodies may have TCs and SCs and WGs, what one might term the 'full abbreviation' for the international Pascal working group is ISO/TC 97/SC 5/WG 4. This notation indicates the various levels in the hierarchy and will not trouble those familiar with programming languages like Cobol or PL/I, or Pascal itself, which have facilities for defining data structures and similar means for identifying parts of a structure. It will not surprise those who have been long in the programming field to learn that, although similar hierarchies exist in various other standards bodies, both national and otherwise, there is no uniformity, or even partial standardisation, either of notation or of identifiers for equivalent parts of similar hierarchical structures.

The relevant parts of the ISO structure are described in more detail in Appendix A, which includes a structure diagram. Their equivalents (if they exist) in national standards bodies are given in Appendix B.

1.3 MEMBERSHIP

It should not be thought that all these committees are filled with full-time standards bodies officials. The committees, both at national and at international level, consist of technical experts, people from industry, government agencies, universities, technical institutions, trade associations and so on, nominated by some sponsoring body. These people need to have their participation approved by their employers, to be given the time to attend meetings, and in many cases obtain from them the necessary financial support for their activities. The actual employees of the standards bodies are primarily there to supply secretarial and administrative support. The delegations to a technical ISO meeting from ANSI, BSI and so on thus almost wholly consist of such seconded experts, rather than officials of the standards bodies. It is common in such meetings, or in correspondence (as when postal votes are taken on particular issues, between meetings), to refer to the delegations by country rather than by member body (that is, 'United States' rather than 'ANSI', 'France' rather than 'AFNOR', and so on), retaining the names of the standards bodies themselves to refer to the various secretariats. This custom will be followed in this book. Nevertheless, it must be remembered that the U.K. delegation to an ISO meeting will be selected through the BSI machinery, and will almost always consist of members of the corresponding BSI committee, and the same will be true of other national delegations.

1.4 ISO/TC 97/SC 5: PROGRAMMING LANGUAGES

The nations that belong to ISO do not necessarily take an active part in all of its technical committees or sub-committees. Those who take part in the work of any committee are divided into two groups: full participating members (P-members) and observing members (O-members). Both O-members and P-members receive documents and may comment, take part in discussions, send delegations to meetings, etc., but only P-members may vote — whether on policy, or on specific standards proposals. Only P-members may nominate members for ISO working groups. At the TC 97/SC 5 meeting in Turin in 1979, there was resistance to creating more working groups on the grounds among others, that this rule precluded participation by O-members and was hence too restrictive. In fact there seems nothing in ISO rules to preclude a P-member nominating a person from an O-member country, but clarification was sought on this point.

The current P-members of TC 97/SC 5 (from now on, 'current' will mean 'as at 1st January 1980') are Canada, China, Finland, France, Germany, Hungary, Italy, Japan, Netherlands, Romania, Spain, Sweden, Switzerland, U.K. and U.S.A., and the O-members are Australia, Austria, Belgium, Czechoslovakia, Denmark, India, Israel, Norway, Poland, Portugal, South Africa, U.S.S.R. and Yugoslavia. (There are also some liaison members — L-members — which we shall come to later.) There was a large influx of new members, especially O-members, towards the end of the 1970s reflecting the growing importance of the subject, though few of the new arrivals are yet participating actively in the standardisation work. It will be apparent that the task of providing administrative services to the many ISO committees and WGs is an enormous one, and in fact the problem is solved by assigning the duties of the secretariat of each of these bodies to one of its member standards organisations. In the case of TC 97/SC 5 it is ANSI that provides the secretariat. Within SC 5 itself, responsibility for given languages or areas is similarly delegated. For many (for example, Cobol, Fortran, PL/I) ANSI again provides the secretariat, but, for example, Pascal is assigned to BSI and graphics to the Netherlands standards body, Nederlands Normalisatie-Instituut (NNI). Appendix A shows which organisations currently provide the secretariat of the various topics within the remit of SC 5.

Mention of SC 5's remit brings us to an important point. While SC 5 has responsibility in the area of programming languages, it cannot decide for itself whether to embark on standardisation of a given language. The decision on whether standardisation is needed and that SC 5 should begin work on it rests with its parent committee, TC 97, which must approve the project as a new 'work item' for SC 5. Proposals for new work items can be put forward from within ISO, or by a member body, or by some interested outside organisation. There would be nothing to stop SC 5 itself proposing its own work items, but the practice to date has been for SC 5 to request the sponsoring body for a project to propose it to TC 97. The procedure then is for TC 97 to vote on the proposal by letter ballot of its P-members — a wider group than the P-members of SC 5. This rather roundabout process may seem cumbersome, but it does ensure that any standardisation activity is seen in a wider context; it prevents an enthusiastic group from generating large numbers of standards, some of which may impinge on related areas, and it enables TC 97 to carry out its responsibilities for co-ordinating standards work over the whole data processing area, and for seeing that work is concentrated in areas where standardisation is most needed.

1.5 THE NATIONAL COMMITTEES

Each of the member nations has some equivalent to the ISO hierarchy, though the details vary depending on the size of the country and of its standards body, and the extent of its involvement in the technical area concerned. Clearly, however, if the national body is heavily involved in related ISO activity, there are advantages if its own internal structure matches, or has a simple relationship to, the ISO structure. Thus in the U.K. the equivalent to ISO/TC 97 is BSI: DPS/– (pronounced 'BSI DPS dash'), which has responsibility for the data processing area. It is a large committee and much of its detailed work is delegated to an executive sub-committee, DPS/–/1. Beneath DPS/– there is a structure of sub-committees similar to that beneath ISO/TC 97; among these is one for programming languages, DPS/13, corresponding to ISO/TC 97/SC 5. Like SC 5 and for similar reasons, DPS/13 has working groups, though these may not always match exactly the working groups under the international committee, since the DPS/13 groups depend also on the national standards work which DPS/13 has on hand at any time. The current working groups of DPS/13 are shown in Appendix B. This pattern is repeated in other members of SC 5, though there are variations — for example, ANSI has a committee (X3) corresponding to ISO/TC 97, but it has no sub-committee equivalent to TC 97/SC 5, instead directly appointing sub-committees for individual languages, corresponding to the WG level in ISO. An extremely useful guide to data processing standards bodies generally, principally in the U.S.A. but also in other countries and at international level, has been published by Sperry–Univac [1]. Appendix B describes the current committee and working group structures in the various member states of ISO/TC 97/SC 5 as far as we have been able to ascertain.

1.6 STANDARDISATION PROCEDURES

It can be seen from this description that, with so many official standards bodies, the possibility exists for there being at any given time for any given language, several different national standards ·and, perhaps, an international standard which is different again. This would clearly not be a desirable situation when so many computers, packages and programs cross national frontiers. In practice the situation would of course never be as bad as that, but it does serve to indicate the need for co-ordination. Perhaps of more importance, however, is the possibility that one national body could 'pre-empt' by producing a national standard without agreement. In such a case either incompatible standards would co-exist or the other nations would be forced to accept a standard they did not like (or do without a standard), at least until the standard was next revised. It would be idle to deny that a main concern on this point as far as programming languages are concerned has been the position of ANSI. For obvious reasons American standards have long led the field in computing. It is natural that people in other countries should, now that computing is becoming so important everywhere, be concerned at the prospect of American dominance being perpetuated or becoming so great that the legitimate requirements of users in other countries would be squeezed out. It must be stressed that this concern is not aimed at the people who have been involved in ANSI programming languages standards. To take just two examples, the ANSI/X3J2 committee has worked closely with others concerned with standardising Basic, and the X3J3 committee was very concerned to obtain views from the international Fortran community on its drafts of the revised standard of 1978 (Fortran 77). Nevertheless, however satisfactory the position may have been, in the long term only conscious, generally agreed policy will ensure that no standards body, whether ANSI or anyone else, will suddenly produce a new standard without consulting others who may have an interest.

The importance of co-ordinating standards in programming languages arises from the frequent need to transfer programs from one computer installation to another across international frontiers. This, and the need for a conscious policy, led to a proposal for co-ordinating the development of programming language standards being discussed at the November 1977 meeting of ISO/TC 97/SC 5 in The Hague. The remarks above about the pace-setting of ANSI should not be taken to mean that the other countries were in any sense 'ganging up' against the Americans — far from it. In fact the U.S. delegation was strongly behind the proposal. It was originally put forward by the Cobol working group, on which ANSI/X3J4, the responsible ANSI committee, is heavily represented. In its original form the proposal referred to Cobol alone, but it was quickly extended to cover all standards within the remit of SC 5. At *ad hoc* Fortran group sessions during the SC 5 meeting, it was agreed that, whatever the fate of the co-ordination proposal for languages in general, it should be adopted for Fortran, and again the U.S. representatives, members of ANSI/X3J3, took a leading part. The move was a result of a generally felt need on which all parties were agreed, not a manoeuvre to restrict the activities of any particular body.

In fact the proposal was agreed, perhaps the most important policy decision which has been taken to date by SC 5. There was much discussion on points of detail, wording and interpretation, but no disagreement on the basic principle. The co-ordination mechanism is based on the fact that the standards procedures of the various bodies, though they vary from one to another, all make provision for a period of public comment. In the case of an ISO standard, agreement is required from the members of the ISO body responsible for the standard, in this case the members of SC 5. The essence of the co-ordination policy is that an SC 5 comment period, and the national comment period of the body responsible for the development of the standard, should as nearly as possible be made to coincide. If these periods coincide, then inevitably the drafting periods leading up to the publication of the drafts for comment also coincide, or at least overlap. Furthermore, after the standard is finally agreed at both national and international levels, the time lag between the publication of the national standard and the corresponding international standard will be minimised. ISO standards invariably, and probably inevitably, take longer to be produced than national standards, but at least with this mechanism the maximum overlap is achieved between national and international procedures.

It can be appreciated that the mechanism also depends on the idea of having a single responsible body for a given programming language, to provide the secretariat for an ISO working group (if any) and probably its convenor also. At first this was little more than recognition that ANSI were going to produce standards for Cobol, Fortran etc. anyway and they might as well be left to get on with it, but it is now a key feature of the programming language standards scene.

1.7 THE PROCEDURE FOR PRODUCING A STANDARD

The procedure whereby a language becomes standardised, assuming that ISO/TC 97 have approved it as a work item for SC 5, is therefore this:

(i) The 'responsible member' announces its intention to develop the standard. The SC 5 co-ordination policy requires at least 12 months notice of this. The wording is slightly ambiguous in that it could be held to mean that no work on standardisation could begin for 12 months; on the other hand 12 months is a very short time in which to produce a publishable final standard of virtually anything, let alone something as complex as a programming language, so in practice this should not cause problems;

(ii) The responsible body will use its own procedures towards the development of a national standard but should keep the other members of SC 5 informed of progress towards a draft, including sending relevant working documents, etc.

(iii) If an international meeting of experts is deemed necessary, one should be called within the 12 month period, either as a full ISO working group, or *ad hoc*. How and by whom it should be decided that a meeting is necessary is not specified, but probably, as with 'keeping other members of SC 5 informed' above, what really matters is that interested members of the international programming fraternity have something to quote if they feel that the spirit of the SC 5 policy is being ignored;

(iv) The responsible body will produce its draft for public comment in its own way, but also circulate it for international comment. By ISO procedures the SC 5 members may vote to approve or disapprove the draft. Comments may be added if wished, and the reasons for disapproval must be given. During the comment period the other SC 5 members can inform their own public, by whatever means they feel appropriate, that the draft exists, and suggest means whereby individuals can obtain copies of the draft and submit comments;

(v) The responsible body will review the public comments and the votes and comments of SC 5 members. As a result they will either recommend that the draft, perhaps with minor amendments, go forward for 'processing' as a final standard, or (more likely in the first instance) revise the draft in the light of comments received, and reissue it for further comment and another round of SC 5 voting.

Rules and procedures for acceptance of a national standard will vary from country to country, and these will not be discussed here. However, those for acceptance of an ISO standard are of interest to all and are worth summarising. General ISO rules state that a proposed standard must be approved by a 'substantial majority' of the responsible technical committee (TC 97 in this case) before it can proceed to the Draft International Standard stage, and the DIS must be approved by 75 per cent of the ISO members who vote before it becomes a full international standard. In practice, in fact, considerable efforts are made to achieve unanimity and a standard will not necessarily be accepted even if there is only one 'No' vote, assuming that it is backed up by explanatory comment. For example, in the first two votes on the draft ISO standard for Minimal Basic (see Chapter 6) the U.K. alone voted against, yet in both cases, even in the second when there was relatively little comment from other members participating in the vote, the responsible committee of experts, effectively a joint committee of ECMA/TC 21 and ANSI/X3J2, was still asked to consider and reply to the U.K. comment.

1.8 THE PROCEDURE FOR REVISING A STANDARD

Both ISO and national procedures include rules governing the revision of a standard. ISO, and other bodies including ANSI and BSI, have a rule requiring that a standard be revised, renewed without change, or withdrawn, after an interval of five years. There is some feeling in the computing community that such a period is inappropriate for programming languages, because of the time lag between publication of a standard and the publication of a working compiler which conforms to it. The problems have been felt most acutely so far in the cases of Cobol and Fortran; these will be discussed later in the book. At the November 1979 meeting of ISO/TC 97/SC 5 this issue was discussed; we shall return to it in Part 2. Whatever the timescale for a revision, the SC 5 procedures follow exactly the same lines as for a new standard. The responsible body announces its intention of revising the standard for the language, but thereafter the same procedures as for a new standard are followed. As can be seen, these procedures are relatively new and have not yet been tested through a complete cycle, though to some extent they represent a codification of what had been happening informally earlier. The chapters which follow summarise what has happened in the past for particular languages, and Chapter 7 on Pascal, the first language to be standardised entirely under new procedures, includes a detailed description of how they have operated at a practical level in that case.

1.9 OTHER BODIES INVOLVED IN STANDARDISATION

Reference to Chapter 7 will show that other bodies besides ISO and its national counterparts have been involved in the standardisation of Pascal, and it was mentioned earlier that such bodies do exist. Of course, many organisations (computer manufacturers, industrial companies, government departments) do produce standards of their own, for their own purposes, one example being the 'Official Definition' of Coral 66 produced by the U.K. Ministry of Defence (see Chapter 8). However, of more interest here are the various bodies involved in collaborative standards, covering more than one organisation. These can be divided into four groups – trade associations, user groups, professional bodies, and organisations especially founded for the purposes of undertaking collaborative work.

Trade associations (whose members are firms making products of a particular kind) may be national – like the Business Equipment Trade Association (BETA) in the U.K., or international, like the European Computer Manufacturers Association (ECMA). Such bodies have an obvious interest in standards, and commonly have committees concerned with standards. In some cases they are content with participating in the work of official standards bodies – for example, BETA nominates members to BSI: DPS/13. In others, they produce standards of their own – for example, ECMA has produced standards in various areas of computing, including, in the field we are discussing, one for Minimal Basic (see Chapter 6).

User groups come in a variety of forms. Some are branches or 'special interest groups' of professional societies, and will be dealt with below. Some are groups of users of particular machine ranges. These have a particular interest in programming languages and in standards, and can bring pressure to bear on manufacturers to provide standard-conforming compilers, or to produce new languages (note, for example, the role of IBM user groups in stimulating the development of PL/I). They can also act as distributors of compilers produced by their own members rather than the manufacturer, and thus help standard-conforming compilers to spread. However, the effective 'standard' for any language within such a group is inevitably not the official standard but the implementation provided by the manufacturer, so there may be little incentive for such a group to produce its own; at most, they may produce a list of requirements for the manufacturer to include in the next version of the compiler. They may demand implementations which conform to national or international standards, to facilitate transfers of programs to and from other machine ranges; on the other hand, they may exert influence in the reverse direction, by demanding non-standard features (for example, to exploit some feature of that particular machine) or by exchanging notes on non-standard 'tricks' which can be exploited with a particular implementation.

A third kind of user group, less common but important where it does exist, is that formed by enthusiasts for a particular language, independently from outside influences such as machine ranges or professional societies. Since its members will have access to different implementations, and will want to exchange programs, interest in standardisation is inevitable. The most notable instance of such a group is the Pascal Users Group (PUG), though others exist or have existed for languages like APL and Algol 60. Groups of this kind may also be content to act as channels for communicating information on standards activity by the official bodies to interested persons among its membership or to exert pressure. They may, however, become more closely involved in standards work in their own right, either voluntarily or by being approached by others to provide expertise. The role of PUG in developing a Pascal standard is described in Chapter 7, and APL groups are being drawn into new standards activity for that language (see Chapter 14).

Professional bodies also have an interest in standardisation. At the international level there is the International Federation for Information Processing (IFIP) which, through its WG 2.1, has particular interest in the Algol languages and holds the copyright on their defining reports. Algol 60 is discussed in Chapter 4 and Algol 68 in Chapter 14.

Many national professional bodies also exist which have an interest in programming languages and standards, for example the British Computer Society

(BCS) in the U.K. and the Association for Computing Machinery (ACM) in the U.S.A. The BCS has a Standards Committee, and it nominates members to various BSI committees, including DPS/13. It also has 'specialist groups' on various aspects of computing, including (among programming languages) Fortran and PL/I. Such groups are an obvious source of expertise both for taking part in standards work and in commenting on draft standards during public comment periods. For example, during the development of the revised Fortran standard (Fortran 77) BSI: DPS/13 did not feel it necessary to set up its own working group corresponding to ANSI/X3J3, since the BCS Fortran Specialist Group could equally well represent and express the interests of Fortran users in the U.K. When it did later set up an *ad hoc* Fortran working group to consider preparations for the next revision, almost all of that group were also members of the BCS group.

While such bodies mostly involve themselves in standards work through participation in the work of the official standards bodies, this does not mean that they never undertake standardisation work themselves. Mention has already been made of IFIP's concern with Algol 60 and Algol 68, and though this work was mainly to develop and define the languages, the standards aspect was an incidental if inevitable consequence. The Institution of Electrical and Electronic Engineers (IEEE) in the U.S.A. did, however, deliberately embark upon standards activity in the case of Pascal in 1978, and there is no reason why professional bodies such as this should not feel the need to take such action with respect to other languages in the future, especially if the official bodies seem disinclined to do so in a particular case. The involvement of IEEE in Pascal standardisation is described in Chapter 7.

The last kind of body mentioned was an inter-organisational body set up specifically to undertake collaborative work of relevance to programming languages. The principal instance to date is Codasyl, the Committee on Data System Languages, in the U.S.A. Codasyl has had considerable influence on standards for Cobol (see Chapter 3) and Database Management Systems (DBMS) (see Chapter 9) and may in the future similarly influence standards in other languages (such as Fortran, see Chapter 2) which have database facilities added to them or are designed with them.

As we have seen, most of the standards activity of these bodies is channelled in some way or another through the official standards bodies, or some formal or informal liaison mechanism is set up, as happened in the case of Pascal. However, it is worth noting that an explicit mechanism is provided at international level for liaison between ISO and other international bodies. The constitution of ISO allows for liaison both with other ISO committees and with two categories of external bodies – category A, who are effectively full liaison members (L-members) receiving all papers, etc., and category B, with whom liaison is maintained on matters of particular interest. These external bodies are not nations, but international organisations. The current full L-members of

ISO/TC97/SC5 are IFIP, ECMA, LTPL-C (Long Term Procedural Language Committee), ITU (International Telecommunications Union), CIRP (International Institution for Production Engineering Research), and the Commission of the European Communities, though only the first three have been active to date in programming language standards.

This, then, is the foundation upon which the standardisation of programming languages rests. If it still seems complicated, this is only because it is indeed complicated. If it still seems confusing, it is hoped that the confusion will diminish as discussion of particular languages, in the chapters that follow, places it in context.

1.10 REFERENCE

[1] Prigge, R. D., Hill, M. F., and Walkowicz, J. L. (1978), The world of EDP standards, GS-4248, 3rd edition, Sperry Univac Corporation.

CHAPTER 2

Fortran

by Walter S. Brainerd

As mentioned in the last Chapter, the remainder of Part 1 describes the current position in the various languages and related subjects within the remit, or potentially within the remit, of ISO/TC97/SC5. We begin with Fortran, since this is the oldest high-level language still in widespread use, and the first to be formally standardised. The author of this Chapter is Walter S. Brainerd, formerly of Burroughs Corporation and now at the Los Alamos Scientific Laboratory of the University of California. He is an officer of the ANSI committee responsible for Fortran, X3J3.

2.1 INTRODUCTION

Fortran was the first programming language to be standardised in the U.S. The standardisation effort dates back to the early 1960s. At this time Fortran and Algol were vying to become the accepted languages for scientific and engineering applications. In the U.S., Fortran became the more dominant of these two languages, due to the emphasis placed on it by IBM and its competitors.

The basic strategy of IBM's competitors was to provide a compiler with the functionality of the IBM 704/709 Fortran, but with some features added as a competitive inducement. While these new features contributed to the development of the language, they also had the effect of creating a myriad of incompatible dialects.

At that time ASA (subsequently to become ANSI, the American National Standards Institute) and BEMA (subsequently to become CBEMA, the Computer and Business Equipment Manufacturing Association) undertook a massive standardisation effort in a variety of data processing areas. Someone had the daring idea of including programming languages, and Fortran, Algol, and Cobol were selected as candidates.

2.2 FORMATION OF STANDARDS COMMITTEE

The ASA/X3.4.3 sub-committee (to become the ANSI/X3J3 Technical Committee) was formed in May 1962 and its first meeting was held on 13-14

August that year in New York City. At that meeting it was decided that Fortran standardisation was needed and that a sufficiently wide representation of interests was participating. The group also adopted the following criteria for evaluation of proposed language features (the importance of each criterion is not indicated by its position in the list):

(i)   ease of use by humans;
(ii) compatibility with past Fortran use;
(iii) scope of application;
(iv) potential for extension;
(v)   facility of implementation, that is, compilation and execution efficiency.

Critics of the Fortran language would probably argue that items (ii) and (v) were weighted too heavily in the development and standardisation process. Yet, in the days of expensive hardware and primitive compiling techniques, it is those features that permitted Fortran to be accepted by IBM and other implementors and become established as the predominant language for scientific computing in the U.S. As will be seen in the discussion of current Fortran standardisation activities, other criteria, such as ease of use by humans, have become more important.

2.3 PUBLICATION OF STANDARD

In October 1964, the proposed draft standards were published [1]. There was a full language, which became the standard X3.9-1966 Fortran, and a subset, which became X3.10-1966 Basic Fortran. As the first standards ever proposed for programming languages, they severely taxed the editing and approval mechanisms of ASA and BEMA. Until then, draft standards rarely contained more than one page of text, usually including diagrams, such as one for a screw thread. By contrast the Fortran standard contained 26 pages, not counting appendices, including many tables, lists, and examples. Furthermore, the inability to check a processor for conformance to the standard was a shattering blow to the approval process. It is not surprising that almost a year and a half elapsed before final approval was obtained in March 1966.

2.4 AN INTERNATIONAL STANDARD

Early in the standardisation effort, the European Computer Manufacturers Association (ECMA) submitted a proposed draft of what they felt the full language should contain. Partly because they were separated from the developments in the U.S., their proposal fell between Basic Fortran and the full language. When Fortran standardisation was undertaken by the International Standardization Organization (ISO), the ASA form and content were chosen as the basis, but the ECMA subset was added as an intermediate level. The three levels were published by ISO as 'ISO Recommendation R 1539, Programming Language Fortran'.

2.5 CLARIFICATION OF THE STANDARD

After producing the 1966 standard, the committee X3.4.3 was disbanded. However, it was revived in 1967 to provide authoritative answers to the many requests for clarification that had been made. The clarification process turned out to be more tedious and demanding than the original standardisation effort. A single comma could not be altered without repeating the same approval cycle gone through by the standard itself. Interpretations had to be based on the actual wording that appeared in the standard, regardless of the intent of its authors. More than three years of meetings were required to produce two interpretational reports published in 1969 [2] and 1971 [3].

2.6 THE BEGINNING OF FORTRAN 77

Even before 1966, many extensions beyond the 1966 standard had already appeared in Fortran implementations. After investigating how these extensions could be standardised, the committee voted in 1968 not to reaffirm X3.9-1966, but to replace it with a revised standard. They also decided that the new standard should be an evolutionary development that would not invalidate programs written in the language of the original standard.

It was in 1970 that it was decided that further clarification work should be abandoned in order to devote all the resources of the committee to the development of the revised standard. At that time it was projected that a draft would be available by the end of 1971. However, the draft proposed standard was not published until the spring of 1976 [4].

2.7 PUBLIC COMMENTS

The main reason for publishing the draft proposed standard was to elicit comments from persons interested in the development and use of Fortran. The response was remarkable. The comments submitted came in 289 letters totalling 1225 pages from individuals and organisations all over the world. Most letters contained several comments and proposals for change. The committee responded to each comment in each letter and made a number of changes based on these comments.

2.8 CRITERIA FOR FORTRAN 77

The main criteria used to develop Fortran 77 were the following:

    (i) inclusion of new features whose utility has been proven by actual usage;
    (ii) inclusion of new features that make programs easier to transport from one processor to another;

(iii) minimal increase in the complexity of the language or of processors of the language;

(iv) avoidance of features that conflict with X3.9-1966;

(v) elimination of features in the 1966 standard only for a clearly demonstrated reason;

(vi) production of a more precise description of the language.

Note that these criteria are quite similar to those used in the development of the 1966 standard. Near the end of the development process, X3J3 did eliminate a major feature in the 1966 standard, Hollerith data. Most members of the committee felt that there was 'a clearly demonstrated reason', namely, that a much better replacement feature, the character data type, had been added. This action was a significant one for X3J3 in that it signalled the beginning of a shift of attitude toward the idea that there *are* good reasons for dropping features contained in previous versions of the standard. As will be seen in a later section, this attitude has become more prevalent during the initial phases of the development of the next version of the Fortran standard.

2.9 NEW LANGUAGE FEATURES

In general, the technical features added in Fortran 77 were those that had already been incorporated into most Fortran compilers. Examples are mixed mode arithmetic, in some places allowing arbitrary expressions where previously only constants or variables were permitted, direct-access input and output, alternate returns, and multiple entries into subprograms. Mixed mode arithmetic supplies a good example of the perils of lack of standardisation. Nearly every manufacturer allowed it, but the rules varied from one to another, so that the same expression could give totally different results. Fortran 77 now says precisely what it does mean, but at the cost of invalidating some existing compilers.

Other features in Fortran 77 were included by X3J3 because the committee perceived a real need for them in spite of the fact that they were not included in a majority of existing Fortran compilers. The most important example of this kind is the character data type. Replacing Hollerith data with character data removes what is probably the single greatest impediment to portability in the 1966 Fortran standard. Since the character data type was not in widespread use, the standards committee was required to do a certain amount of language design in this area. The IF–THEN–ELSE construction was another feature that was obviously needed, but one that had not been included in many Fortran compilers. Fortunately, an IF–THEN–ELSE construction had been included in a large number of preprocessors, and these served as an excellent model for standardisation.

In the case of the DO statement, the committee actually went counter to a large body of existing implementations by specifying that a DO loop could be executed zero times. In this case, X3J3 felt that the superiority of language design outweighed the argument in favour of incorporating a feature, even if it were implemented already in a number of compilers. It should be noted, in spite of what some people seem to believe, that the new version is not contrary to the 1966 standard.

A more detailed discussion of both the history and the technical content of Fortran 77 may be found in reference [5].

The American Fortran 77 standard [10] has been adopted verbatim as the ISO Fortran standard.

2.10 STANDARDISATION ISSUES

Several issues that are of central importance to all programming language standardisation efforts are discussed in Part 2 of this book. It is interesting to see how the Fortran standardisation committee in the U.S., X3J3, handled some of these problems in the development of the 1966 and 1978 Fortran standards.

2.11 LANGUAGE DEVELOPMENT UNDER A PERMISSIVE STANDARD

One of the most important issues is the potential conflict between standardisation and language development. Strict adherence to a standard could mean that experimentation and innovation would be suppressed entirely. The Fortran solution to this difficulty is that the standard is *permissive*. It describes what a standard-conforming program is and how it must be interpreted by a standard-conforming processor. As long as a processor interprets standard-conforming programs correctly, it is still considered standard-conforming even if it accepts additional language constructions. Thus, an implementor of a Fortran system may include any features thought to be advantageous to the Fortran programmer (and hence, to the implementor), and still produce a standard-conforming Fortran processor. These features then become candidates for future standardisation and their acceptance or rejection can be based in part upon the results of their actual use.

Another way to look at this same approach is to state that the standard describes what the programmer can do to create a standard-conforming program, not what the implementor must do to create a standard-conforming processor. Consider an example. Suppose the programmer wants to put the statements:

```
REAL A(100)
A = 0
```

in a Fortran program. Examination of the standard will reveal that putting an array name on the left-hand side of an assignment is not permitted. (It is of interest to note that a *prohibition* in the standard and an *omission* from the standard have exactly the same effect.) Thus, if the programmer puts the above statements in a program, it will not conform to the Fortran standard. However, it is possible that an implementation may allow that particular combination of statements. If this implementation processes all standard-conforming programs correctly and also allows the above statements, it is still standard-conforming. One might hope that, if a processor allows the statement:

A = 0

where A is an array, it would execute the statement by setting all elements of A to zero, but as far as the standard is concerned, the processor could give a diagnostic, execute the statement by setting A(1) to zero (as some implementations have done), or even print a line of asterisks!

The implementors, and users, of such extensions have to take the risk that the extensions will not conform to a future standard.

2.12 LANGUAGE DESCRIPTION

Standard Fortran is described using natural language (English). This description uses many words that are given a special technical meaning in the document. For example, in the assignment statement:

X = B(I,J)

the *subscript* for the array B is '(I,J)', whereas in more common usage, I and J are subscripts.

Many syntactic constructions are described using an informal notation incorporating some of the characteristics of BNF and regular expressions. Accompanying the standard is an appendix that describes most of the syntax using 'railroad' charts[†]. These charts are thought by some people to be much easier to read than BNF or regular expressions, but also have the weakness that certain context-sensitive properties of the language cannot be described.

The X3J3 committee did not use a more formal description of the language semantics because it felt that the standard should be accessible to programmers as well as to those who must understand it well enough to implement the language.

The informal description of the language had another important effect. It permitted a large number of interested persons to comment on the draft proposed standard and thereby contribute significantly to the final description of the language. As was stated earlier, 289 individuals and organisations submitted comments on the draft proposed standard. Many of the comments caused changes to be made. This would not have been possible if the language had been described using a completely formal mechanism.

2.13 THE FORTRAN ENVIRONMENT

The current Fortran standard does not address issues that are not considered to be part of the language itself. For example, there are no processor directives,

† See, for example, Fig. 12.11, page 144.

such as those relating to optimisation and source listings. The standard is written in a manner that allows the maximum freedom to the implementor. An example of this principle is that, subject to the over-riding precedence of parentheses, expressions may be evaluated in any manner as long as the result is mathematically equivalent (but not necessarily computationally equivalent) to the expression written. Another example is the prohibition of the program:

```
CALL S(X,X)
PRINT *, X
END
SUBROUTINE S(A,B)
A = 1
B = 2
END
```

because different implementations might produce different results. For example, in a 'copy in, copy out' implementation of the argument passing, the first dummy argument A might get copied to actual argument X after the dummy argument B is copied to the actual argument X, with the result that X = 1. Prohibition of any program like this in the standard allows passing of arguments by reference or by a 'copy in, copy out' mechanism.

The standard has been written so that minimal demands are placed on the environment in which the programs are executed. In particular, there are no requirements for dynamic storage allocation. Indeed, a Fortran processor could be implemented in an environment with no operating system, even though many systems choose not to implement input and output within the Fortran language system.

2.14 THE NEXT STANDARD

As soon as the ANSI committee X3J3 finished work on the Fortran 77 standard, it began considering if and how a next revision should be made. With a remarkable change of working methods, the committee spent most of the year establishing goals and criteria for revising the standard and discussing major problem areas that needed to be attacked.

The committee then spent more time seeking general solutions to these major problems. In place of proposals, tutorials and position papers were presented. Questionnaires on several major topics were submitted to interested groups of Fortran users. It has been only after the major problems have been studied thoroughly in this manner that specific proposals have been made. These proposals have attempted to cover an entire major problem area. For example, rather than consider a proposal to add a DO WHILE statement, the entire area of control structures has been studied in order that any proposals made will fit into one overall plan for control structures in Fortran.

Based on the committee's recent actions, there has been a significant shift in attitudes concerning the objectives of Fortran standardisation. One reason for this has been the realisation that the language is becoming too large by adding new features and almost never removing any old ones. The committee is also faced with the difficult problem of interfacing with collateral standards. A standard data base management system for Fortran has been proposed [6]. The Instrument Society of America has produced standards for Fortran programs used for process control [7, 8, 9].

2.15 THE CORE AND MODULES ARCHITECTURE

X3J3 has responded to these challenges by proposing a language architecture consisting of a 'core' language plus 'modules'. The core is to be a complete general purpose programming language, but will not contain features that are redundant or obsolete just because they are in Fortran 77.

There are two types of module, 'language' modules and 'applications' modules. Process control, data base management, and graphics are examples of possible applications modules. It is likely that X3J3 will not specify these modules directly, but will establish rules about how these modules interface with the core language.

On the other hand, the language modules will be designed by X3J3. One of these modules will contain all of the features in Fortran 77 that are not in the core. This is important in order to support the huge investment in Fortran programs written using these features. Other candidates for language modules are those features that may be somewhat special purpose, but are used enough to justify establishing a standard way of implementing them. Some possibilities are comprehensive array processing or data structure features.

This next version of the Fortran standard is due to be completed in the middle of the 1980s. It will be interesting to see whether these new approaches to standardisation being tried by X3J3 will be successful.

2.16 REFERENCES

[1]   ASA (1964), A programming language for information processing on automatic data processing systems, *Commun. ACM.*, **7**, 591-625.

[2]   USASI (1969), Clarification of Fortran standards − initial progress, *Commun. ACM.*, **12**, 289-294.

[3]   ANSI (1971), Clarification of Fortran standards − second report, *Commun. ACM.*, **14**, 628-642.

[4]   ANSI (1976), Draft Proposed ANS Fortran, *SIGPLAN Not.*, 11, No. 3.

[5]   Brainerd, W. ed., (1978), Fortran 77, *Commun. ACM.*, **21**, 806-820.

[6]   Codasyl Fortran data base facility, Journal of Development, Department of Supply and Services, Canada.

[7] ANSI ISA 61.1, Industrial computer system Fortran procedures for executive functions, process input/output and bit manipulation.

[8] ANSI ISA 61.2, Industrial computer system Fortran procedures for file access and the control of file contention.

[9] ANSI ISA 61.3, Industrial computer system Fortran procedures for the management of independent interrelated tasks.

[10] ANSI (1978), ANSI X3.9-1978: Programming Language Fortran.

CHAPTER 3

Cobol
by John M. Triance

*If Fortran is the most widely used language for scientific and engineering appli-
cations, Cobol is certainly by far the most widely used commercial language.
For that reason it is not surprising that standardisation of Cobol quickly followed
that of Fortran, in 1968. It was also the first language to pass through a complete
revision cycle, the revised standard appearing in 1974. As will be seen, this has
brought problems as well as benefits. The author is John M. Triance, of the
Department of Computation at the University of Manchester Institute of Science
and Technology.*

3.1 BACKGROUND
Cobol is generally regarded as the most widely used programming language.
Surveys of the European Economic Community [1] and the U.S.A. [2] reveal
that more than half the programs written in these regions are in Cobol. It also
holds the record, or comes a close second, in the following areas:

(i) the most implementations;
(ii) the largest language;
(iii) the greatest effort expended on standardisation;
(iv) the most successful standardisation.

Cobol differs from other languages in that the functions of development
and standardisation are separated. Codasyl has always been responsible for
development and ANSI for standardisation.

3.1.1 Codasyl
Codasyl, the COmmittee on DAta SYstems Languages, resulted from a meeting
in the Pentagon in May 1959 between American private and government users
and computer manufacturers. They decided to design 'a COmmon Business
Oriented Language independent of any make or model of computer, open

ended and stated in English notation and a narrative form'. The first version of Cobol appeared seven months later.

Since then Codasyl has continued to develop Cobol. Currently the Codasyl Cobol Committee meets eight times a year for three or four days at a time. Its membership varies in size, with representatives from approximately ten computer manufacturers including all the major ones, and approximately ten (government and private) users. All members are from the U.S.A. except ICL and the Canadian Federal Government. As a result of all this effort Cobol has been kept up to date — it was, for example, the first major language to include database handling facilities. Also it continues to grow in size — the Codasyl Cobol specifications (known as the Cobol Journal of Development [3]) now occupy over 600 pages.

3.1.2 ANSI

Implementing a fast evolving language was soon recognised to be a problem. It would of necessity prevent Cobol from being common to all machines since each implementation would depend on the date the compiler was written. This problem was ameliorated by ANSI's publication in 1968 of the first Cobol standard [4]. This was based on Codasyl Cobol as it stood on 1st January 1967.

Virtually all compilers for the next six years were based on this standard. This level of conformance is due largely to the U.S. Government's procurement policy, which insists that any data-processing machine supplied to them should have a standard Cobol compiler. This means that all the American manufacturers are obliged to supply a standard Cobol compiler or forego all sales to the world's largest user. Since this results in all the world's dominant manufacturers supporting standard Cobol there has been strong pressure on other manufacturers to produce compatible compilers to ease the transition of programs from their competitors' machines. The next standard [5] in 1974 was adhered to even more strictly and the situation has now been reached where all new Cobol compilers of any significance are based on the current standard. To this extent Cobol standardisation has been very successful.

The inevitability of each ANSI standard becoming the *de facto* world standard has now been recognised by ISO. In fact the current ISO standard [6] consists of a single page which cross-refers to the ANSI document. In return for this recognition ANSI have agreed to consult international opinion during the production of the next standard. This is done by holding international Cobol experts' meetings at which representatives of ANSI discuss the contents of the next standard with representatives from other interested countries. At the time of writing Canada, France, Germany, Japan, Netherlands, U.K. and U.S.A. have participated in these meetings. Such democracy inevitably delays the production of a new standard.

Even without it the 1974 standard appeared nine months after the expiry of the 1968 standard (ANSI standards are valid only for five years). This delay is insignificant however compared with the seven year delay in the production of the successor to ANSI 66 Fortran. A major reason for Cobol's relatively good record is the restricted input permitted to each standard. For each standard the features can be drawn only from the previous standard and the current Codasyl specifications. Thus ANS 74 Cobol is made up entirely of features from ANS 68 Cobol and Codasyl Cobol as defined on 31st December 1971.

The effect of this can be seen in the following example. With the advent of structured programming the need was recognised for an explicit scope terminator for nested IF statements. Some of the suggestions were:

    (i) END-IF
    (ii) FI
    (iii) statement blocking with BEGIN ... END as in Algol 60
    (iv) statement blocking with brackets (....) or [....] or {....}

These alternatives were debated for many hours and the first was eventually accepted into Codasyl Cobol. This left ANSI with the far simpler task of deciding whether or not it wanted an explicit scope terminator for IF. It quickly decided to have one so END-IF was automatically included. So ANSI avoids many lengthy arguments which could delay the publication of a Cobol standard. These arguments can, however, result in the total omission of a feature from the standard if it was not incorporated in Codasyl Cobol in time.

3.1.3 Compiler validation

The U.S. Federal Compiler Testing Center has produced a set of programs which check compilers for conformance with the ANSI standard. This is done by submitting the programs, known as the Cobol Compiler Validation System, to the compiler being tested. The object programs are then executed and the output is analysed. The results of these analyses are published as 'Validation Summary Reports'. A list of all the Validation Summary Reports is also published by the Testing Center [7]. At the time of writing 52 compilers have been tested, half of them for ANS 68 and half for ANS 74 Cobol.

When a compiler is first tested it is issued with a certificate which is valid for 12 months. This certificate indicates whether or not the compiler deviated from the standard. If it did deviate the compiler is retested in 12 months' time and another certificate is issued only if the previously identified deviations have been corrected. An error-free compiler is issued automatically with another 12 month certificate on the expiry of the previous one unless the compiler or the Compiler Validation System have been modified in the meantime. In either of these cases the compiler will be re-validated. These certificates are the mechanism for ensuring that compilers used by the U.S. Government conform to standard. They will only buy compilers which have been certified.

Since the validation system checks most of the standard (report writer and communications modules are not currently checked) it ensures that errors in the implementation of ANS features of Cobol are corrected within 12 months. This seems a reasonable requirement, but in the past some implementors have preferred not to correct errors unless they are a major cause of inconvenience to a number of users.

The validation suite makes no checks on extensions to the standard and does not ensure that invalid syntax is correctly identified by the compiler. It does however play a vital role in ensuring that programs written in Standard Cobol are accepted by compilers and correctly executed.

3.2 PROBLEMS WITH THE COBOL STANDARD

As a result of the efforts of the U.S. Federal Compiler Testing Center there is a high degree of conformance to the Cobol Standard. This does not however mean that a Cobol program can be expected to produce the same results regardless of the machine on which it is compiled and run. In fact the level of portability of Cobol programs is poor. This results from the limitations of the standard. The standard:

    (i) permits the implementation of subsets;
    (ii) permits non-standard additions;
    (iii) leaves the specification of many features to the discretion of the implementor;
    (iv) cannot control some deviations from the standard;
    (v) has no control over supporting documentation; and
    (vi) takes many years to replace its predecessor.

We shall now examine each of these problems in turn.

3.2.1 Freedom to implement subsets

ANS 74 Cobol consists of a nucleus and eleven modules as shown in Fig. 3.1. The compiler writer has the freedom to implement each of these at various levels (including complete omission for those modules where 'null' is shown as a level). In all cases level 2 is a superset of level 1.

	Levels
Nucleus	2 1
Table Handling	2 1
Sequential I-O	2 1
Relative I-O	2 1 null
Indexed I-O	2 1 null
Sort-Merge	2 1 null
Report Writer	1 null
Segmentation	2 1 null
Library	2 1 null
Debug	2 1 null
Inter-program Communication	2 1 null
Communication	2 1 null

Fig. 3.1.

Thus statements such as those shown in Fig. 3.2, although correct Cobol according to the ANS 74 specifications, would not be acceptable to a compiler that implemented only minimum ANS Cobol (that is the nucleus, table handling and sequential I-O each at level 1). This is because the VARYING option of PERFORM is a level 2 feature of the nucleus and SEARCH is a level 2 feature of table handling. Furthermore 'GREATER THAN' and 'EQUAL TO' must be used instead of '>' and '=' in minimum Cobol. These of course are just a few of the standard features which are optional to the compiler writer (only about one third of the standard is obligatory) and in fact, the freedom offered by this modular structure permits more than 100 000 possible versions of Standard Cobol. Moving Cobol programs from one of these versions to another which is not a superset of the first will involve conversion problems.

```
PERFORM ADD-DIGIT
    VARYING POINTER FROM 1 BY 1
    UNTIL POINTER > FIELD-SIZE.
SEARCH SALESMAN
    WHEN SALESMAN-CD (SALES-IND) = INSALES
    PERFORM ADD-SALES.
```

Fig. 3.2.

In fact a move from a subset to a superset can also cause problems. For example the PERFORM statement in Fig. 3.2, although perfectly acceptable to many compilers, would be rejected by any compiler which implements the STRING verb. This is because POINTER is a reserved word used with the STRING verb.

ANS 74 does not require the implementor to support the full list of reserved words specified in the standard. Most compilers support only those reserved words used in the subset of features they implement.

Most compilers take advantage of the opportunity to omit optional modules — the report writer and telecommunications are frequently omitted. Indeed the complete language is very large and thus carries compile time overheads which are prohibitive on some computers.

3.2.2 Non-standard additions

Provided a compiler writer implements one of the approved versions of ANS Cobol described above, the compiler is regarded as standard. This status is not forfeited by any further additions of non-standard features. Thus various computer manufacturers have added EXHIBIT, EXPUNGE, FILL, TRANSFORM and ZIP verbs each of which performs a useful purpose but none of which is ever likely to be standard and thus supported by more than a handful of compilers. These extensions should not however be condemned out of hand, since extensions such as the CALL verb and indexed sequential files provided these two facilities to programmers years before they appeared in the standard. In fact such extensions play an important part in the Cobol development process by allowing features to be tested prior to incorporation in the standard. Additional problems arise only if the standard version of indexed files, for example, is incompatible with its forerunners.

These extensions obviously are a potential cause of incompatibility in Cobol programs. But for the users who want their programs to be portable, some implementors provide a compile time option to reject any non-standard features used in the programs.

3.2.3 Implementor-defined features

In addition to the freedom already described, more subtle variations in the language are introduced by certain features in the standard which are left for the compiler writer to define. Many of these features are listed in the standard as being 'implementor-defined' but others result from ambiguities in the standard.

The most noticeable implementor-defined variations occur in the Environment Division. It has, however, always been intended that such variations be confined to this division, where they can easily be located for conversion. The more serious variations are those which occur in other Divisions. A cross-section of these follows:

(i) On some computers non-numeric literals must be bounded by quotation marks (for example, "SALES REPORT"); on others the programmer is permitted or required to use apostrophes (for example, 'SALES REPORT');

(ii) Standard compilers are required to allow a number of destination fields in a MOVE statement but no upper limit to this number is specified. Thus there is no guarantee that the statement

> MOVE 0 TO ITEM-COUNT
> NO-OF-REJECTS
> CLASS-A-COUNT
> CLASS-B-COUNT
> CLASS-C-COUNT.

is acceptable to all computers. The same problem arises wherever a list is indicated by ellipsis (...) in a Cobol format. The compiler writer usually tries to permit the list to be 'as long as anyone could reasonably want';

(iii) Consider the following example:

> 1 ITEM-COUNT PIC 9 VALUE 9.
>
> :
> :
>
> ADD 1 TO ITEM-COUNT.

According to ANS 74 the value of ITEM-COUNT is 'undefined' after the above ADD statement. This is because a SIZE ERROR has occurred but has not been checked for. Most programmers would probably expect the leading digit of the resulting 10 to be truncated and 0 stored in ITEM-COUNT. But the standard does not prevent compilers from leaving ITEM-COUNT unaltered as would happen if a SIZE ERROR clause had been specified.

Ideally when the contents of a data item become undefined access should be prevented by the compiler. But most implementors consider the overhead in doing this to be prohibitive. The programmer is thus able to find out, from the reference manual or by experimentation, the result in these circumstances and write his program accordingly. The standard offers no safeguards against bad programming practice such as this.

The standard contains a list of items which are implementor-defined but has no such list for situations which are 'undefined' or 'unpredictable'. It is planned however to include this latter list in the next revision of the standard.

3.2.4 Deviations from the standard

Many implementations which claim to be standard infringe rules stated in the standard.

The following syntax, for example, is taken from the 1974 standard:

OCCURS [integer-1 TO] integer-2 TIMES [DEPENDING ON data-name-1]

The appearance of this in a manufacturer's manual is no guarantee that it is implemented in a standard manner or indeed implemented at all. The following paraphrased extracts are taken from two different manuals:

'The DEPENDING ON option is for documentation only'
'ANS COBOL does not permit the omission of integer-1 when the DEPENDING ON option is used. This compiler has no such restriction'.

The U.S. federal compiler tests do not prevent deviations such as these, which could be supported by a conforming implementation by any of the following means:

(i) *Explicit extension*: The standard says nothing about how a compiler should process non-standard code. The relaxation of rules can thus be regarded as a valid extension which does not prevent the compiler from conforming to the standard;

(ii) *Implicit extension*: The compiler could recognise the omission of integer-1 as an error, issue a warning message and then proceed as if integer-1 had been specified;

(iii) *Infringement at optional level*: The format of the OCCURS clause shown above is in level 2 of the table handling module. This means that its implementation is optional. If a compiler claims conformance only at level 1 of table handling it is free to vary the syntax and semantics of any level 2 features;

(iv) *Pre-processors*: Pre-processors, which convert an extended form of Cobol into Cobol which is acceptable to the compiler, are subject to no standards. A large number of pre-processors are in use for implementing database handling, telecommunications, structured programming and many other extensions. Their use can be justified when no equivalent facility is yet available in the standard but, on the other hand, they can be used blatantly to circumvent the standard.

3.2.5 Transition between standards

At any one time there is only one American National Standard for Cobol. The transition from one standard to another occurs instantaneously as far as the standardisation body is concerned. But manufacturers cannot be expected to provide a new compiler overnight or indeed discard a compiler, based on the superseded standard, which contains enough extensions to make it adequate for most users. The result is that it is several years before a standard is widely applied. For example, as late as 1979 the use of ANS 68 compilers was still widespread.

Standards are scheduled for revision every five years. So this time lag will mean that for a period after each standard is published there will be, in common use, compilers based on three different standards.

Thus in practice, there are two or three Cobol standards not one. Furthermore they are incompatible. For example, the ANS 68 EXAMINE verb was replaced by the INSPECT verb in ANS 74 and conversion from ANS 74 to its successor will involve transferring certain clauses associated with the description of files between the Environment and Data Divisions.

The advantage of a single standard is thus lost to any user who uses two compilers based on different standards. The transition from the ANS 74 compilers will however be somewhat eased by the delayed deletion facility. If a deletion from ANS 74 is judged to cause significant portability problems it is placed in the delayed deletion category [8]. This means that the feature will temporarily be retained in the next standard thus allowing approximately five years in which it can be phased out of applications programs.

3.2.6 Accompanying documentation

Undoubtedly the most effective way to enforce programming standards is with software. But the absence of a single rigorous standard for Cobol makes this infeasible. As a result the documentation which accompanies an implementation assumes greater significance. The documentation can usefully support the implementation by:

(i) Clearly indicating which optional parts of the standard have been implemented;

(ii) Highlighting the features which are non-standard (that is, extensions to the standard);

(iii) Not specifying the values or results in situations where the standard states that they are 'undefined' or 'unpredictable'.

Furthermore the compiler could usefully include in any source listing an indication of the standard and its level of implementation.

It should be possible for a programmer to determine the relationship of a compiler to the standard. This should be possible in outline by consulting a source listing and in detail by consulting the appropriate manual.

3.2.7 The wider scene

To a significant extent the success of Cobol standardisation is tied up with the degree of standardisation in hardware, software and programming techniques. The motivation for most extensions to the standard is to take advantage of some special feature in one of these areas (for example, floating-point hardware, special file organisations and structured programming techniques). The users can thus often confine themselves to standard Cobol only by ignoring some language features which are highly desirable in their environment.

The general lack of standardisation in related areas also causes problems with the Cobol standard itself. Even when there are standards such as the American Standard Code for Information Interchange (ASCII) it is not as rigorously applied as the Cobol standard. In fact incorporation of a feature into Cobol is one of the most effective ways of standardising it and making it generally available. The Cobol debugging feature and source text manipulation facilities (COPY and more recently REPLACE) are arguably operating-system functions. A standard job control language, which would automatically define a minimum set of operating-system functions, would greatly ease the task of specifying a Cobol standard (see Chapter 11).

Many of the implementor-dependent features in Cobol are for the purpose of getting most efficient use of the hardware. As hardware prices fall these features become less important and their removal from the language could result.

In the longer term, programming techniques are likely to pose the greatest problems. The favoured techniques can change very rapidly and it is impossible for the standard to keep up to date. This is demonstrated by the widespread use of modular programming and structured programming long before features to support these techniques appeared as standard.

3.3 EFFECTS OF THE COBOL STANDARD

Despite the problems discussed in the previous section the standard has, to a large extent, ensured that Cobol is indeed a common language. Successive revisions of the standard have solved many portability problems and eased many others.

Any reservations about the portability of Cobol programs do not apply to Cobol programmers. Cobol courses are mounted and Cobol books are written for programmers using a variety of hardware. Furthermore many employers are prepared to recruit experienced Cobol programmers from any background. When they do require experience on a specific machine it is more likely to be experience of the operating system, rather than the particular version of Cobol, that is required.

3.4 REFERENCES

[1] Commission of the European Communities (1978), Cost benefit study of transfer of technology problems of Cobol − Cobol user requirements − initial study.

[2] U.S. National Bureau of Standards, Report NBSIR 76-1100.

[3] Codasyl (1978), Cobol Journal of Development, Department of Supply and Services, Canada.

[4] ANSI (1968), ANSI X3.23-1968: Programming Language Cobol.

[5] ANSI (1974), ANSI X3.23-1974: Programming Language Cobol.

[6] ISO (1978), ISO 1989 Programming Language − Cobol.

[7] FCCTS-NTJS Information, Federal Compiler Testing Service, U.S.A.

[8] Triance, J. M. (1976), Cobol is too big. *Datamation*, **22**, No. 7, 156-160.

CHAPTER 4

Algol 60
by Dr. I. David Hill

In the early 1960s the main rival to Fortran in 'scientific' computing was Algol 60, a language immensely influential in later developments of programming languages (notably PL/I, Algol 68, and Pascal) and still in widespread use, especially in educational establishments. Based on a generally recognised defining document, the Revised Report of 1962, Algol 60 achieved formal standardisation at national level (in the German Federal Republic and Japan) but has not yet achieved full standardisation at ISO level. This chapter explains why, and describes the work on Algol 60 standardisation which continues. The author is Dr. I. David Hill of the Medical Research Council's Clinical Research Centre, a member of BSI:DPS/13 and of IFIP/WG 2.1.

4.1 ORIGINS OF ALGOL

Algol started life rather differently from some of the other languages in this book, appearing in the form of a report by a committee, without reference to any particular computer, and without having been implemented on a computer. Indeed in its early days some doubts were expressed on even the possibility of implementing some features.

There was first a Preliminary Report [1] leading to a language called Algol 58 which some computer manufacturers set out to implement. Their efforts were overtaken, however, by a much improved language, Algol 60 [2], only two years later. Those who decided not to implement this, on the grounds that such rapid changes made it uneconomical to do so, were not to know that the language would remain remarkably stable from then on.

Those who did implement it found certain difficulties, obscurities, ambiguities and errors in the report and consequently a Revised Report [3] was issued in 1962 with minor corrections and clarifications, but no attempt to extend the language. It also listed five points that had yet to be settled, in the hope that then-current work would help to resolve them.

4.2 IFIP AND ISO BECOME INVOLVED

Immediately following the Revised Report, responsibility for Algol was given to IFIP/TC 2/WG 2.1, while ISO interest in producing a standard on the language became evident at about the same time. In September 1962 the chairman of WG 2.1 (Professor W. L. van der Poel) was authorised by IFIP to submit to ISO/TC 97 the revised Algol 60 report as officially approved by IFIP.

ISO/TC 97/SC 5 at a meeting in Berlin in June 1963 decided that 'the IFIP ALGOL 60 Report was not sufficient by itself for standardization' and 'resolved to invite IFIP to further submit specifications of a subset language, input-output facilities, and graphics and media codes of ALGOL symbols' [4].

A little explanation may be desirable on two of these matters on which extra specifications were required. The first is input-output, of which the revised report makes no mention at all, it having been thought at the time that the language should concentrate on specifying algorithmic processes within a computer, and that input and output were too hardware-dependent to be part of it. Since every implementation needs input-output facilities, implementors each devised their own, with a consequent unstandardised jungle that contrasts strangely with the uniformity of implementations in most other respects. It is not surprising that ISO should have required some discipline to be brought to this area.

On graphics and media codes the point is that Algol 60, in its purest form, is represented by a 'reference language' that is not immediately usable on most computers but must be translated to a 'hardware representation' for the particular implementation.

Thus a piece of reference language text:

begin array $x[0:5]$;

might have to be punched for four different computers as:

    BEGIN ARRAY x[0:5];
    'BEGIN' 'ARRAY' X [0:5];
    'BEGIN' 'ARRAY' X (/0:5/);
    .BEGIN. .ARRAY. X (/0..5/).,

according to the character sets available. The important point here is that each hardware representation has to be accompanied by rules for unambiguous translation to and from the reference language. Provided that this is so, different representations on different machines cause little trouble as translations between them can be automated. Nevertheless it is again not surprising that ISO should have desired a standard hardware representation.

At the next SC 5 meeting, in New York in May 1964, an *ad hoc* working group on Algol agreed some detailed proposals [5] that there should be 'a unique subset' and 'two levels of I/O procedures'. The proposal for a unique subset was subsequently modified to allow three levels of subset.

The aim was to base these additions on work that was in progress outside

ISO at the time, IFIP/WG 2.1 making proposals on a subset [6] and elementary input/output [7], ECMA a proposal on a less restrictive subset [8] and a committee of ACM (under the chairmanship of D. E. Knuth) a proposal for extended input/output [9]. An ISO working group added these proposals to the revised report, making sure that the subsets were properly nested, introducing a new subset (to be identical to the ECMA subset except for allowing recursion in procedure calls), and expressing the extended I/O in terms of the elementary I/O.

Final agreement was reached, subject to the preparation of a new draft proposal, at the SC 5 meeting in Copenhagen in September 1965, while TC 97 gave approval in Tokyo in October 1965.

Meanwhile, within ISO, there had been discussions on whether it was right to put out a number of standards for rival languages rather than to standardise one only. It was decided to go ahead with ISO Recommendations rather than ISO Standards for the three languages then under consideration (Algol, Cobol and Fortran), and await developments in the computing world before proceeding further. It should be noted here that nowadays ISO no longer has Recommendations, but only Standards and Technical Reports.

4.3 THE RECOMMENDATION APPEARS

Finally the drafting work was complete, and in April 1967 draft ISO Recommendation No. 1538 was ready in typescript [10]. In general this draft shows evidence of careful editing and errors are very few. It was approved by IFIP/WG 2.1 and by ISO/TC 97/SC 5 and was taken into the inner workings of ISO for processing. Before 1967 was finished there were already rumblings that the standardisation effort appeared to have entered a 'peculiar state of limbo'. Indeed it had, for the final printed version [11] did not appear until March 1972, having been processed under ISO's 'accelerated procedures'!

Worse, however, even than the time that had been taken was that the document had been changed in significant ways from the draft that had been agreed, the careful editing of the draft had come to nothing the printed version being riddled with errors, and a price had been put on the publication almost guaranteed to ensure that hardly anyone would buy it [12].

The worst of the deliberate changes was that the five points that had yet to be settled, mentioned above, had been omitted. It is very understandable that a standards body would not wish to publish a document containing a list of matters yet to be settled, and it would have been quite reasonable at an earlier stage to have said that the language was not suitable for standardisation until they had been settled; but, not having done so, arbitrarily to omit them from an agreed document was deplorable.

4.4 HARDWARE REPRESENTATION

A standard representation of the Algol basic symbols in terms of the ISO 7-bit character set [13] did not appear in ISO/R 1538, but a separate document was being circulated with some proposals. However, a number of disagreements were expressed to this document, partly because it did not sufficiently define the requirements for all circumstances, partly on technical grounds.

The most serious of the latter concerned the representation of the $_{10}$ symbol, used in numbers so that, for example, $1.5_{10}3$ means 1.5×10^3. The suggestion had been made to use the letter E for this purpose, as in Fortran and various other languages; but in Algol $_{10}5$ is a valid number (meaning 10^5) while E5 is a valid identifier. A different symbol was therefore required.

To resolve this and various other comments a meeting of experts was called in Berlin in January 1972. Unfortunately this was attended by only two countries, the U.K. and Western Germany, plus two members of the SC 5 secretariat. A proposal was worked out, subject to detailed drafting and incorporating a number of compromises.

Subsequently I was asked to chair a drafting committee which, working by correspondence, produced three drafts and submitted the third, together with a discussion paper on two remaining points of difficulty, to SC 5 member bodies for ballot. The resulting votes were two affirmative and six negative. Some of the negative votes were on matters where deliberate compromises had been made at the Berlin meeting, and it does point to one of the difficulties of international (or any other) standardisation if parties who do not attend a meeting, do not hear the arguments, and do not know where other parties have compromised by trading one point for another, are subsequently able to exercise a vote in ignorance of these matters.

In the absence of agreement, it was decided that a Technical Report should be issued instead of a Standard and this appeared in 1977 [14]. A French version was prepared by M. D. Suty, on behalf of AFNOR, for ISO.

4.5 WASHINGTON, 1972

Returning to 1972, there was a meeting of SC 5 in Washington in November of that year, at which I acted as chairman of the *ad hoc* working group on Algol. This group produced a document [15] listing 104 errors in the ISO Recommendation, and among SC 5's resolutions [16] were:

'15. That a new edition of ISO/R 1538 be produced incorporating the corrections contained in document N 313. The UK will undertake the editorial function.'

and:

'17. That IFIP is acknowledged to be the responsible organization for developing and maintaining ALGOL.'

It was known at the time that IFIP/WG 2.1 was planning to set up a maintenance committee for Algol 60, under Professor C. A. R. Hoare, to overhaul the language as a result of ten years of experience since the revised report. The Washington working group therefore took the chance to put together an informal document listing 23 questions of Algol 60 maintenance.

Shortly afterwards I was asked by Professor Hoare to join the maintenance committee and was faced (together with R. M. De Morgan and B. A. Wichmann) with the task of answering these questions.

4.6 THE JAPANESE STANDARD

In 1972 JSA produced a national standard [17] based on the Revised Report, translated into Japanese writing, and a companion standard [18] specifying an input-output system based on the Knuth proposals [9]. These standards also defined various levels of subset of both the language and the input-output.

4.7 NEGOTIATIONS

No action was apparent from ISO in response to SC 5's call for a new edition of R 1538, other than a suggestion that the list of errors might be issued as an amendment slip.

At a 1973 meeting of IFIP/WG 2.1, it was resolved [19] that IFIP should request that ISO withdraw R 1538, and that failing this 'IFIP should disassociate itself explicitly from the ISO Recommendation'. Possibly as a result of this, I was asked by the SC 5 secretariat to form an editorial committee to re-edit the document to satisfy both ISO and IFIP.

Meanwhile the maintenance committee was proceeding with its task — without Professor Hoare who, having set it up, had to resign from it because of absence abroad. In addition to the document from SC 5 it had also to consider a number of other documents relating to Algol 60 difficulties [20, 21, 22]. R. M. De Morgan and I attended, as observers, the WG 2.1 meeting in Breukelen (Netherlands) in August 1974 to present an interim report.

Knowing that I was due to attend this meeting I thought it wise to postpone starting work on the re-editing for ISO until I had had a chance to discuss it with the WG 2.1 members.

It was agreed that: (1) we must start from the draft document of 1967. This was the one that had received the international vote, so any major revision would require a repeat of the international exercise causing years of delay; (2) there was no real difficulty about the printing errors since it was agreed what they were and there was nothing controversial about them; (3) the tricky part of the exercise lay in the deliberate amendments that had been made, so we should start by trying to settle them.

Correspondence with the ISO secretariat seemed to be very slow and getting nowhere, when the situation was changed again by the news of a new ISO procedure in cases where standards were bulky documents whose technical content already existed as a national standard or some similar document. To save expense ISO agreed to refer to such other documents instead of reprinting them, but there was a difficulty in trying to adopt this procedure for Algol 60, since there was no one publication that included everything needed.

However, while the correspondence was taking place, DIN had gone ahead on their own and brought out a standard, DIN 66 026 [23] that reproduced ISO/R 1538 (in a reduced size: 2 ISO pages to 1 DIN page) with nearly all the errors corrected. Being reproduced from the ISO document it could not, of course, include the omitted matter, but an ISO reference to this document, while not a perfect solution, might have been a reasonable way out of the difficulties. ISO felt this to be impossible though on the grounds that 'it would look rather odd if ISO, when re-editing one of its publications, referred to a national standard which in turn refers to the original ISO publication', so this way was blocked too.

The Algol 60 maintenance effort was now making rapid progress and it became questionable whether the negotiations were worth continuing rather than starting again with the new version that was about to appear.

4.8 MAINTENANCE

The maintenance committee found the language to be, in general, in a sound state needing only minor tuning in places. They tried, as far as possible, to settle outstanding points and queries in such a way as not to invalidate existing implementations if it could be avoided. This led in a number of places to the taking of decisions that would have been taken differently if the language were being designed from scratch. For example, all the members would have preferred a looping mechanism in which the step-expression and the until-expression were evaluated once only each time the loop was entered, rather than re-evaluated for every cycle of the loop, but the dynamic, rather than the static, interpretation was too heavily settled into Algol folklore for this to be possible.

The aim was 'not to gratify this or that party in any their unreasonable demands; but to do that, which to our best understandings we conceived might most tend to the preservation of Peace and Unity' [24].

There was one area, however, where a more major change was made. This was to remove the extended input-output procedures, which were judged not to have been a success, and to be too clumsy compared with the general elegance of Algol. Most manufacturers had ignored them and continued to supply their own input-output. It was thought that the best that could be done was to re-write the elementary input-output (to remove certain difficulties) and to hope that this would supply the basic requirement for interchange between machines, while leaving extended procedures to be implementation-dependent.

The conclusions having been circulated for comment [25], a revised version was approved by IFIP/WG 2.1 at Munich in 1975 and subsequently by IFIP/TC 2. It was published in the form of a supplement to the revised report [26], and resulted in a modified report [27] to which an erratum has subsequently been published [28].

4.9 WITHDRAWAL OF ISO/R 1538

In October 1976, IFIP adopted a resolution:

'In view of the length of time which has elapsed since the start of the attempts by ISO to standardize ALGOL 60, and in view of the confusion caused by R 1538 with its many and serious errors, and of the difficulties apparently inherent in rectifying them, and in view of the fact that the Working Group has recently released the specification of a modified form of the language, IFIP WG 2.1 recommends to ISO that all attempts to standardize ALGOL 60 in its original form should be abandoned, and that R 1538 should simply be withdrawn. Should ISO now be prepared to standardize the modified language, IFIP WG 2.1 would be willing to co-operate, provided that the standardization were done by a reference to the modified Report to be published in the November 1976 issue of the Computer Journal.'

The secretariat of ISO/TC 97/SC 5 then held a letter ballot, and the withdrawal of R 1538 was approved, leaving a vacuum in international standardisation of Algol 60 for the time being.

4.10 WHAT NEXT?

In November 1977, ISO/TC 97/SC 5 met in The Hague, and it was agreed [29] that:

'15. ISO/TC 97/SC 5 wishes to consider the IFIP documents "Modified Report on ALGOL 60" and "Revised Report on ALGOL 68" as potential draft International Standards, and requests its secretariat to inform IFIP of this fact....'

Consequently, IFIP submitted the Modified Report and a suggested wording that ISO could use to refer to it. The ISO meeting in Turin in November 1979 resolved to accept these as a Draft Proposal, and asked the secretariat to conduct a letter ballot [30]. It also set up an 'experts group' under J. W. van Wingen to take care of the remaining stages but the resolutions (8 and 9) were passed by only small majorities and further progress must be doubtful.

This is not only because it is thought in some quarters that Algol 60 is now outmoded and no longer sufficiently alive, but also because of a strong feeling among professional standardisers, particularly in BSI, that a document such as the Modified Report is not adequate for their purposes. In particular it does not address questions of the definitions of standard-conforming implementations and standard-conforming programs.

Furthermore it seems to be very difficult to meet the requirements of both the language designers and BSI editorial practice [31]. BSI require standards that are worded precisely enough to survive challenge in a court of law, and for most things that are subject to standardisation this causes no real difficulty, the technical committee members deciding on the requirements while the BSI staff put them into their particular brand of precise wording; but language designers have equally precise wording of their own, and any modification introduced by someone who is not fully conversant with the language can have serious consequences. A good example can be found in the unsatisfactory ISO/R1538, where ISO editorial staff changed 'specificator' to 'specifier' in a number of places.

At the beginning of 1980, it appears somewhat unlikely that enough support will be available for any further progress, and that Algol 60 will have to remain without such benefits as international standardisation might bring. Whatever happens, let us hope that those concerned with other languages in the future may be forewarned by reading this sad tale, and thus be able to avoid some of the difficulties.

4.11 REFERENCES

[1] Backus, J. W. *et al.* (1958), Preliminary report — international algebraic language, *Commun. ACM.*, **1**, No. 12. 8-22.

[2] Naur, P. *et al.* (1960), Report on the algorithmic language Algol 60, *Commun. ACM.*, **3**, 299-314; *Numer. Math.*, **2**, 106-136.

[3] Naur, P. *et al.* (1962), Revised report on the algorithmic language Algol 60, *Commun. ACM.*, **6**, 1-17; *Comput. J.*, **5**, 349-367; *Numer. Math.*, **4**, 420-453.

[4] ISO (1964), Chairman's report on the work of ISO/TC 97/SC 5, Paper ISO/TC 97/SC 5 (Secr-13) 59.

[5] ISO (1964), Brief minutes of *ad hoc* working group on Algol, Resolutions 2 and 4, Paper ISO/TC 97/SC 5 (NY 64-14) 83.

[6] IFIP (1964), Report on subset of Algol 60, *Commun. ACM.*, **7**, 626-628; *Numer. Math.*, **6**, 454-458.

[7] IFIP (1964) Report in input-output procedures for Algol 60, *Commun. ACM.*, **7**, 628-630; *Numer. Math.*, **6**, 459-462.

[8] ECMA (1963), Subset of Algol 60, *Commun. ACM.*, **6**, 595-597.

[9] Knuth, D. E. *et al.* (1964), A proposal for input-output conventions in Algol 60, *Commun. ACM.*, **7**, 273-283.

[10] ISO (1967), Draft ISO Recommendation No. 1538: Programming Language Algol, Paper ISO/TC 97 (Secretariat-97) 150E.

[11] ISO (1972), ISO/R 1538: Programming Language Algol, 1st Edition.

[12] Hill, I. D. (1972), Algol 60 — the ISO disaster of 1972, *Comput. Bull.*, **16**, 542-543.

[13] ISO (1973), ISO 646: 7-bit coded character set for information processing interchange.

[14] ISO (1977), ISO/TR 1672: Hardware representation of Algol basic symbols in the ISO 7-bit coded character set for information processing interchange.

[15] ISO (1972), Corrections to ISO/R 1538, Paper ISO/TC 97/SC 5 (Wash. 72-5) 313.

[16] ISO (1972), Resolutions, Paper ISO/TC 97/SC 5 (Wash. 72-7) 315.

[17] JSA (1972), JIS C 6210: Programming language for computers Algol (level 7000).

[18] JSA (1972), JIS C 6215: Programming language for computers Algol input-output (level 70).

[19] IFIP (1973), WG 2.1 Resolution Dresden 2.

[20] Knuth, D. E. and Merner, J. N. (1961), Algol 60 confidential, *Commun. ACM.*, **4**, 268-272.

[21] Utman, R. E. *et al.* (1963), Suggestions on the Algol 60 (Rome) issues, *Commun. ACM.*, **6**, 20-23.

[22] Knuth, D. E. (1967), The remaining trouble spots in Algol 60, *Commun. ACM.*, **10**, 611-618.

[23] DNA (1975), DIN 66 026: Programmiersprache Algol.

[24] Book of Common Prayer (1662), Preface.

[25] De Morgan, R. M., Hill, I. D., and Wichmann, B. A. (1974), A commentary on the Algol 60 revised report, *Algol Bull.*, **38**, 5-38.

[26] De Morgan, R. M., Hill, I. D., and Wichmann, B. A. (1976), A supplement to the Algol 60 revised report, *Comput. J.*, **19**, 276-288; *SIGPLAN Not.*, **12**, No. 1, 52-66.

[27] De Morgan, R. M., Hill, I. D., and Wichmann, B. A. (1976), Modified report on the algorithmic language Algol 60, *Comput. J.*, **19**, 364-379.

[28] De Morgan, R. M., Hill, I. D., and Wichmann, B. A. (1978), Modified Algol 60 and the step-until element, *Comput. J.*, **21**, 282.

[29] ISO (1977), Resolutions, Paper ISO/TC 97/SC 5 N427.

[30] ISO (1977), Resolutions, Paper ISO/TC 97/SC 5 N559.

[31] BSI (1975), A standard for standards, Part 4: BSI editorial practice, BS 0: Part 4.

CHAPTER 5

PL/I

by David Beech and Michael Marcotty

All the languages dealt with so far were originally designed with limited design aims – Fortran for scientific calculation, Cobol for business data processing, Algol 60 for the expression of algorithms. PL/I was the first major language to be designed as a general-purpose language. At first, like Fortran, a purely IBM product, it was standardised by ANSI and ECMA in 1976 and the standard was recognised by ISO in 1979. The authors of this chapter are David Beech of IBM United Kingdom Laboratories and Michael Marcotty of General Motors Research Laboratories.

5.1 HISTORY

During 1976, after more than ten years of co-operative work, a standard for PL/I was adopted by ECMA [8] and ANSI [2]. This was followed in 1979 by the approval by ISO [12] of the same standard for use worldwide. We shall briefly outline the events that led to its publication, and then touch on the subsequent activities of ANSI and ECMA in this area.

5.1.1 Global view

The first step in the standardisation process is a reconnaissance of the terrain to establish the desirability and feasibility of the work. ECMA started exploration in 1965 and ANSI followed suit in 1966. The timing of the start of the development of a new standard is critical; there is only a short period while there is sufficient implementation and usage to justify standardisation but not yet too much entrenched divergence to permit reasonable compromise. For PL/I this period fell at the end of 1968. At that time, both ECMA and ANSI, as a result of their studies, decided that a PL/I standard should be developed in concert. Accordingly, in March 1969, the 'Joint Project' between the technical committees ECMA/TC 10 and ANSI/X3J1 was born. The goals were the development of PL/I for standardisation, the definition of standard subsets, and the generation of a rigorous definition of the language. A fuller account of the early history of the standardisation of PL/I is in reference [16].

The transatlantic scope of the Joint Project provided an escape from a problem that besets much standardisation work, namely the synchronisation of various national and international efforts in the same area. The nature of data processing is such that the value of international agreement is clear. Consequently, the Joint Project sent regular reports to ISO through ISO/TC97/SC5. As we have seen, the result has been that a single standard for PL/I has now been adopted worldwide. The Project's mailing list reached around the world and many helpful comments from outside the Project were received and acted upon.

ANSI procedures call for review of a draft proposed standard during a four-month public comment period. This was done in March 1975. Because of the international nature of the PL/I project, ISO member countries were also given the opportunity to comment at this stage. In all, about 1000 copies of the document were requested. As a result, 46 sets of comments were received, containing a total of 951 items (including duplicates from different sources). Some 575 of these items were essentially editorial, but 221 were requests for language change, plus 11 more patient ones for extensions after the initial standard. Given that about 90 per cent of the requests for change in the proposed language were for extensions, it is remarkable that the committee were able to respond positively to as many as 72 of the requests by making two noticeable extensions (a source-text inclusion facility and a group of mathematical built-in functions) and various minor adjustments.

Alongside this pressure for extension, there were six requests for definition of standard subsets. However, most of those who lamented the size and complexity of the language when asking for subsets also asked for extensions.

Since the adoption of the standard, two activities that were postponed during its development have been taken up by X3J1: the definition of a general purpose subset suitable for implementation on small machines, and the development of extensions for real-time use. A draft of a proposed general-purpose subset was distributed for public comment early in 1979. Several extension proposals arising from the comment period, or deferred earlier within the project, still await consideration together with other proposals that may be generated during the five-year phase ending in 1981, when ANSI expects its committee to present recommendations for revision of the original standard. Despite the care that has been taken over the definition of the latter, there may be some corrections or clarifications to be made as a part of the committee's maintenance activity. During this period, TC10 has maintained its links with X3J1 and has recently started work on extensions for interactive devices and full-screen processing. Both committees expect to work together to process corrections and clarifications to the standard and in development work for the revised version of the standard for 1981.

5.1.2 Membership and procedures

The makeup of the membership of the two committees differed somewhat, reflecting the difference between their parent organisations. Since ECMA is an association of computer manufacturers, the membership of TC 10 consists solely of representatives of computer manufacturers. On the other hand, the rules of ANSI require a diversity of viewpoints to be represented in its technical committees, and the maintenance of the right balance is important in seeking new members. Users, implementors and academics all took part in the work of X3J1. The requirements for membership are technical expertise and an ability to attend at least one meeting in three.

The committees held regular meetings approximately every seven weeks and these usually lasted three days. In addition, there were 'Coordination Meetings', with representatives of both committees present, held twice a year, once each side of the Atlantic. At several stages during the development of the standard, small '*ad hoc* committees' were established to carry out specific tasks and report back to the main committee.

A standardisation project needs well thought-out and understood working procedures, and a considerable part of the early history of the Project was concerned with establishing these. The Joint Project had the added complication of two separate groups that had to agree both to common procedures and to internal procedures for their own meetings. One achievement of the Project was to demonstrate that it is possible to succeed in this type of work with two co-operating committees separated by a large body of water.

The main vehicle of co-operation was the working version of the language definition, 'Basis/1'. The Project came to regret the name Basis/1 because of its confusion with Basic and the clash between its Arabic '1' and the Roman 'I' of PL/I — itself a subject of much hot debate.

The first version of Basis/1 was obtained by slightly subsetting the 1968 IBM PL/I Language Specifications [10]. The work of the Project was to transform Basis/1 into the definition of the standard language by a sequence of agreed amendments. The document was maintained in machine-readable form, and the actual mechanics of amendment were under the charge of a succession of three Basis editors, who, although members of TC 10, served the whole Project in their editorial capacity. Their accuracy and vigilance were crucial to success, as was the close collaboration between the committee secretaries and the editor in tracking the status of all amendment proposals.

Before a change could be made to Basis/1, a detailed proposal that specified the exact text and point of insertion had to be approved by the whole project. The Project's joint procedures specified how a proposal could be approved by the whole Project without having each committee consider every proposal individually. This was important, since over 3000 proposals were processed during the development of the standard. A proposal was first considered by one committee or the other, depending on the part of Basis/1 affected. This committee's decision to accept, modify, or reject the proposal was distributed to all Project members. If there was no objection to this decision by any member within six weeks, the proposal reached 'Joint Final Approval' and was incorporated by the Basis editor at the next six-monthly update. There is no doubt in our minds that the use of detailed proposals was essential as it ensured scrutiny and discussion of the actual text before approval and modification of Basis/1.

An objection to an initial decision on a proposal forced the same committee to reconsider it and, in the light of the objection, possibly reverse its decision. Even after the second decision, it was still possible for members to make what was called a 'hot objection'. If the hot objection was supported by the objector's parent committee, then the other committee had to make a decision on the proposal. If the two committees agreed, then the matter was resolved. Otherwise, the problem had to be decided by the chairmen of the two committees in a manner that was deliberately left unspecified. The tortuous path for a controversial proposal to reach Joint Final Approval ensured that all objections received thorough airing. As a measure of success, only about one per cent of the proposals exercised all the escalation procedures before being resolved.

As the work progressed, the joint procedures became more formalised and were eventually expressed algorithmically — illustrating the extent to which technical people had come to recognise the value of sound administration.

Both the drafting of proposals and their intelligent discussion demanded much careful work between meetings. Over and over again, it was found that attempts to take short cuts by processing proposals on the spur of the moment cost dearly in correcting errors later. Members of the two committees had to be prepared to do a considerable amount of homework. We also found that this could be done only by insisting on a three-week deadline for agenda and proposal distribution before a meeting. Despite this rule, the mails, both transatlantic and transcontinental, occasionally prevented members from receiving the material early enough to be useful.

5.1.3 Technical development

During the preparation of the standard, the language went through alternate contractions and expansions:

the deletion of some items from the original IBM definition [10];

the development of extensions for aggregate handling, tasking, defaults and dynamic loading;

the deletion and simplification of some parts, including the newly developed tasking features;

the reinstatement, in response to public comments, of some previously deleted items.

Probably the quickest way to appreciate what happened as a result of this ebb and flow is to compare the outcome with the IBM version of the language [11]. This may be summarised as follows (for more detail and discussion, see references [6, 9]):

Deletions: Compile-time facilities (except %INCLUDE)
     48-character set version
     CONTROLLED parameters
     I through N default rule
     CHECK condition
     Tasking and event I/O
     plus about 20 other items

Extensions: More general RETURNS attribute (aggregates, dynamic strings,
      entries)
     DEFAULT statement
     String handling built-in functions
     Dynamic BASED extents without REFER
     DO ... REPEAT (control expression evaluated each iteration)
     Remote FORMAT statements outside block where referenced
     plus about 30 other items

Changes: True aggregate operations
     Arithmetic default FIXED BINARY
     Order of evaluation of multiple assignments
     plus about 18 other items

Of course, the quantifications are approximate, depending upon what is considered to be an 'item'. The overall effect was probably some expansion of the language, although this was not very great since deletions such as those of the compile-time facilities, tasking and event I/O, and the CHECK condition, effected a substantial reduction. The general-purpose subset has been constructed by deletions and restrictions applied to the complete language.

5.2 TECHNICAL PROBLEMS

5.2.1 Language content

A few examples will illustrate some typical problems of programming language standardisation as they have arisen in the PL/I work.

5.2.1.1 *Existence versus alteration*

An existing language has already acquired a body of users who have been pioneers in demonstrating its viability. They deserve to be spared the impact of numerous alterations and yet some alterations may definitely benefit posterity.

Almost all proposals for deletions from PL/I led to lengthy debate, and examples of successful proposals have been listed above. On the other hand, attempts to change the fixed-point division rule, or to change the name of the language from PL/I to PL/1, could not demonstrate enough improvement to justify the pain and confusion they would cause.

Incompatible changes were the most controversial alterations, but even deletions raised doubts in users' minds as to whether new compilers would support the deleted features for the benefit of programs that had used them. Thus event I/O, for example, found many defenders and this complicated the deletion of the tasking language since many of those in favour of deletion insisted that the closely related event I/O be deleted also, to have the way clear for a new approach to synchronisation.

5.2.1.2 Extension

One of the first questions to ask about a proposed extension is whether it adds a new primitive to the language. Does it enable programs to be written whose semantics could not have been achieved within the language previously? This turns out to be a surprisingly difficult question to answer in the affirmative. If the language already has the power of a Turing machine, it must be a matter of extending its semantics in terms of practical effects rather than computational power. However, it is precisely at this boundary between the program and the real world that a loosely specified mapping is performed. Thus a new statement intended to cause the ringing of a bell might not be a functional extension if a specially mapped 'write' statement in the existing language already achieved this.

Assuming more generous criteria such that a new primitive affecting the world outside the program may be identified, there are still likely to be serious obstacles to adding it to a language due to the aim of system-independence. The outside world is even less standardised than programming languages, and the languages have limited ability to impose their semantics upon it.

It is hardly surprising, therefore, that few of the extensions made to PL/I could be classified as strictly primitive. Most of the features added, such as true aggregate (array and structure) expressions and functions, were introduced for greater convenience, clarity or efficiency. The case for each extension had to be strong enough to outweigh its dangers. Even so, there is bound to be somewhat piecemeal consideration of separate extensions, and the question naturally arises as to whether a general extensibility mechanism can be introduced, at least for this repackaging of non-primitives. Although this was not considered feasible in the time-frame of the initial standard, the developers of any major language need to monitor the state of the art in this area. Extensions previously made, or newly proposed, should be taken as test cases to see how many of them could be handled by any given extension mechanism, and with what ease and efficiency.

Apart from those concerns about the impact that extensions can have on the overall size and redundancy of the language, there must also be doubts as to the practicality of untried extensions, especially when designed by a committee.

5.2.1.3 Interchange

There is a danger that concentration on desirable alterations and extensions may obscure the objective of a standard to allow interchange of programs and programmers between different implementations. PL/I had always shown some awareness of this problem by its insistence on the UNSPEC built-in function to identify dependence on the internal representation of a data value, and the ENVIRONMENT attribute to contain system-dependent information about file usage. The exercise of producing rigorous definitions of the language served to focus attention further on other problems with implementation-dependence. We shall begin by noting some topics related to machine-dependence, irrespective of the operating system, and then move on to the more general questions of system-dependence.

The numerical results produced from arithmetic operations and built-in functions and conversions are liable to be strongly influenced by the underlying machine, since it becomes very inefficient to simulate algorithms other than those employed in the hardware. This especially affects floating-point computations, and conversions between binary and decimal fractions, and the best that can be done is to state that these results are approximate. The standard distinguishes between those results that must be exact and those that are implementation-defined approximations.

Other influences of the machine show through in the use of main storage. Besides the explicit use of UNSPEC, there are cases where the mapping of objects in memory is significant for the use of based variables and areas. The based variable situation occurs with the use of 'left-to-right equivalence' between two descriptions of aggregate variables, one of which is supposed to be some leftmost part of the other (typically used in the analysis of self-describing record structures). Rules were developed to specify when implementation-independence was guaranteed − see reference [14]. Likewise, the mapping of variables allocated within areas was constrained such that comparisons of offset values would produce implementation-independent results for the most useful cases.

Many of the problems of the tasking extensions were concerned with system-dependence, and these vanished for a while when this part of the language was deleted. However, the real-time extensions reintroduced the questions. The concern here would be not so much whether a system can give compatible results, but whether its underlying structure is a good enough fit with the superimposed language for implementation to be reasonable, reliable and efficient.

An example of a statement that was deleted from the full language due to system-dependence was DISPLAY. This was originally conceived as relating to a unique operator terminal in a system, but became corrupted in some implementations to apply to a user terminal, so that its semantics were becoming dependent on the configuration of the system. This leads us to more general questions of input/output, which is where most of the system interfaces of PL/I occur. Apart from the ENVIRONMENT attribute, most of the attributes of a file were accepted as having system-independent semantics, although BUFFERED and UNBUFFERED were dropped because, as defined, they were of little interest to many systems. Of course, the biggest residual interchange problem concerns the data in files rather than the programs themselves. PL/I provides STREAM files in character form, which require only a little goodwill between systems in order to provide an interchange medium, but the representations and mappings used in RECORD files are allowed to be implementation-defined in the interests of efficiency rather than being constrained for the purposes of interchange.

5.2.1.4 *Optimisation*

In addition to keeping a general eye on performance, the committees studied various additional optimising attributes. These were intended to allow a language processor some latitude to improve performance for the normal case, at the cost of some possibly different results in what the compiler writers would claim were pathological cases. The general problem is clear — the more tightly a standard defines the language in the interest of uniform results, the harder it is liable to become to achieve those results efficiently on a variety of machines. Therefore, some legitimate way of relaxing the requirements appears an attractive option to offer to the user. However, it becomes difficult to give a precise definition of the effect of an optimising attribute, even for a single compiler, and almost impossible to do so in a way that is satisfactory across different implementations.

5.2.2 Method of definition

5.2.2.1 *Readership and emphasis*

It is the defining document itself that creates the first immediate impression of a standard, and there is bound to be great diversity among the readers and their expectations. It is almost certainly impossible to satisfy the whole range, from a beginner's tutorial to precise definition, in a single document. Which, then, is the more important in a standard?

The Project chose to emphasise precise definition in the belief that the primary purpose of a standard is to serve as an authoritative reference. The greatest service that a language standard can perform for its users is to lead to consistent implementations. We contend that a higher degree of correctness can be achieved by providing a good definition in advance rather than by trying to detect variant interpretations afterwards. This may not remove the need for validation of standard compilers, but it does limit that validation to comparison of the compiler with the standard rather than requiring the validation procedures to complete the definition of the standard.

Given that the standard is in the nature of a paper implementation of the language, the question of the conformance between actual implementations and this definitive one had to be addressed, and section 1.2 of the standard does this with some care. The standard defines only what happens to error-free programs, and for these, despite all the internal mechanism required to achieve the results, it is only the sequence of changes to the datasets that is relevant. This is the sole visible effect of a program-run, and an implementation is free to achieve it by any means.

5.2.2.2 *Methodology development*

The refinement of the method of definition [5, 15] and the actual rewriting of the whole document were the responsibility of the Ad Hoc Editing Committee of ANSI/X3J1 and the I/O Subgroup of ECMA/TC 10 — about ten people scattered over two continents. The aim was to achieve precision without undue formalisation. Every increase in formality had to be justified by showing how it improved the actual definition work in progress. We concentrated on how to solve the specific problem of defining standard PL/I rather than developing a metalanguage in a vacuum, and right from the start wrote drafts of parts of the definition to see what situations would have to be dealt with in the metalanguage, and where it would have proved inadequate, imprecise or inconvenient. In the overall approach, there was obvious indebtedness to the pioneering work in the IBM Hursley [1] and Vienna [13] Laboratories.

The first stage was to cut-and-paste the existing document into the desired organisation. This aimed to describe systematically the translation and interpretation of any given sequence of characters supposed to represent a PL/I program. Already it dispensed with the redundancy that had been natural in a user manual, but had been presenting a maintenance problem as changes were made. Moreover, it began to remove the aura of mystery from the language — the lurking suspicion that it could not be understood without initiation into some folklore that was incapable of being captured in writing.

A first draft of the translator was written in which the algorithmic language was fairly free. However, the writing of the interpreter raised many problems that led to a more fully developed metalanguage. The interpreter chapters were necessarily introduced into the document all at once, since they were so interrelated. Finally, the translator was rewritten in the same metalanguage, and the translator and interpreter were united as phases of a complete definitional algorithm.

Reflecting on the experience, we have to admit that it is preferable not to have to develop a new metalanguage on the critical path of a standard. Furthermore, if the definition is being produced by authors around the world, much more precise written guidance is required than we began with. Even those present when a decision is taken cannot be relied upon to remember it. A 'Manual of Style' eventually helped but had to compete for resources with the actual writing of the definition — not unlike the implementation of a compiler while the language is still being defined.

The orderly and detailed algorithmic approach justified itself in bringing to light many errors and omissions that would otherwise have lain buried until implementers had to cope with them. As regards the notation, we felt that the advantage of a semi-formal, higher-level metalanguage over a totally formal one should in principle be like that of everyday mathematical notation over its expansion into formal logic — see reference [7]. If one accepts this, then one must beware of the slippery slope that leads to more formalisation to achieve a tiny increase in precision at the expense of general utility. Clearly, further study of the approach to semi-formal definition is needed – should a formal definition be produced first, then the semi-formal version be derived from it? Or is it possible to stay informal and come up with a result less formal than the present one? Can one take the existing definition and reduce the formality without essential loss of precision?

The method is obviously applicable to other procedural languages. It would be a worthwhile test of its utility to apply it to the definitions of Basic [4] and Fortran [3] to see whether it revealed significant errors and omissions, and, if so, whether these are easily remedied within an informal document or call for the semi-formal style. A more ambitious undertaking would be to define an operating system command and response language in this way by means of a suitably abstracted machine-state.

5.2.2.3 *Results and comments*

The result of an exercise like this almost always turns out to be less simple and elegant than envisaged. It was also in this case less complete, due to the absence of informal explanation and examples. This was largely attributable to the shortage of resources to provide these without unreasonably delaying the standard, and to some turnover in committee membership. However, another important contributory factor was the difficulty of writing this informal text – most prose was found to be misleading where not actually incorrect, and this is highly dangerous since such prose may easily gain wider currency than the correct definition. Examples were usually irrelevant to elucidation of the dark corners of the definition. Their redundancy also presented a maintenance problem if written too early, and we missed the split second before it became too late.

Among the 103 comments received on various aspects of the presentation of the standard, two were opposed to the definitional method as a whole, but most were seeking detailed improvements or supplementary material, and several explicitly commended the approach. The committees were also encouraged by the implicit evidence of understanding revealed by many of the perceptive and accurate comments about the language, including those from readers whose native tongue was not English, or who were remote from other sources of information about the content of the proposed standard.

As just indicated, there was general agreement that more explanatory notes and examples would have been desirable. These should be to assist in reading the standard as a precise document, and we do not believe that it can or should attempt to serve also as a tutorial on how to use the language. However, it is important to note two more ways in which the document is positively intended to help the user. Firstly, it should lead to the production of some unusually accurate tutorial texts by authors who are skilled at teaching programming languages. Secondly, many competent PL/I programmers will develop the ability to find in it answers to questions not covered in their everyday reference books.

5.3 CONCLUSION

The work proved to have more similarities than we anticipated to a large programming project, carried out on an industry-wide basis. It called for many of the same management and technical skills. It had the additional problems of part-time, geographically dispersed participants who belonged to different companies, some of them competing, yet it brought the stimulus of meeting distant and, on the whole, remarkably like-minded colleagues. Even the most vigorous disagreements left few hard feelings, a tribute either to the fairness of the decision-taking procedures or to the cooling-off time between meetings. The members of the project may have experienced some feeling of professional prestige in serving on an industry committee in this way — that is certainly the image we believe that future standardisation needs to have if it is to be successful. Increased awareness, respect, and participation will be steps along the road to true professional maturity.

Acknowledgements

We are grateful to many members of ANSI/X3J1 and ECMA/TC 10 whose work provided the factual basis for this chapter. All commentary expresses solely our personal opinions.

5.4 REFERENCES

[1] Allen, C. D. *et al.* (1966), An abstract interpreter of PL/I, TN3004, IBM Hursley.

[2] ANSI (1979), ANSI X3.53-1976: Programming Language PL/I.

[3] ANSI (1978), ANSI X3.9-1978: Programming Language Fortran.

[4] ANSI (1978), ANSI X3.60-1978; Programming language Basic.

[5] Beech, D. (1973), On the definitional method of standard PL/I, Conference record of ACM symposium on principles of programming languages, ACM SIGACT/SIGPLAN, 87-94.

[6] Beech, D. and Marcotty, M. (1973), Unfurling the PL/I standard, *SIGPLAN Not.*, 8, No. 10, 12-43.

[7] De Millo, R. A., Lipton, R. J., and Perlis, A. J. (1979), Social processes and proofs of theorems and programs, *Commun. ACM.*, 22, 271-280.

[8] ECMA (1976), ECMA-50: Standard for PL/I.

[9] GUIDE (1976), Guide PL/I group analysis of ANSI Standard PL/I, GUIDE International, Chicago.

[10] IBM (1968), PL/I language specifications, IBM GY33-6003.

[11] IBM (1976), OS PL/I checkout and optimizing compilers: language reference manual, IBM GC33-0009-4.

[12] ISO (1979), ISO 6160 Programming Language – PL/I.

[13] Lucas, P. and Walk, K. (1969), On the formal definition of PL/I, *Annu. Rev. Autom. Program.*, 6, 105-182.

[14] MacLaren, M. D. (1970), Data matching, data alignment and structure mapping in PL/I, *SIGPLAN Not.*, 5, No. 12, 30-43.

[15] Marcotty, M. and Sayward, F. G. (1977), The definition mechanism for standard PL/I, *IEEE Trans. Softw. Eng.*, SE-3, 416-450.

[16] Steel, T. B., Jr. (1975), The impact of standardisation, Proc. PL/1 symposium, Keystone, Colorado.

CHAPTER 6

Basic
by Dr. Gordon M. Bull

Basic, the first important language designed for use from an interactive terminal, has existed in various forms for many years, but did not begin to achieve major significance until the emphasis in computing began to shift noticeably away from batch processing. It started to become prominent with the spread of multi-access systems based on mainframes and minicomputers in the 1970s, and its use has mushroomed with the advent of microprocessors and personal computers, for which Basic has become the lingua franca. *This growth in use increased the importance and the urgency of standardising the language. The work to date is described in this chapter by Dr. Gordon M. Bull of the Department of Computer Science at Hatfield Polytechnic in the U.K., who, although from Britain, is a member of the ANSI/X3J2 committee which is responsible for Basic, as well as of BSI:DPS/13.*

6.1 HISTORY OF THE LANGUAGE

BASIC (Beginners All-purpose Symbolic Instruction Code) [1, 2] was invented by John Kemeny and Tom Kurtz of Dartmouth College in 1963–64. It was first implemented on a GE265 system – the original Dartmouth Time-sharing System. This same system was the basis for General Electric's initial world-wide time-sharing service. Basic has been implemented on almost every computer from major main-frames to the smallest micro-computer.

Each implementation of Basic has its roots in the various versions of the language produced at Dartmouth, so it is most instructive to trace these versions from 1964 to the present.

The first and second editions (they differed only marginally) consisted of those statements which may be regarded as the core of the language – LET, READ, DATA, PRINT, GOTO, IF–THEN, FOR, NEXT, GOSUB, RETURN, REMARK, DIM, single line DEFs, STOP and END. It is this set that almost all implementations include. It is also within this first version that four of the most important aspects of the language are to be found:

(i) Variables are self typing.

(ii) Line numbers serve both for editing and as statement labels.

(iii) There is only a single numeric data type of type 'number'.

(iv) The print statement automatically provides a simple formatted output suitable for a wide range of applications.

The third edition of the programming manual appeared in January 1966. By this time the INPUT and MAT statements had been added, and the language included RESTORE and a few more functions, and a few more commands had been added to the environment. By March 1967 the language included the RANDOMIZE and ON statements and the TAB function. The most significant advance at this stage was the inclusion of string variables.

The next significant advance was in July 1967 when multiline DEFs (at one time allowing recursion) were introduced, and more importantly, files. The inclusion of files, both terminal format and random access, meant adapting the READ, PRINT and INPUT statements and the inclusion of WRITE, RESET, SCRATCH and FILES statements. A further facility was provided with the introduction of the CHAIN and GOSUB file-number statements.

By February 1969, file input/output using MAT statements had been added as had LINPUT, IF-END, IF-MORE, MARGIN, CHANGE, and TIME statements. A number of standard string functions had also been added.

The fifth edition of the manual was published in September 1970, by which time LINPUT and MAT LINPUT from files were added. A version of subprograms was also included. The sixth edition which appeared in 1971 saw major changes to subprograms, files, the string package and output format control. The introduction of the CALL, SUB and SUBEND statements was the most significant change. The FILES statement was replaced by the FILE statement which provided run-time binding of file names to channel numbers. New string functions were added for substringing, and image formatting by including a string variable in the PRINT statement.

The seventh, and most recent version of the language which is due to appear towards the end of 1979 includes some radical changes to the language:

(i) Multicharacter identifiers.

(ii) Graphics statements.

(iii) Multi-line control structures including:

> IF-THEN-ELSE
> DO-LOOP with WHILE and UNTIL modifiers
> SELECT CASE

(iv) Revised substring notation.

(v) Revised matrix statements.

Thus we see a constant evolution of Basic, over a period of fifteen years. This is summed up by Kurtz [2] in the following way:

'Our goal was to provide our user community with friendly access to the computer. The design of BASIC was merely a tool to achieve this goal. We therefore felt completely free to redesign and modify BASIC as various features were found lacking. We have always remained loyal to our overall goals, while at the same time we allowed the language to grow to meet increasingly sophisticated tastes.'

6.2 HISTORY OF THE STANDARDISATION OF BASIC

In 1969, I was sponsored by the U.K. Department of Trade and Industry to conduct a survey on the uses of Basic and the need for a standard. The survey showed widespread use of the language in industry, commerce and education and strong support from users and implementors for a standard. Further support allowed me in 1973, in collaboration with others, to produce a specification for Basic as a candidate standard which was published by NCC [3]. In parallel with this work in the U.K., similar pressures were being exerted in the U.S.A. which led to a proposal being laid before ANSI/X3 for a sub-committee on Basic to be formed. This committee (X3J2) held its inaugural meeting in Washington DC in January 1974, and has met quarterly since then.

In Europe, partly due to the work in the U.K., ECMA set up a technical committee (TC 21) to work on Basic standardisation. This committee first met in Geneva in June 1974 and has been meeting quarterly since.

The International Purdue Workshop on Industrial Computer Systems operates as WG 5.4 of IFIP/TC 5, 'Common and/or Standardised Hardware and Software Techniques'. It set up a number of technical committees, one of which, TC 2, was concerned with Industrial Real-time Basic. This committee, working primarily in Europe and to a lesser extent in Japan, held its first meeting in April 1974; it has been meeting three times a year since. Finally, in 1974 the European Standards Organisation on Nuclear Electronics (ESONE) in collaboration with the U.S. Nuclear Instrumentation and Measurements Committee (NIM) set up a committee to standardise the use of Basic as applied to CAMAC interface systems.

Thus we see much activity on Basic standardisation throughout the world, starting in 1970, with a flurry of committees being set up in 1974, and continuing to the present day. Clearly if a 'standard' Basic was to emerge the work of the various committees had to be co-ordinated and a common goal agreed. The CAMAC standard was produced in 1975 (and amended in 1977) [4], and the principal authors of this document, being also members of TC 2 working on Industrial Real-time Basic, were able to feed into this committee their work on CAMAC, thus bringing together these two streams of development. Early in 1976 X3J2 and TC 21 agreed to co-operate in the production of a common standard for Basic; by May 1977 TC 2 were included in this agreement. The final version of this working agreement is summarised below [5].

The parties would work through an enhancements sub-committee whose membership consisted primarily of the chairmen of the various enhancement area working parties with myself in the chair. The next document X3J2 and TC 21 would produce would be the level 1 enhancements to Minimal Basic. The object of the co-operation was to attempt to produce compatible standards which subsequently could be submitted to ISO as the basis for an international standard. It was recognised that, however desirable this objective was, it might not be possible to achieve it. The working parties on each enhancement area were charged with producing the working documents in an agreed format.

In addition to this it was agreed to hold an annual joint meeting of the committees to resolve inter-committee problems, and these have been most successful. I have liaised between the three committees, attending most of the meetings of each, and acting as rapporteur. The initial outcome of this collaborative work was a common standard for Minimal Basic. The ANSI standard [6] and the ECMA standard [7] were both published in January 1978. These two standards differ in minor ways primarily reflecting the different approaches ANSI and ECMA take to standards, but also taking account of such minor things as the names of characters. (ECMA calls the character '.' 'point' whilst ANSI calls the same character 'period'.) The ANSI standard also has an appendix which gives the background to many of the decisions. This standard for Minimal Basic is currently being voted upon as an ISO standard [8]. A set of validation routines for this standard has been produced by the National Bureau of Standards in the U.S.A.

The current activity of the three committees is to produce a draft Basic standard enhanced beyond the minimal version.

6.3 FORM OF THE STANDARD

The ANSI standard for Minimal Basic describes a very simple language and includes those statements of Basic with which all users are familiar — LET, PRINT, READ, DATA, RESTORE, INPUT, IF, GOTO, GOSUB, RETURN, FOR, NEXT, ON, RANDOMIZE, DEF, DIM and REM. The standard consists of a number of sections, each of which defines a statement or related group of statements. The following description is taken from the standard [6]:

'General. This standard is organized into a number of sections, each of which covers particular features of BASIC. Most sections are divided into subsections, as described below.

Subsection 1: General Description. This subsection briefly describes the features of BASIC to be treated and indicates the general syntactic form of these features.

Subsection 2: Syntax. The syntax of BASIC is described by means of an extended Backus-Naur Form (BNF) notation.

For the sake of comprehensibility, the syntax in this standard occasionally describes constructions that are incorrect according to this standard; for example, the syntax allows the generation of the statement

100 LET X=A(1)+A(1,2)

in which the array A occurs with differing numbers of subscripts.

The primary goal of the syntax is to define the notion of a 'program' and its constituent parts. In addition, the syntax defines several other items that are not needed for the definition of a 'program'. These items are 'keyword', which denotes the set of keywords used in program statements; 'input-prompt', which denotes an element generated by the execution of an input-statement; 'input-reply', which denotes strings supplied by users in response to an input-prompt; 'end-of-input-reply', which denotes the termination of an input-reply; and 'end-of-print-line', which denotes a special character generated by the execution of a print-statement.

This standard does not include requirements for reporting specific syntactic errors in the text of a program. Implementations conforming to this standard may accept programs written in an enhancement language without reporting all constructs not conforming to this standard. However, whenever a statement or other program element does not conform to the syntactic rules given herein, either an error must be reported or the statement or other program element must have an implementation-defined meaning.

Subsection 3: Examples. A short list of valid examples that can be generated by certain of the rewriting rules in subsection 2 is given. The numbering of the examples corresponds to the numbering of the rewriting rules, and will not be consecutive if examples are not given for all rules.

Subsection 4: Semantics. The semantic rules in this standard serve two purposes. First, they rule out certain constructions that are permitted by the syntax but have no valid meaning according to this standard. Second, they assign a meaning to the remaining constructions.

Subsection 5: Exceptions. An exception occurs when an implementation recognizes that a program may not perform or is not performing in accordance with this standard. All exceptions described in this subsection must be reported unless some explicit mechanism provided in an enhancement to this standard has been invoked by the user to handle an exception. Additional exceptions may arise, for example, if an implementation runs out of resources while processing a program.

Where indicated, certain exceptions may be handled by specified procedures; if no procedure is given, or if restrictions imposed by the hardware or the operating environment make it impossible to follow the given procedures, then the exception must be handled by terminating the program.

Enhancements to this standard may describe mechanisms for controlling the manner in which exceptions are reported and handled, but no such mechanisms are specified in this standard.

This standard does not specify an order in which exceptions must be detected or processed.

Subsection 6: Remarks. Thus subsection contains remarks that point out certain features of this standard as well as remarks that make recommendations concerning the implementation of a BASIC language processor in an operating environment.'

The syntax of the language is defined in an extended BNF, designed so as to be printable on most computer printing devices, and first used in the specification published by the NCC [3]. An innovation in language standardisation, again based on [3], is the identification by the standard of exceptions which can arise at run-time, the specification of the recovery procedure for each such exception, and the inclusion of the requirement for conforming implementations to process exceptions as specified by the standard. The full conformance rules are as follows [6]:

'**Conformance.** There are two aspects of conformance to this language standard: conformance by a program written in the language, and conformance by an implementation that processes such programs.

Conformance by a program. A program is said to conform to this standard only under the following conditions:

(1) Each statement contained therein is a syntactically valid instance of a statement specified in this standard.

(2) Each statement has an explicitly valid semantic meaning specified herein.

(3) The totality of statements composes an instance of a valid program that has an explicitly valid meaning specified herein.

Conformance by an implementation. An implementation is said to conform to this standard only under the following conditions:

(1) It accepts and processes programs conforming to this standard.

(2) It reports reasons for rejecting any program that does not conform to this standard (although it need not reject all such programs if it implements a superset of the BASIC language described herein).

(3) It detects and processes exceptional circumstances according to the specifications of this standard.

(4) It interprets the semantics of each statement of a standard-conforming program according to the specification in this standard.

(5) It interprets the semantics of a standard-conforming program as a whole according to the specifications in this standard.

(6) It accepts as input, manipulates, and can generate as output numbers of at least the precision and range specified in this standard.

(7) It is accompanied by documentation that describes the actions taken in regard to features referred to in this standard as 'undefined' or 'implementation-defined'.'

6.4 SCOPE OF THE PROPOSED STANDARD

The draft standard for Enhanced Basic (this is not necessarily the title of the standard; that has yet to be decided) includes a number of functional areas. These areas are listed below in a way that reflects the way that three committees carried out the work rather than the way the conformance rules will be written. That is, it is unlikely that the conformance rules will demand that a conforming implementation provide all the features described in Enhanced Basic. It is planned that rules will be written which allow implementors to select sections of the language much in the way Cobol identifies sections and levels. At the time of writing the conformance rules had not been decided.

The main areas are: Graphics, Files, Subprograms, Chaining, Strings, Matrices, Mathematical Functions, Editing, Debugging, Exception Handling, Real-time, Alternative Data Types, Formatting, and a general extension to the core of the language (called Nucleus). In producing the draft standard for Enhanced Basic, each working group produced formal definition documents for their given area in two levels, where level 1 was that set of minimal capabilities which made the enhancement area viable, and level 2 was an extension to this set of capabilities. Such loose definitions have on the whole served the committees well and enabled the level 1 language to be kept as small as possible. The draft standard contains only the level 1 items. The object of producing the level 2 documents was primarily to enable discussion to take place as to what was level 1 (and would therefore be a candidate for inclusion in the current draft) and what was level 2.

Since producing the standard for Minimal Basic, a number of suggestions for improvements have been made on the method of presentation. One, which is also included in the ISO version at the suggestion of Japan, is to print in boldface in the semantics all references to metanames from the syntax productions. In this way it is clear when a given English word, or group of words, is being used in a specific rather than general way. Another recent suggestion is to extract from the semantics those descriptive sections which are limitations on the syntax, and include them in the syntax section.

6.5 CURRENT PROBLEM AREAS

One of the main reasons for the worldwide interest in standardising Basic was the realisation that the name 'BASIC' was becoming meaningless. In 1974 it was possible to buy translators for languages calling themselves Basic which ranged from Minimal Basic through to well beyond what is likely to appear in the Enhanced Basic standard. With such a wide variety of Basics available it was decided that it was sensible to standardise Minimal Basic first since it was assumed that everyone would agree on this, and later produce a standard for an enhanced version of the language. In the event it took four years to complete the standard for Minimal Basic and even now this standard contains a construction – OPTION BASE – that is very contentious.

The OPTION BASE statement provides an interesting insight into the problems of standardisation. Given that the standardisation process is primarily to adopt current practices, at least one aspect of Basic, the lower bound of arrays, had given rise to two common practices – a lower bound for all array subscripts of 0 and of 1. Whenever X3J2 voted on the matter the vote was split equally. The various arguments used in support of their position are summarised below [6]:

'The problem of whether the default lower bound for array subscripts should be zero of one proved to be the most difficult problem for the committee to resolve. Briefly, the arguments revolved around the following considerations:

(1) *User convenience.* Those in favour of zero as the default felt that many mathematical applications, such as the evaluation of polynomials, made natural use of the zeroth element of a vector, and that to disallow this use in Minimal Basic or to permit it only through the inclusion of a statement to override the default in the program would defeat the pedagogical advantage of Basic. Those in favour of one as the default felt that the number of users who needed a subscript value of zero was too small in comparison to the total number of Basic users that this concern should not dictate the choice of the default.

(2) *Storage requirements.* Those in favour of one as the default felt that reserving space for the zeroth row and column of arrays, when most programs did not use them created an inefficient use of core storage, thereby making it difficult for minicomputer implementations to handle programs of a reasonable size. Those in favour of zero as a default felt that the needs of novices wanting to use a subscript value of zero came before those of the presumably more sophisticated programmer trying to squeeze a large program onto a small machine.

(3) *Conformance to the standard.* Those in favour of a default of zero argued that all current programs, whether written for implementations with a default of zero or for implementations with a default of one, would conform to a standard that set the default at zero but not to one that set the default at one. Those in favour of one

as the default argued that since most programs did not use subscripts whose value was zero, conformance was not a problem.

Both sides eventually agreed that the choice of the default would make no difference to the majority of users of Basic, since their programs neither used subscripts with a value of zero nor had stringent space requirements. However, it is equally clear that neither side would accept a standard that refused to deal with its concerns. Hence the X3J2 Subcommittee sought to find a compromise solution acceptable to both sides.

The compromise chosen was to have the standard specify the default lower bound, but also to have it give the user a means of overriding this default. It was recognized that no such mechanism for overriding the default was commonly implemented at the present time, and that ordinarily such a state of affairs would exclude any such mechanism from inclusion in any standard for Minimal Basic. On the other hand, there appeared to be no other solution to the impasse, and such mechanisms did exist in some current Basic implementations, as well as in several other common programming languages such as Algol 68 and PL/I. Hence it was finally decided to include a mechanism in Minimal Basic for specifying both the upper and lower bounds for array subscripts, and to set the default lower bound to zero. Originally a variant of the DIM statement was proposed for setting the lower bound of each array subscript individually; later discussion resulted in a preference for a mechanism which would set all lower bounds to one or to zero simultaneously.

In this case, as in several others, it was felt that user convenience was a more important factor than consistency, either with other programming languages or with other constructions in the same programming language. Furthermore, there is an important difference between indices of elements in an array and indices of columns in a print line or line-numbers in an on-goto-statement. In the case of print lines or on-goto-statements, users are forced to use the indexing positions sequentially, starting from the first; hence they must be aware of what the smallest possible index is and they must use it. In the case of arrays, users are not forced to use any particular indexing positions at all, and so they need not be aware of the smallest possible index. The default lower bound of zero was chosen so that no user need be aware of the lower bound for array subscripts; if one had been chosen as the lower bound, then those who wanted to use a subscript of zero would have to be aware of the default lower bound, in violation of the Basic tenet that users must learn only what is absolutely necessary.

It was decided to use an option-statement, OPTION BASE 1, rather than a simpler base statement, BASE 1, to override the default lower bound since such a statement could be used for similar purposes in enhancements to this standard, thereby reducing the potential number of new statements to be added to the language.'

The OPTION BASE statement was reluctantly accepted by TC 21 and appears in the ECMA and ANSI standards for Minimal Basic. It is interesting to note that when the standard for Minimal Basic was circulated as a draft ISO standard this was the only aspect to cause a country to vote against the adoption of the draft.

In working towards a draft for Enhanced Basic, some areas proved to be relatively simple to reach agreement on and others very difficult. The various areas in the draft can be broadly classified into three categories:

(i) *Straightforward*

Areas in this category are those where, like Minimal, a large amount of agreement existed amongst the various implementations, or, where there was more than one version, one of these was seen to be superior in some way. Areas in this category are strings, array handling, formatting, mathematical functions (although the spelling of some were hotly contested), chaining, subprograms and editing (although ECMA may not include editing commands as part of their standard since they believe only the language itself should be standardised).

(ii) *Contentious*

Areas in this category are those which exhibit the widest divergence in the various implementations and where the committees find it difficult to identify the 'best' way of providing a given facility. Areas in this category are files (often reflecting the underlying filing system provided by the operating system), exception handling (a complex aspect of any language and one which no other language has satisfactorily solved), debugging and alternative data types (such as decimal, extended real, integer, etc. the main disagreement being whether simple variables in Basic should be self typing or declared).

(iii) *New functional capabilities in the language*

Basic is by no means a static language, and within the period of standard-isation, two major areas have emerged — Graphics and Real-time. Although few implementations exist which provide these functional capabilities, the decision was taken to standardise in these areas. The real-time feature has gone through many iterations but commands a good measure of agreement. The graphics feature after some early disagreements seems to be progressing well. The proposal introduces the PLOT statement, which is modelled on the PRINT statement, to control the drawing device. This approach is in contrast to other languages which use subroutine calls to achieve the same end.

A recent inclusion in the core of the language has been comprehensive control structures along the lines of the seventh edition of Dartmouth Basic.

6.6 SUMMARY

In summary I would make the following observations on the Basic standardisation process:

(a) A wordwide need was felt for the standardisation of the language and led to a number of independent activities.

(b) International co-operation and a distribution of the work between national and international committees is possible and has been most fruitful.

(c) The use of a widely available (in the U.S.A.) time-sharing system for document production and maintenance greatly simplified the work and ensured a consistent form of presentation.

6.7 REFERENCES

[1] Bull, G. M. (1971), Basic – its growth and development, *J. Inst. Comput. Sci.*, 3, No. 3.

[2] Kurtz, T. E. (1978), Basic. Proc. ACM Sigplan history of programming languages conference.

[3] Bull, G. M., Freeman, W., and Garland, S. J. (1973), Specification for standard Basic, NCC.

[4] ESONE (1977) Real-time Basic for CAMAC, ESONE/RTB/02 (published simultaneously by NIM as TID–26619).

[5] ANSI (1977) Cooperation between ECMA, ANSI and Purdue on enhancements to Minimal Basic, X3J3/77-25 (published simultaneously as ECMA/ TC 21/77/18E).

[6] ANSI (1978), ANSI X3.60: Programming Language Minimal Basic.

[7] ECMA (1978), Standard ECMA-55 Minimal Basic.

[8] ISO (1978), Draft standard for Minimal Basic, ISO/TC 97/SC 5 N447 Part 1, DP 6373.

CHAPTER 7

Pascal

by Anthony M. Addyman

Another language which, having been in existence for some years, has been the subject of a recent upsurge of interest, is Pascal. Again this led to a need for work on standardisation, as implementations multiplied and variations and extensions began to creep in. One of those principally involved in the Pascal standardisation effort is Anthony M. Addyman of the Department of Computer Science at the University of Manchester in the U.K., who became chairman of BSI: DPS/13 in 1978, has acted as co-ordinator of the international work on Pascal and is convenor of ISO/TC97/SC5/WG4. In this chapter he describes the current state of progress of this work.

7.1 INTRODUCTION

The standardisation of a programming language is a long and complex activity. In the attempt to clarify my description of the standardisation of Pascal I would like to consider a number of different aspects, as independently as possible.

To give an impression of the timescale and the non-technical work involved a brief history of the project is given, considering the activities in several different countries. The second part of the chapter describes, without going into great detail, the technical issues facing the drafting group. The third part of this chapter describes some very important factors which have contributed to the success of the project to date. The final part describes what effects the standardisation has had, in my opinion, so far.

7.2 HISTORY

7.2.1 U.K. activities

To assist BSI: DPS/13 a system of informal working groups has evolved. Each working group is responsible for one topic, usually a single language. A working group is organised by a member of the committee, who is designated the 'rapporteur' for the topic by DPS/13. The working group consists of a number

of willing, technically competent computer professionals from industry, government organisations, universities and polytechnics. Since voting is not used to
resolve differences within BSI committees, there is not the need to ensure that
each vested interest has the appropriate number of people. The main problem in
recent years has been the lack of available manpower within the BSI itself, which
has resulted in a far smaller involvement by the professional standardisers in the
efforts of the computer professionals.

The standardisation of Pascal within DPS/13 began in a very small way in
March 1976, when I asked at a meeting why Pascal was not on the agenda of
DPS/13. This resulted in a request that I should provide the committee with a
brief note concerning Pascal. Several members also suggested that the views of
Professor Wirth, who originated the language, should be sought on the subject
of its standardisation. In June a letter was received from Professor Wirth [13]
welcoming the idea of declaring an official standard. The note on Pascal was
presented at the September meeting of DPS/13 by which time a rapporteur had
been appointed.

At the June 1977 meeting it was proposed that there should be a project
whose aim was the production of a British/International Standard for Pascal.
The request was forwarded by DPS/13 to the committee responsible (DPS/-/1)
and I was asked to convene a working group designated DPS/13: WG/4. The
request for a project for Pascal was approved in September, but the remaining
DPS/13 meetings held in 1977 were largely concerned with the preparation for
and results of the ISO/TC 97/SC 5 meeting held in The Hague in November.

7.2.2 International activities

At the request of the U.K., Pascal was added to the agenda of the meeting in
The Hague. A move by the British delegation to have Pascal added to the work
program of SC 5 was prevented on procedural grounds. It was stated that it was
necessary to refer the matter to TC 97 who would conduct a letter ballot. The
British delegation indicated its intention to follow this course of action, and
consequently the December meeting of DPS/13 requested DPS/-/1 to take the
necessary action. DPS/-/1 referred the matter back to DPS/13 stating, not
unreasonably, that its approval of the British project implied its approval of an
international one. A proposal [3] to be sent to ISO was drafted by the rapporteur
and presented to the March 1978 meeting of DPS/13, and after minor alteration
was sent to ISO.

In October 1978 the result of the letter ballot was announced. Eight member
bodies had supported the proposal and one (Japan) did not support it. There
were ten abstentions. The countries voting in favour were Brazil, Canada,
Germany, Italy, Netherlands, U.K., U.S.A., and U.S.S.R. Two of the countries
added comments to their votes; the Netherlands expressed doubt as to whether
the usage of Pascal was great enough to justify standardisation: the U.S.A. vote
was conditional on the deletion of the last sentence of the proposal, which

stated 'It is not intended that the standardisation effort will involve any development of the language'.

In February 1979, the British draft for public comment (79/60528 DC) was sent to ISO for circulation to member bodies as an ISO working draft (ISO/TC 97/SC 5 N462). The ISO working draft was also published by the IEEE [12].

In September 1979, the fourth working draft (ISO/TC 97/SC 5 N510) was sent to ISO for circulation prior to its discussion at the ISO Pascal Experts Group meeting in Turin, Italy in November. The meeting in Turin resulted in changes to be incorporated in a fifth working draft, which was to be circulated to the members of the Experts Group in December, and a recommendation that the document after correction of any typographical errors, etc. should become a Draft Proposal, and a recommendation to the SC 5 plenary session concerning the formation of an ISO Working Group. These recommendations formed resolutions of the plenary session and were subsequently approved. The Draft Proposal was sent to ISO for comment and letter ballot in February 1980. The first meeting of the ISO Working Group is expected in late June 1980 to consider the outcome of the ballot. The draft Proposal also appeared in SIGPLAN Notices [7].

7.2.3 U.S. activities

In the United States, two standardising bodies have been involved in what were initially separate projects, namely the Institute of Electrical and Electronic Engineers (IEEE) and the American National Standards Institute (ANSI). The development of their projects will be described separately.

7.2.3.1 *IEEE activities*

In July 1978 the Computer Society of the IEEE began a project concerned with Higher Level Languages for Microprocessors. Following the Pascal Workshop at the University of California, San Diego (UCSD) several members of the IEEE became convinced that the production of an IEEE standard for Pascal, which could be produced more quickly than an ANSI standard, would be of benefit to the computer industry. Their activities resulted in the Higher Level Language group limiting itself to Pascal, and to the formation in December 1978 of a Standard Co-ordinating Committee on Higher Order Languages. In January 1979 the Computer Society submitted a Project Authorization Request (PAR) to the IEEE Standards Board for approval.

The IEEE Pascal committee held its first meeting on 29th January 1979 in Los Angeles, chaired by Bruce Ravenel. The meeting resulted in the passing of two motions (both unanimously) and the formation of two sub-committees. The first motion concerned the preparation of a review document on the U.K. draft — N462; and the second offered support to the corresponding ANSI committee. X3J9. The two sub-committees, to be chaired by Bill Price and

Craig Snow, were formed to review the BSI/ISO document and to consider language extensions to Pascal, respectively. Thus the IEEE Standards Committee has associated itself very closely with the BSI activity. Their stated intention [12] was to use the British draft, revised as a result of the comments received during the comment period, as a basis for a proposed IEEE standard.

7.2.3.2 *ANSI activities*

The ANSI involvement in the standardisation of Pascal came as a direct result of the BSI proposal to ISO concerning a Pascal project. In October 1978, X3 voted in favour of the U.K. submission to ISO concerning the formation of a Pascal project. At this same meeting a motion was passed to establish an X3 Technical Committee which would write an SD-3 (the term used to describe a proposal for initiating a standards development project) to develop an American National Standard for Pascal and to provide the U.S.A. focal point for input to the development of the corresponding international standard by ISO. The SD-3 was to be submitted for approval by X3 at its meeting in February 1979. The committee thus formed was designated X3J9.

The first meeting of X3J9 was held in Washington DC in December 1978. The meeting was primarily concerned with matters of administration and organisation. A group of volunteers was formed to work on the SD-3, led by Justin Walker of the National Bureau of Standards. In addition, the following motion was passed unanimously: 'X3J9 accept the BSI: DPS/13: WG/4 working draft 3 as an initial input for consideration in the development of an American National Standard for Pascal'.

The second meeting of X3J9 was held on February 1979 in Costa Mesa, California. This meeting was, in fact, also a meeting of the IEEE Pascal Committee. This meeting resulted in the formation of three Task Groups — two *ad hoc* and one standing — subject to the approval of X3. The *ad hoc* groups were concerned with production of an SD-3 and a technical review of the BSI draft which had been circulated to ISO member bodies. The standing task group is concerned with language extensions. It was decided however that no evaluation of extensions was to take place before June 1979. Also at the second meeting nominations were made for the officers of X3J9 — the chairman, vice-chairman and international liaison. Jess Irwin had volunteered to be secretary at the first meeting.

In March, Marius Troost of Sperry-Univac and Scott Jameson of Hewlett-Packard were appointed as chairman and vice-chairman respectively. The third meeting of X3J9 was held in April in Boulder, Colorado. Much of the meeting was spent discussing the interim report of the Technical Review Task Group (TRTG). This report received tentative approval. Final processing of the report was deferred to the June meeting to give members a greater opportunity to study the report and the BSI draft. The April meeting did, however, result in the passing, unanimously, of a motion requesting us to avoid enhancement of the language.

This motion was their response to the suggestion that the language be extended to permit the passing to a procedure, as a parameter, an array whose bounds were not determined by the declaration of the procedure. Several important organisational changes also took place at the April meeting. Firstly, the effective absorption of the IEEE committee by X3J9 was ratified by both committees. A standing TRTG was established to replace the *ad hoc* one, the chairman remaining as Bill Price of Tektronix.

The June meeting was devoted to consideration of N462. The fifth meeting, in September, was given over almost entirely to procedural matters – mostly the correct name for the committee! The sixth meeting, in November, reviewed the Turin meeting which preceded it and an *ad hoc* meeting which had been held earlier in November, before the SC 5 meeting, to examine the fourth working draft.

7.2.3.3 *The Pascal Standard Co-ordinating Committee*

In January 1979, the IEEE hosted a meeting in San Francisco in an attempt to resolve some of the problems caused by the two U.S. activities. This meeting was held between various individuals from X3J9, IEEE, PUG and myself. It was suggested that this group establish itself as a self-recognising Steering Committee to work on co-ordinating the technical efforts within X3J9 and IEEE. However, the two written reports [8, 11] of the meeting differ, with each other and with my recollections. Fortunately, either as a result of the efforts of those involved, or in spite of them, a single U.S. activity has been created.

7.2.3.4 *The Joint ANSI/X3J9–IEEE Pascal Standards Committee*

The Joint Pascal Committee is the result of the merger of X3J9 and the IEEE Pascal Committee, using X3 rules and procedures. Although the two committees from which it was formed still exist, they are now inactive.

7.2.4 European activities

My knowledge of activities on Pascal standardisation in the rest of Europe is somewhat limited. Three countries are known to be active – Sweden, France and Germany. The Swedish Technical Committee on Pascal has been in existence since 1977. Liaison between the Swedish Committee and DPS/13: WG/4 was established as a result of the ISO/TC97/SC 5 meeting in The Hague in November 1977. The *official* activities in France and Germany are very new, their first meetings being in Paris in April 1979 and West Berlin in May 1979, respectively. Both countries have, however, the equivalent of nationally organised Pascal User Groups. The French group has had a standards sub-committee since mid-1977.

7.2.5 The work of DPS/13: WG/4

Although it has achieved much since its creation in June 1977, this working group has only actually met on five occasions. Most of the progress has been due to individual members' efforts.

The first meeting was held in September 1977 in London. This meeting decided that the group should begin by identifying the problems with the current definitions of Pascal rather than their solutions. Several members presented Attention Lists styled after the original one published in Pascal News [4]. As a result of the lack of progress during the meeting the convenor was given the responsibility of combining the Attention Lists of the members together with those received from other members of the Pascal Users Group (PUG) and with performing a literature search to examine all published criticisms of Pascal. This effort resulted in the production of Attention List No. 2 in January 1978.

The second meeting of DPS/13: WG/4 took place in London in April 1978. This meeting welcomed a representative from the Swedish Technical Committee with whom DPS/13: WG/4 had been exchanging papers since the meeting in The Hague. The main result of this meeting was the decision to produce a draft, for which a timetable was proposed by Brian Wichmann and accepted by the group. This proposal made each section of the draft, which at that time corresponded with a section of the Revised Report [9], the responsibility of two members of the group. They would produce a draft for their section(s) by the end of May, members would then correspond during June and July to attempt to resolve any differences, and a revised draft would be produced by the end of August. A meeting would be held in September to discuss this draft and resolve any remaining differences. What actually happened was rather different!

The sections which together made up the first working draft were in my hands by mid-July 1978 (six weeks later than intended) but only a small number of them in machine-readable form. In late June I accepted an invitation to attend the UCSD Pascal Workshop, which took place in the second half of July, when the working draft was discussed informally and a number of valuable contributions were received. On my return to the U.K. in August, with the agreed timetable in ruins, I unilaterally decided to produce the second working draft, to incorporate suggestions made during the San Diego discussions. A certain amount of editing and reworking was also necessary, as might be expected, to produce a single document from the contributions of eleven individuals. These two working drafts were converted into machine readable form and sent to members in late August.

The third meeting, in September 1978, adopted the second working draft as a basis for its work and decided upon a number of changes. The meeting instructed me to make these changes and create the third working draft, which was to be sent to the BSI secretariat for editorial comment.

While in the U.S.A. I had undertaken to make the draft produced by DPS/13: WG/4 available to certain interested parties, in particular the IEEE and the Pascal Users Group, in an effort to stimulate some U.S. comments on the document. There was at the time no forum in which the matter could be discussed in the U.S.A. and it was felt to be unlikely that many people there would send to BSI for their draft for comments. The third working draft was published in Pascal News, and in Software − Practice and Experience [1, 2].

The BSI secretary completed his editorial corrections by January 1979. These were implemented and the resulting document formed the draft for public comment (79/60528 DC).

As a result of the comment period I received a considerable amount of correspondence. A proportion of this was through official standards channels but much of it came about as a result of the publication of the draft in Pascal News, IEEE Computer and Software – Practice and Experience. These comments were collected into two reports [5,6] with considerable assistance from my mother and my wife. The first of these reports helped to shape the fourth working draft. The second report consists of very late comments.

In September 1979, DPS/13: WG/4 met to prepare the fourth working draft and consider the controversial issues thrown up by the comment period. The group was under considerable pressure to produce a revised draft because of the proximity of the ISO experts meeting in Turin. So although a revised draft was produced it did not really satisfy the group as a whole.

Immediately before the Turin meeting the group met again to review the decisions of the previous meeting. Assisted by the presence of Arthur Sale, the group came to doubt the correctness of some of the alterations which the fourth working draft contained, and suggested alternatives. Arthur Sale and I went to Turin armed with this knowledge. In particular the group preferred the Sale proposal for 'conformant arrays' to the one incorporated in the fourth working draft.

7.3 THE TECHNICAL ISSUES

The central issue facing the drafters was that concerning language extensions. At the suggestion of Brian Wichmann each item on the Attention List had been classified as a clarification, a modification or an extension. The convener of DPS/13: WG/4 gave an undertaking to the Pascal Users Group they would not 'fiddle' with the language. Fortunately this was in accord with the views of a majority of its members.

It will be, of course, impossible to discuss all the technical issues exposed by the standardisation process in the space available here, but I have undertaken to try to produce such a discussion elsewhere when the Draft Proposal has been accepted and becomes a Draft International Standard. To enable the reader to obtain an impression of the issues, I shall briefly examine two of some importance. These two issues are quite different: the first is essentially a clarification – an attempt to answer the question 'When are two objects of the same type?'; the second is nothing less than a language extension – the syntax has been altered so that the language may be used in applications where it could not previously.

7.3.1 When are two objects of the same type?

It is rather surprising, if not amazing, that such a fundamental question should be in need of clarification; nevertheless before the draft standard was produced the only answers (and there were several) to this question were to be found in the source code of the compilers. There are quite a few different ways in which this question may be answered. For simplicity let us restrict the discussion to two approaches when applied to variables:

(a) *By name*

This is also known as 'Name Equivalence'. Two variables are of the same type if they were declared using the same type-identifier (allowing for the effect of the scope rules) or in the same declaration. This is a fairly strong rule because objects exhibiting the same structure (for example, two arrays with the same index-type and the same component-type) need not be of the same type. This approach offers the user good type security and as a bonus ensures that packed and non-packed forms are distinct.

NOTE (For those unfamiliar with Pascal) — a programmer may specify that a particular type should be packed, to indicate that objects of that type should have their storage requirements reduced even at the expense of greater code complexity. To permit the unrestricted mixture of packed and non-packed forms, for example as procedure parameters, would introduce unacceptable overheads into the compilers.

(b) *By structure*

This is also known as 'Structural Equivalence'. In this case two variables are of the same type if they have the same structure. So all arrays with the same component-type and the same index-type (or number of components) are considered to be of the same type. This approach can have its problems. For example, one must decide whether packing alters the structure. Another difficulty is the fact that the protection offered by types is reduced. So, for example, all records with two components of real type are of the same type and may have their values assigned to one another. Yet in the program they may represent a rectangle, or a complex number (in Cartesian form), or a complex number (in Polar form) or a bank balance with a credit limit etc.

The issue is further complicated by the realisation that there are further questions to be asked, leading on to the definition of 'type compatibility' between two types and 'assignment compatibility' between a value and a type.

7.3.2 Conformant array parameters

In the Pascal of Jensen and Wirth [9] the index-type of an array is part of its type. Since the declaration of a procedure necessitates the specification of the types of the parameters, it is clear that a procedure parameter of an array type can only accept objects of that type. In particular, a general procedure to do matrix multiplication could not be written. To allow such procedures to be written, a new form of parameter was needed, one which did not specify the type of the actual parameter. Instead it simply specifies the characteristics to which the actual parameter must conform. Hence the term Conformant Array Parameters.

Here then the problems are quite different. Firstly, there is the decision as to whether or not to bow to pressure to extend the language to solve this problem; then there are the language design issues of how best to provide such a facility. Dynamic arrays as in Algol 60? Parameters with adjustable bounds as in Fortran? If the latter, should value parameters be allowed? What about packed arrays? Should the bounds be available to the program (as in Algol 68) and if so how should this be done? Or should the programmer pass extra parameters as in Algol 60? etc. etc.? Whether the solution arrived at in such circumstances is 'correct' or not is very often a matter of taste rather than of fact. Fortunately, as a result of the policy that 'There shall be no change!' these language design issues have been rare in the standardisation of Pascal.

7.3.3 Resolution of the issues

For the record, the two issues have been resolved thus: (i) a variation on Name Equivalence has been chosen; (ii) a decision was taken to extend the language to introduce conformant array parameters in which the bounds are available to the program; value parameters are not permitted and neither are packed arrays. These two restrictions are currently the subject of debate.

The only way fully to appreciate the work done by DPS/13: WG/4 and the many people who have assisted them is to compare the Revised Report with either the third working draft or the draft for public comment. The most noticeable differences between the documents are the section on lexical issues, the clarification of the scope rules, a statement of the rules governing type compatibility, the very detailed specification of the input and output procedures and the use of the terms implementation-defined, implementation-dependent and error.

7.4 CONTRIBUTORY FACTORS

Although the standardisation of Pascal has progressed as the result of the efforts of those working to that end, these efforts have been assisted significantly by the actions of others.

7.4.1 The Pascal Users Group

This group, which now has about 5000 members in over 40 countries, is not a representative body; rather it is a special interest group which produces a quarterly newsletter. Nevertheless it was possible to conclude from the correspondence of members that there was no opposition to the production of a standard. In addition it was possible to identify interested people in several countries who would be willing to contribute.

7.4.2 The Southampton symposium, March 1977

A symposium was held at the University of Southampton on 'Pascal — the Language and its Implementation'. At the symposium the final afternoon was given over to the subject of standardisation [10]. The proposal made at the June 1977 DPS/13 meeting was a direct result of this discussion. The symposium also brought together many Pascal users in the U.K. and Europe. As a result, many of the members of DPS/13: WG/4 knew one another in advance.

7.4.3 The UCSD workshop on systems programming extensions to Pascal, July 1978

This workshop made significant contributions to the international effort. It gave an opportunity to a number of people from the U.S. to discuss the first working draft with the convener of DPS/13: WG/4 and with Arthur Sale and Jeff Tobias from Australia. Arthur Sale later became the chairman of the Australian Pascal Committee. In addition it allowed many of those present to build up a working relationship with the convenor of DPS/13: WG/4. As many of those actively involved in the ANSI and IEEE efforts attended the UCSD workshop, this has facilitated international co-operation. A final contribution of the workshop was to convince many people that it was difficult if not impossible to achieve any consensus on extensions to Pascal!

7.4.4 The international working group on Pascal extensions

This group was formed in January 1979 by Professor Wirth at the suggestion of Professor J. Steensgaard-Madsen, and was made up almost entirely of implementors of Pascal. It was formed in the hope that agreement could be reached among them on the form that a limited number of extensions to Pascal might take. It also discussed clarifications. These discussions, especially the letters from Professor Wirth, influenced the drafts produced by DPS/13: WG/4.

7.5 THE EFFECTS OF THE STANDARDISATION EFFORT

Even though the standard has not yet been completed, the standards project has had a significant impact both inside and outside the U.K.

Inside the U.K. the effect has been to increase the awareness of Pascal within the U.K. computer industry. In this regard it should be noted that in my view the production of a British Standard for Pascal, in isolation, could not be justified when the project began. The BSI activity was seen by its supporters as being on behalf of the international computing community.

In the U.S.A., the draft for public comment has provided a large number of computer manufacturers and software houses with a better definition of Pascal than any previously available. It has helped to prevent unnecessary differences from appearing due to differing interpretations of those matters which were in need of clarification. It is my firmly held belief that a standard for Pascal would have proved impossible had the BSI project not started when it did and spawned the ISO project, because the creation of X3J9 has uncovered a large number of companies (in excess of 200) involved in the production of Pascal products. Many of these are still in the formative stages.

If the formation of X3J9 had had to await the announcement of these products and an awareness of the need for standardisation caused by their differences, the task would surely have been impossible.

7.6 A PERSONAL NOTE

So much has happened during the standardisation effort to date, that I find it difficult to recall my original, personal motives for wanting a standard for Pascal. I was undoubtedly influenced by a desire to have a good definition from which to write a compiler — a compiler whose writing is still being prevented by my standards activities! I was also made aware of inadequacies in the User Manual and Report [9] during discussions to introduce a new programming language for initial teaching at Manchester.

7.7 REFERENCES

[1] Addyman, A. M. *et al.* (1979), A draft description of Pascal, *Softw. Pract. Exper.*, **9**, 381-424.

[2] Addyman, A. M. (1979), The BSI working draft 3, *Pascal News*, **14**, 7-54.

[3] Addyman, A. M. (1979), The ISO Pascal proposal, *Pascal News*, **14**, 58-60.

[4] Addyman, A. M. (1977), An attention list, *Pascal News*, **8**, 30-32.

[5] Addyman, A. M. (1980), Comments on a draft description of Pascal, JPC/ 80-012, AD Micrographics.

[6] Addyman, A. M. (1980), Further comments on a draft description of Pascal, JPC/80-013, AD Micrographics.

[7] Addyman, A. M. (1980), A Pascal draft proposal, *SIGPLAN Not.*, **15**, No. 4, 1-66.

[8] ANSI (1979), Minutes of the IEEE/Pascal Committee meeting, X3J9/ 79-064.

[9] Jensen, K. and Wirth, N. (1975), Pascal user manual and report, Springer Verlag.

[10] Mickel, A. B. (1977), The future of Pascal, *Pascal News*, **8**, 28-30.

[11] Miner, J. (1979), Review of Pascal standardization effort, ANSI X3J9/ ·79-012.

[12] Ravenel, B. W. (1979), Towards a Pascal standard, *Computer*, **12**, No. 4, 68-82.

[13] Wirth, N. (1976), Private communication.

CHAPTER 8

Real-time languages
by Nicholas J. F. Neve

An application of computers of increasing importance is that of real-time control of processes, such as industrial automation. Various languages have been developed to assist in programming real-time systems, and again standardisation is an important issue. ISO/TC 97/SC 5 has a working group, WG 1, to cover this area, and the author of this chapter, Nicholas J. F. Neve, was until 1979 a member of the working group and its U.K. equivalent. He is at the Royal Signals and Radar Establishment at Malvern, which originally developed Coral 66 and continues to provide validation and support services for it on behalf of the British Ministry of Defence.

8.1 SCOPE

This chapter, unlike Chapters 2–7 which each discuss a single language, covers a number of real-time high level languages or real-time extensions to existing general purpose high level languages that have become the subject of some form of standardisation activity in recent years.

The description 'Languages for Industrial Process Control' or 'Industrial Real-time' (IRT) are often used in place of 'real-time languages' and this is reflected in the informal title given to ISO/TC 97/SC 5/WG 1 which is known as PLIP (Programming Languages for the control of Industrial Processes). This is the international group responsible at working level for processing real-time languages submitted to ISO for consideration as international standards. It first met in April 1976 and has continued to meet at approximately yearly intervals ever since. Throughout its existence four countries – U.K., U.S.A., France and Germany – have taken the lead, and hence this chapter examines the languages developed and used by these four nations. In the U.K., Working Group 2 of the BSI committee DPS/13 performs a similar role to PLIP. In the U.S.A. no group specifically tasked with the role of examining real-time language standards exists, and extensions to base languages intended for use in real-time systems are handled by the committee responsible for the base language, for example

X3J3 for Fortran. In France AFNOR set up a working group AFNOR Z6/SC 5, known as LPCPI (Langages de Programmation pour la Commande des Processus Industriels) to liaise with ISO/TC 97/SC 5 whilst in Germany the relevant DIN committee is NI-5.8 'Programming Languages for the Control of Technical Processes'.

To cover all the high level languages that have been used to implement real-time systems would not be possible in a single chapter, so the scope of this chapter will be restricted to those languages that have been the subject of formal standardisation activity. However, the reader should at least be aware of some of those other languages, which despite falling outside the defined scope of this chapter, have found favour and had considerable use in the real-time field. Some are in fact 'standards' within the particular organisations that have adopted them for their use.

They are:

in France: CPL 1 [1], Maxiris [2], Procol, and PAPE;
in the U.S.A.: HAL/S [3], Jovial [4], CS 4 [5], Tacpol, CMS 2 [6], and
              SPL/1 [7];
in the U.K.: Algol 68-RT [8].

8.2 CATEGORIES OF REAL-TIME LANGUAGES

The remainder of this chapter is devoted to the detailed discussion of the languages that do fall within the defined scope, in other words that have been the subject of standardisation activity. They are first classified into three broad categories:

(i)   Special purpose languages that are commonly used to implement real-time systems but rely on some or all of the real-time features that are necessary to support the system, being present outside the language itself. Examples are Coral 66 [9] and RTL/2 [10].

(ii) Languages that have real-time features built in as part of the syntax of the language. Examples are Pearl and Basic Pearl [11], Pascal, LTR [12], which has been developed in France, and the U.S. Department of Defense language – Ada [17].

(iii) General purpose languages for which an extension, in the form of a set of standard real-time features, has been defined by recognised working groups. Into this category fall the real-time extensions to Fortran and Basic.

8.3 GENERAL CHARACTERISTICS

There are three general characteristics of real-time systems that should be noted, since they influence the choice of an implementation language. Firstly the computer system contains some processes (which while being executed are sometimes called tasks) that are capable of execution in parallel in a multi-processor or multi-computer system or in pseudo-parallel with interleaved execution in a single processor. In each case the control of the execution of the tasks, called tasking, is under control of a scheduler. Secondly the external system is expected to establish a time response requirement on the computer system. Lastly the system will be controlling some external physical process frequently via non-conventional I/O devices.

Clearly, then, a real-time language must be capable, to some degree, of supporting a system with these characteristics by providing the user with the facilities he requires to construct, test and run it. In addition it is often claimed that the use of a real-time language that is also a standard offers additional benefits. These claims are reviewed at the end of this chapter.

8.4 CRITERIA TO BE MET

Much of the discussion that has taken place in the PLIP group has centred around the criteria that should be met by a prospective standard for IRT. To date the only tests that have been applied to submissions have been to establish whether the prospective standard lies within the scope of the Working Group. It is important therefore to note that the current scope of PLIP is confined to standardisation of one or more high-level languages (or extensions to languages) intended for general applicability in IRT computer systems. In the case of more than one language, PLIP currently requires that there shall be differences of a nature and extent that justify additional language standards. The languages shall be machine independent, although 'extensibility features' included in the language may allow the optional definition of machine dependent functions or implementations. In the establishment of such standards, highest priority is given to suitable variants of proven standardised (or draft standard or widely used) general purpose or IRT languages or proper subsets thereof. Similar priority is given to languages intended for writing application programs, although the desirability of languages suitable for writing system control programs (possibly by extension) is a major consideration. Excluded are languages or language features oriented towards specific application areas (for example, continuous processes, as opposed to batch processes) or particular industries (for example, steel, as opposed to paper). Also excluded are features that conflict with the base language, if any such exists. These then are the 'scope' criteria that have been applied by PLIP until now. However PLIP has also been developing a more detailed set of acceptance criteria [13] on which agreement has not yet been reached.

In addition to the scope criteria described above, the additional criteria will cover general items such as the defining documentation, availability of the language, extent and effectiveness of use, transportability, support, verification, security, overall technical criteria and specific criteria. The overall technical criteria cover, amongst others, algorithmic language features, tasking, I/O, file handling, extensibility, reliability and safety whilst the specific criteria set down specific language features that should be available. Clearly the intention in developing this set of criteria is to prevent the proliferation of too great a number of standards by providing a means of discriminating between candidates and to ensure that those that meet the criteria are worthy of the status of being an ISO standard. What has not yet been agreed within PLIP is how the criteria should be applied. For example, which are to be mandatory and which are not, and what weighting if any should be applied to each. The extent to which a candidate language has to meet the criteria in order to be recommended as a standard has also not yet been agreed.

8.5 A CATEGORY 1 LANGUAGE – Coral 66

Now let us return to the three broad categories of language described earlier and examine a language that falls within each of them in a little more detail. The examples are chosen because they are, or have been, the subject of international standardisation activity already. They are examined to see what features they contain and how they are used to meet the requirements of real-time systems.

Coral 66 is widely used by implementors of systems with small dedicated computers where hitherto the use of high-level languages has by no means been universal. For a high-level language to replace machine code in this type of system it is desirable but by no means essential that the compiler should be small enough to run in the production system or its standby system. It must produce efficient code comparable in size to that which would have been produced by an assembler. Languages in this category should allow full use of the target machine's hardware and any other special facilities, but at the same time be capable of implementation on a wide range of different architectures. To achieve any wide degree of availability, which in turn is a prerequisite for a standard to be widely accepted, the language must be cheap and quick to implement on new machine ranges.

Four approaches that the real-time system designer can adopt when using this first category of language are:

    (i) to use existing features in the language to gain access to other standard real-time facilities in the system software;

   (ii) to use a standard machine-independent real-time software kernel;

  (iii) to use standard existing real-time library procedures;

  (iv) to implement the complete system from scratch on a bare machine.

To allow any of these approaches to be adopted the draft Coral 66 standard calls for the provision of:

(i) code inserts, which allow the programmer to have access to the addressable hardware of the machine, such as the interrupt handling mechanisms, peripheral handlers, and device drivers. At a higher level, Coral 66 also allows access to machine addresses via an 'anonymous reference' feature;

(ii) macros, with parameters, which can be used to embed kernel or supervisor calls within the body of the program. This can be done via calls on macro libraries, which can be maintained by systems programmers;

(iii) communicators named EXTERNAL, ABSOLUTE and LIBRARY. EXTERNAL enables a Coral 66 program to refer to objects declared in other modules, by means of an identifier, which would otherwise be outside the scope of the program. ABSOLUTE allows access to objects having any absolute addressable location in the machine in which the program is running and LIBRARY allows for the use of libraries of procedures, which are often provided to perform mathematical, I/O, synchronisation and timing facilities;

(iv) a defined procedural interface. Procedures can be local, global or held in libraries. This interface for example enables the real-time facilities provided on a PDP 11 running under the RT-11 operating system to be used from within the body of a Coral 66 program via a LIBRARY communicator. For example a Coral 66 program could call the ISA-61.1 Fortran procedures, discussed later in this chapter, for executive functions, and for obtaining date and time information.

Recently Coral 66 has been extended to allow it to interface more easily with Mascot, (Modular Approach to Software Construction, Operation and Test). Mascot provides a formal method of dealing with the interconnection and intercommunication between subsystems containing parallel processes. To this end basic modules are defined which are independent even after compilation. These modules can be connected together at load time to construct subsystems which can communicate with each other only via defined data channels or data areas. The Mascot approach is supported by a basic software kernel, which may itself be written in Coral 66. The kernel allows software synchronisation both within and between subsystems, to ensure an orderly and sustained flow of data through the system. The kernel also includes a monitoring facility, which records the time-ordered sequence of its actions. Mascot can be implemented on a bare machine, or on top of an existing operating system. It provides the designer with the capability of producing transferable software, thus enabling him to engage in an evolutionary approach to system design, on machines other than that on which the final system is expected to run. In this way the existence of powerful program development facilities can be exploited on large host machines, and the software can then be transferred to the target machine by down line loading, a particularly useful technique when the target machine is inaccessible.

Lastly there are no features in Coral 66 which prevent the designer from implementing his system directly onto a bare machine. In fact the language has been used in the past as a system implementation language. This approach gives a high degree of efficiency in that a special-to-task system can be designed with an optimum mix of facilities for a given application, but such an approach is time consuming, highly machine-dependent, difficult to extend at a later date and non-portable. Whilst it can provide a sound, and in theory a highly efficient, solution to a variety of real-time problems, it should be considered only when all other options have been rejected as infeasible.

Although the discussion here has been with reference to Coral 66, the points made are in most cases applicable to RTL/2 as well. Both Coral 66 and RTL/2, which is the more modern and somewhat higher level language of the two, have been the subject of formal standardisation activity retrospectively. Coral 66 was originally a Ministry of Defence standard, and RTL/2 was an in-house standard for ICI Ltd. They have now both become draft British standards. The draft standards [14,15], have been widely circulated for comment and it seems certain from the responses that the standards will be accepted as the first language standards processed by the BSI. At the international level there now seems little likelihood that Coral 66 will become an ISO standard. The reasons for this are that it is no longer considered by PLIP to be a modern language, it contains no explicit real-time features and is said not to be extensively used internationally. Whilst the last point is open to doubt, it is unlikely that the BSI will press the case for Coral 66 further in the international arena.

8.6 CATEGORY 2 LANGUAGES – (1) Ada

Now let us consider high level languages that belong to the second broad category, namely those with built-in real-time features. Ada is one of these, being the new language under development by the U.S. Department of Defense (U.S. DoD) and whilst at the time of writing it is neither a standard nor yet implemented it is highly probable that it will at the least be a *de facto* standard in the near future due to its backing and support. It is really an example of a prospective standard, in contrast with say Coral 66 or RTL/2 which were both proposed as standards retrospectively. The U.S. DoD document entitled 'Requirements for High Order Computer Programming Languages' commonly known as 'Steelman' [16] which gave rise to Ada [17] clearly sets out the technical requirements for the U.S. DoD language. In this chapter it is the language features to support parallel processing that are of interest. They are specified in the following terms (somewhat abbreviated here):

It shall be possible to:

(i) define parallel processes;
(ii) mark variables that are shared among parallel processes;
(iii) perform mutual exclusion in programs efficiently;
(iv) access a real-time clock and to delay until at least a specified time before continuing execution;

  (v) terminate another process asynchronously;

  (vi) pass data between processes that do not share variables;

  (vii) set a signal (without waiting), and to wait for a signal (without delay if already set);

  (viii) wait for, determine, and act upon the first completed of several wait operations.

Finally it is specified that the semantics of the built in scheduling algorithm shall be first-in first-out within priorities.

It should be stressed that there is still a need for an Ada run-time support system comparable to Coral's Mascot or RTL/2's family of multi-tasking systems MTS, but by calling for this type of explicit real-time feature in the language the presence of a general purpose real-time operating system is no longer necessary. The requirements for run-time support modules for Ada are set out in another U.S. DoD document entitled 'Requirements for the Programming Environment for the Common High Order Language' commonly called 'Stoneman' [18]. Stoneman describes the requirements laid down by the U.S. DoD for the environment in which Ada will be used. This environment includes all supporting activities and includes aids to develop programs for all applications. Such aids and activities include the following:

  (i) organisation and methods to develop Ada and promote development of tools;

  (ii) translators for converting Ada into executable programs for the target computer;

  (iii) tools to aid in the design, testing and debugging of application programs;

  (iv) organisations and methods to research future uses of Ada;

  (v) materials and techniques for training users of Ada;

  (vi) methods and organisations for collecting, cataloguing and disseminating information about Ada, about programs written in Ada, and about compiler techniques useful for implementing Ada;

  (vii) project management aids to achieve successful implementation and maintenance of software prepared in the Ada environment;

  (viii) techniques for rigorously defining Ada and verifying Ada translators.

Stoneman is one of a series of iterative documents which successively refine the requirements in these areas. Previous iterations were called Sandman and Pebbleman.

The run-time support system for Ada is just one small part of the Ada environment. The requirement is for run-time support packages to provide the necessary executive, mathematical, and I/O routines. These packages will provide all the necessary support routines for language elements which are neither directly compiled nor available on the respective target machine. Such a package will provide an adaptation to existing operating systems and other run-time packages, or will extend the capabilities of a bare machine to match the requirements of the language.

The languages that fall into this second broad category are more recent than those in the first. They have come about through the recognition by the computing community that just to have a high level language standard is not enough and what is required is a standard, or a number of related standards, that in addition to the language itself, cover the complete interaction between the user and the machine, thus enabling movement from machine to machine with the minimum of adjustment or new learning. Ada is not yet available but there exist examples of languages in this group that are: Pearl is one.

8.7 CATEGORY 2 LANGUAGES – (2) Pearl

The language Pearl (Process and Experiment Automation Real-time Language) has been under development in Germany by a group of some twenty industrial firms and research institutes since 1969. The Pearl workshop, as it was originally called, first met within the framework of the Study Group on Nuclear Electronics, a working group funded by the Federal Ministry of Education and Science. The project PDV (Processlenkung mit Dataverarbeitungsanlagen) took over the Pearl project and in 1973 published a provisional language definition. Early implementations resulting from this were called PAS-1 and ASME-Stage-1 Subset. Later the development group became the working group A4.4 of section 4 (Process computers) of VDI/VDE–GMR (Society for Measurement and Control). In 1977 the definition was frozen. It is now the subject of both national and international standardisation activity. Pearl has both a full definition and a subset. called Basic Pearl, which is the subject of a current draft international standard and has already been published as DIN 66253 in June 1978 by working group FNI-5.8.

Pearl provides facilities for:

(i)   the explicit control of the time behaviour of a system;
(ii) interrelations between its parallel activities;
(iii) a description of the hardware configuration;
(iv) handling non-conventional peripheral devices for process control;
(v)   the organisation of man-machine communication via graphic devices.

In effect the Pearl language embodies a Pearl operating system whose functions include interrupt handling, scheduling, task control, input/output, process control, file management and storage control. One advantage of having this functional level in the language standard is that the user has to learn to use these aspects once only compared to say Coral 66 plus whatever is provided on the system on which it is running. It does however lead inevitably to larger and more costly compilers and run-time support systems. In 1979 Pearl and Basic Pearl were formally submitted to ISO/TC 97/SC 5/WG 1 as candidates for international standardisation.

A third language, falling within this category, has recently been put forward by AFNOR to PLIP following a decision taken by LPCPI in early 1979. The language is LTR (Langage Temps Réel) and is the subject of a draft AFNOR standard NFZ 65-350. LTR uses the concepts of tasks, events, resources, time delays, interrupts and primitives to control multi-task real-time systems. It was originally designed to handle the needs of the Service Centrale des Télécommunications et de L'informatique (SCTI) for the French Military. It is based on Algol and PL/I. The language is not owned by any company or agency and hence any organisation that desires to use LTR is free to do so.

8.8 CATEGORY 3 LANGUAGES – (1) Fortran

Now let us turn to the last broad category, embracing those general purpose languages for which additional standard facilities have been designed for use in process control. The best example to examine is Fortran and the work done by the Instrument Society of America (ISA) in collaboration with ANSI and the 'Purdue Workshop'. But first a brief explanation of the activities leading up to this collaborative effort is necessary. The first co-ordinated effort towards language standardisation in the U.S.A. developed within the Purdue Workshop which was established in 1969, largely through the efforts of Purdue University, Indiana. It currently consists of three regional organisations in the Americas, Europe and the Far East (principally Japan). The regional groups meet annually in the spring and each autumn the International Workshop meets as a single body at Purdue.

In its early days the workshop was devoted solely to the standardisation of software. It recognised that an immediate problem existed but that a better, long-term solution was also required for continued progress in the application of industrial computers. As a consequence, it established an Interim Procedural Language Committee to deal with the immediate problem and a Long Term Procedural Language Committee (LTPLC) to consider a long range solution. The interim committee did a survey of current practice in the industry and concluded that Fortran was the most widely used common language. It further concluded that acceptance of standard extensions to Fortran would be easier and more effective if proposals did not involve changing the syntax and semantics of the base language. As a result they concentrated on designing a set of standard Fortran calls that could be invoked using standard Fortran syntax and semantics. They have been responsible for three draft standards describing extensions in the form of procedures. Two of these extensions are of relevance here; the third (ISA 61-2-1978) covers file access and control of file concatenation, and although it has been discussed in PLIP and is equally applicable to both real-time and other types of system, it is not discussed further in this chapter. Of the remaining two the first, the most recent version of which is ANSI/ISA S61-1-1978, covers:

(i) the executive interface;

(ii) process input/output;

(iii) bit string manipulation;

(iv) date and time information.

They are intended for use with programs written in Fortran conforming to the ISO full Fortran (R 1539-1972). These programs are expected to be executed either in a solitary or in a multi-programming environment under the control of a real-time executive.

These functions were originally developed by the ISA Standards Committee on Industrial Computer System Fortran Procedures SP61 and were issued as ISA S61-1-1972 (which has also become a Japanese standard JEIDA-20). This standard was reviewed as a result of extensive use and a revised version was issued in 1976 as ISA S61-1-1976. In 1977 the standard was submitted to the American National Standards Board of Review and was approved as an American Standard ANSI/ISA S61-1-1976.

The executive interfaces provide the facility to control operation of the programs within the system. Through these external procedures one may start, stop or delay programs. The process input/output interfaces allow access to data related to specific analogue and digital sensors and outputs. The procedures for bit string manipulation, whilst they do not relate specifically to real-time systems, do provide an example of a means of extending a language in a standard manner without invalidating existing compilers.

ISA/S61.3 described industrial computer system Fortran procedures for the management of independent but interrelated tasks. When it was first put forward to PLIP for discussion, it became apparent that there was a considerable divergence of opinion between the European experts who had done some related work within TC1 of Purdue Europe, and the American work within X3J3. To date these differences have not been entirely resolved; however it has been agreed to remove those parts from S61.3 where technical conflict exists. This trimmed draft standard may in due course be put forward to ISO and with more certainty it will be processed as an ISA and ANSI standard. The current European view is that further work should be done to produce an internationally agreed and comprehensive standard, but this is not supported by the U.S. experts who are reluctant to support further work.

8.9 CATEGORY 3 LANGUAGES – (2) Basic

For Basic the approach has been to define extensions to the draft standard language in terms of new syntax and semantics. Like Fortran, the communities on both sides of the Atlantic have not yet agreed on a common technical approach. The current European thinking, as discussed within TC 2 of Purdue Europe, is to standardise on an approach that in essence defines three levels of language. The lowest level can be described as a special language which enables a precise description of the environment to be made in the form of a set of declarations. These declarations are capable of being compiled by a small and possibly separate compiler, whose function is to produce a number of descriptor blocks capable of being referenced by the main Process Basic compiler but at the same time being transparent to the main program. The second level consists of the algorithmic part of the language and the third level is in fact a built-in system description language which describes the connectivity and dynamic behaviour of the system in terms of a number of single thread modules. Documents formally defining this approach were due to be circulated by the end of 1979 and are expected to take the place of previous attempts to agree a real-time extension to the Basic standard.

8.10 THE WORK OF LTPL-E

This chapter would not be complete without some reference and description of the work of the Long Term Procedural Language-Europe group known as LTPL-E, which is a regional group that was formed in 1969 under the organisational umbrella of the Purdue Workshop. On the formation of Purdue Europe in 1974, now known as the European Workshop on Industrial Systems, it became known as TC 3 of Purdue Europe and in January 1975 it was recognised as LTPL-E by the Commission of European Communities. From this time onwards it received Commission support primarily for meetings in Brussels but also for some liaison activities with the U.S. DoD in connection with Ada. In 1971, LTPL-E adopted a set of language requirements, produced within the International Purdue Workshop, and these became the basis for further work. Tasking, input/output and algorithmic elements were identified and developed as major facets of the language.

In 1973 an approach known as the 'meld of best features' was adopted. The principle was to identify significant features of languages already being used, or being developed for use in the European industrial control field, to extract those features judged the best for LTPL-E requirements and to mould these with further development into the new language. The results of this work were published in 1974 [19] in a language comparison document. From 1974 onwards language synthesis proceeded using results of the language comparison and other associated material which became available. However, progress was slow and it became clear that, whilst the work being undertaken had great merit and was useful in the development of new constructs and concepts, it was never likely to lead to an agreed definition even within the long-term time scales without considerable funds and effort becoming available on a continuous basis. After a brief attempt to establish a funded project under the Commission, which failed to gain the necessary national support, LTPL-E in 1977 decided to suspend its own development plans and to give support to the then newly initiated DoD activity which was eventually to lead to the Ada definition, by using its considerable pool of experience to provide constructive input in the form of comments on the DoD's four, and later two, preliminary designs. More recently LTPL–E has also been studying the 'Pebbleman' document which described the environmental requirements necessary to support a modern real-time language.

8.11 THE BENEFITS OF STANDARDISATION

In conclusion it is worthwhile considering what benefits can be expected to accrue from this vast amount of seemingly disjoint and at times unco-ordinated worldwide activity to develop real-time language standards. The benefits can be summarised as follows:

- (i) a language, as a result of its adoption as a standard, will inevitably become available on a wider range of machines. Thus for a system, the choice of language should not impose limitations on the choice of machine and vice versa;
- (ii) compilers can be assessed for conformity to the standard and their efficiency measured. Thus the overall performance of a compiler can be predicted, and the effect of its adoption assessed in the system definition phase;
- (iii) the cost and time taken to implement systems is reduced;
- (iv) the output of programmers is increased since they do not have to adapt to unfamiliar dialects;
- (v) the standard of documentation is higher, and the program structure more visible and comprehensible;
- (vi) systems are easier to hand over to the user since they will be in a language understood by all parties. This results in a reduction in the time taken for handover;
- (vii) systems can be more easily maintained by the user;
- (viii) systems can be more easily extended or modified by the user, rather than by the contractor, whose original team is probably dispersed;
- (ix) estimates of software cost and development time can be better assessed, based on cumulative experience;
- (x) the time to train key engineers and programmers is reduced and courses are available on a national basis;
- (xi) programmers become more transferable and thus fit in better with company requirements;
- (xii) some degree of program transferability may be achieved, particularly with the more modern languages.

8.12 REFERENCES

[1] CAP Sogetti Logiciel, CPL 1, Language reference manual: Gen–1002-9.
[2] Compagnie internationale pour l'informatique, MAXIRIS, Description manual: 5341/P/EN.

[3]   Intermetrics Inc., HAL/S, Language specification: IR–61-7.

[4]   Shaw, C. J. (1963), Jovial — a programming language for real-time command systems, *Annu. Rev. Autom. Program.*, **3**, 53-119.

[5]   Intermetrics Inc., CS 4, language reference manual: IR–130-2.

[6]   Fleet Combat Direction Systems Support Activity (U.S.A.), CMS 2, Users' reference manual: M-5035; Vol. 2.

[7]   Intermetrics Inc., SPL/1, Language primer: 5490-120: EF: ekm.

[8]   Royal Signals and Radar Establishment (U.K.), Parallel processing and simulation, Algol 68–RT.

[9]   Inter-Establishment Committee on Computer Applications (1970), Official Definition of Coral 66, HMSO.

[10] SPL (1974), RTL/2 language specification.

[11] Beuth Verlag GmbH, Pearl, DIN 66253, Teil 1.

[12] Centre de programmation de la marine, LTR language manual.

[13] ISO, ISO/TC 97/SC 5/WG 1 (PLIP) papers N45 and N72.

[14] BSI (1979), Draft standard Coral 66, BSI: DPS/13 paper 79/63650.

[15] BSI (1979), Draft standard RTL/2, BSI: DPS/13 paper 79/63337.

[16] DoD (1978), Requirements for high order computer programming languages, 'Steelman'.

[17] Ichbiah, J. D. *et al.* (1979), Preliminary Ada reference manual, *SIGPLAN Not.*, **14**, No. 6, Part A.

[18] DoD (1980), Requirements for the programming environment for the common high order language, 'Stoneman'.

[19] Roessler, R. and Schenk, K. (1975), LTPL–E language comparison document.

CHAPTER 9

Data base management systems

by Dr. T. William Olle

The first of our topics which is not an actual language or related to particular languages is that of data base management. Specifying structure and organisation of data bases is, however, a task sufficiently akin to specifying a programming language for it to have been placed within the remit of ISO/TC97/SC5 for standardisation purposes, and it is the 'related area' on which, so far, most standards work has been done. It is described by Dr. T. William Olle, an independent consultant and lecturer, who is a member of the relevant ISO working group, SC5/WG3, and of its U.K. counterpart, BSI: DPS/13: WG/1.

9.1 INTRODUCTION

The aim of this chapter on data base management is to review the topic from a standardisation point of view. It must be remembered that at the time of writing there is no standard at all available in the data base field. Nevertheless, different data base management systems (hereinafter referred to as DBMS) are in widespread use throughout the world of commercial data processing.

Data base management systems have been with us for a long time, although when Charles Bachman announced his pioneering system in 1964 [1], he did not use that term. The term was probably created by the Codasyl Systems Committee in 1969 [2], although the prefix 'generalised' fell into disuse quickly when it was recognised that all DBMS are generalised. This implies that any DBMS is applicable to a wide range of applications in exactly the same sense as a programming language such as Cobol or PL/I.

Since this book will presumably be read by people with an interest in programming languages, I shall start with an attempt to bridge the gap between programming languages and data base management by giving a short analysis of what data base management is all about. This section is followed by a review of current practice, a short exposé of the Codasyl work, leading into presentation of what kind of standards are currently emerging from that work. In conclusion, this chapter will examine the potential impact of relational theory, of current work on data dictionaries and of other activities also associated with the field of data base management.

9.2 ESSENCE OF THE DATA BASE MANAGEMENT APPROACH

There is an unfortunate tendency to regard data base management as an advanced *pot pourri* of data storage techniques. For this reason, many researchers in the field of information systems tend to dismiss data base management as something which enters the information systems design process at a fairly late stage.

It is indeed true that a DBMS provides an effective tool for handling data stored on direct access storage devices. It is furthermore true that each DBMS has its own technique or choice of techniques for representing the data on the direct storage devices. However, the main insight that has emerged in some fifteen years of DBMS usage is that use of a DBMS leads to a more complete and realistic logical representation of the application data. This in turn leads to a more effective and more complete information system.

The use of the phrase 'logical representation of the application data' must quickly be explained in the context of data base management. At the same time, we focus on the essential differences between what we tend to call the conventional approach to commercial data processing and the DBMS approach. The conventional approach is epitomised by Cobol (before the anticipated addition of the Data Base Facility). The programmer prepares his Data Division File Section by identifying the record types and data items appropriate to the application. However, when using any DBMS commercially available today, there is an extra problem to consider at data definition time, namely the definition of relationships between these record types.

What does 'relationship' mean here? This is a most important question because the facilities for defining data relationships and the facilities for making use of them in application programs once they have been defined are without doubt the essence of data base management.

The concept of a relationship is best illustrated by an example. Suppose that the definition of the data includes the definition of two record types called DEPARTMENT and EMPLOYEE. Using a DBMS, it would also be possible to specify the fact that a relationship exists between these two. (How this is done varies from one DBMS to another).

The relationship as specified conveys two assertions as follows:

(i) Each DEPARTMENT contains zero, one or many EMPLOYEES.
(ii) Each EMPLOYEE is assigned to one DEPARTMENT.

The relationship can be illustrated as shown in Table 9.1.

Each row has one cross (that is, each employee is attached to one department). Each column contains zero, one or more crosses.

This relationship between EMPLOYEE and DEPARTMENT is a one to many relationship. There are other kinds of relationships (such as many to many and zero or one to many) which play an important role when recognising the relationships between record types. Commercially available DBMS tend to be built around the definition of one to many relationships.

Table 9.1.

DEPARTMENT / EMPLOYEE	Purchasing	Sales	Production	Planning
Smith	X			
Jones			X	
Brown	X			
Williams		X		
Edwards		X		
Hill			X	
Dale			X	
Jackson			X	
Johnson	X			

It must be emphasised that without a DBMS, the kind of constraint implied in such a one to many relationship has to be taken care of in the application programs which update the data.

In a typical commercial data base, one might define some thirty to forty record types and about the same number of relationships. Inevitably, the data base approach tends to integrate previously distinct applications. Technically, a data base with three record types and two relationships must still be called a data base, but it is not a particularly interesting one.

Another essential aspect of data base management is the complete separation of the process of defining the data from that of defining the processes to be performed on the data. (It should be noted that this was not provided in Bachman's pioneering IDS system, but was recognised as important a few years later).

This definition of the data (that is, the record types, items and relationships between record types) is defined using what we call a Data Definition Language (or DDL). This language has its own translator which is used to translate a data definition into object form. The term 'schema' is widely used in this context. One writes a source schema. It is processed by a Schema DDL translator producing an object schema. This results in a computerised description of what a data base looks like — but no data base!

A data base has to be loaded, rather like a file, the only difference being that, as the records are being loaded into the data base, the system takes into account the relationships defined in the schema, and checks that the records satisfy the constraints implied in the relationships.

Application programs which perform this data base loading, plus subsequent updating and retrieval, are usually written using one of the standard programming languages suitably enhanced with extra facilities. These extra facilities are frequently referred to collectively as a Data Manipulation Language (DML), but it must be emphasised that a DML is not a programming language in itself — merely an appendage to one.

9.3 CURRENT PRACTICE IN DATA BASE MANAGEMENT

Although there is no standard yet available in data base management, there are several packages commercially available, and many of these are in widespread use among commercial installations. If one analyses different packages in use, it is quickly apparent that most claim some kind of compliance with the various proposals which have been published by the Codasyl organisation since 1969 [2, 3, 4].

However, there are three of four other packages, each of which can claim considerable usage worldwide. These are the following:

Software AG's	Adabas
IBM's	IMS
Cincom's	Total
MRI's	System 2000.

Only one of these, namely IMS, is limited to one hardware vendor, but IMS has numerous variants and versions running under the different IBM operating systems.

Cincom's Total is available on the hardware lines of some ten computer manufacturers and it is claimed that its worldwide market runs well into four figures.

Adabas and System 2000 are available for several different manufacturers' hardware lines. It is notable that in the case of each of these two systems, the number of users is well into three figures.

The commercial data processing user who is planning to start to use a DBMS often has a choice of DBMS available, especially if he is a user of IBM hardware. Almost all hardware vendors other than IBM tend to offer a Codasyl-compliant DBMS, although in the absence of a standard, there are often significant differences between one such system and another. A highly respected Codasyl-based DBMS, namely IDMS, has been available on IBM hardware for many years.

For an analysis of how Adabas, IMS and Total compare with the Codasyl approach, the reader is referred to my full length text [5].

9.4 CODASYL'S ROLE IN DATA BASE STANDARDISATION

The Codasyl Cobol Committee started to grasp the data base nettle in 1966, even before the term 'data base management systems' was created. The aim of the List Processing Task Force (as it then was) was to add list processing facilities to Cobol based on Bachman's chaining techniques in IDS. The group was renamed the Data Base Task Group in 1967 and it produced three reports [2, 3, 4] before it was disbanded in 1971. By that time, it had laid the foundation for the facilities which are now moving towards acceptance as an ANSI standard.

The cornerstone of the Codasyl approach to data base management is the complete freedom to define relationships between record types. This freedom is best illustrated by an example of a data structure diagram, often popularly called a Bachman diagram (especially in Europe). Bachman was one of the first to recognise the need to be able to agree on the logical data structure with the users at the time the data base was being designed [6].

Fig. 9.1 illustrates a purchasing example with 10 record types and 14 relationships. Each record type comprises one or more items of data in the same way as in Cobol or PL/I. The data items are not discussed further here. In a Codasyl-based DBMS, the data base designer would be able to define the data base in terms of these 10 record types and 14 relationships. Depending on the kind of processing he wishes to perform on the data base, he might find it

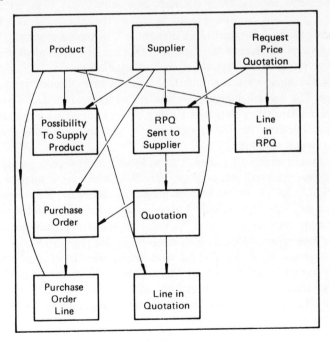

Fig. 9.1 – Purchasing example.

necessary to add extra record types and relationships to make such processing easier, faster or even possible at all.

This adding of extra record types and relationships is conceptually analogous to 'programming one's way around' a shortcoming in a programming language. Situations in which it is necessary to add these extra record types and relationships are far more prevalent in DBMS such as IMS and Total than in Codasyl-based systems. In IMS, the data base is defined as a number of separately identified hierarchical structures with the possibility of defining extra relationships between a record type in one such structure and a record type in another. In Total, the data base is restricted to a two level structure. The example in Fig. 9.1 is a four level structure. The techniques for flattening out such a structure into two levels by added extra record types and relationships are well known to designers of Total data bases.

In terms of the facilities provided for logically structuring the data in the data base, Codasyl-based systems are clearly superior to their commercial competitors. The fact that the picture or template of the data base can be so much closer to reality than is the case with the competitors means that Codasyl data bases are easier to design and it is easier to write applications programs to process them.

Another aspect of the Codasyl approach which must be mentioned here is the sub-schema facility. Once the data base schema has been prepared and translated, programs can be compiled to process the data in that data base. The data base definition is regarded as independent of the programming languages used to process the data in the data base. One can in theory prepare a suite of application programs in a mix of Cobol, Fortran, PL/I, etc.

A sub-schema serves as an interface between an application program and a data base. The Sub-schema Data Definition Language is regarded as part of each programming language's Data Base Facility. So far Codasyl has proposed detailed Data Base Facilities for Cobol and Fortran, and both are being prepared by ANSI for standardisation.

A sub-schema has a number of rules. Firstly, one selects from the schema's record types, items and relationships, only those which are of interest to a given application program (or set of such programs). Secondly, the selected record types and data items are re-defined as necessary to conform with the rules of the programming language to be used. This may mean different naming conventions, different item types or possibly different intra-record type structures.

A final aspect of the Codasyl work which merits attention has recently emerged in the 1978 Journal of Development [7] of the Data Description Language Committee. This committee was founded in 1971 to take over responsibility for the Schema Data Definition Language. As a result of some very active work by the U.K. based BCS Working Group [8], the Schema DDL has now been divided into two data definition stages. The first stage is still called the Schema DDL and the second is called the Data Storage Definition Language (DSDL).

The Schema DDL now contains the logical aspects of the data base definition. Previously, it contained many data definition factors which were quite physical. Most such factors have now been expediently moved into the DSDL. Examples of such factors are the following:

(i)   representation of relationships in storage;
(ii) control over physical contiguity of records of the same type;
(iii) control over physical contiguity of records of different types;
(iv) control over techniques used to represent the primary key for a record type.

It should be noted that, at the time of writing, this important breakdown of the data definition into two stages has yet to manifest itself in commercially available systems. However, most implementors are probably awaiting the ANSI standards planned for release in 1981.

9.5 PAST ACTIVITIES IN DBMS STANDARDISATION

In late 1972, ANSI/X3/SPARC established an *ad hoc* Study Group on DBMS charged with the task of investigating the subject of data base management systems and determining which aspects of such systems were, at that time, suitable candidates for the development of American National Standards.

This Study Group published its so-called interim report in 1975 [9]. This report must be recognised as one of the most unreadable documents ever produced on the topic of data base management and its effect on the standardisation effort represented a strange mixture of confused negativism coupled with some extremely valuable insight. It was left to two non-members of the Study Group, Klug and Tsichritzis, to separate the wheat from the chaff and in 1977 to publish a shorter, more readable edited version [10].

The principal piece of valuable insight with which this Study Group is often credited is the idea of a conceptual schema. (In fact, Sibley suggested this in 1973 [11], but it is not clear whether he, as a member of the DBMS Study Group, contributed the idea or borrowed it.)

A conceptual schema is many things to many people. For the present discussion, it consists of a data model defining the data of interest in a given environment, irrespective of whether the data will be handled using a DBMS or not, and even irrespective of whether the data will be computerised or not.

Many people like to use the term 'representation of reality' when talking of a conceptual schema. However, it is useful to recognise that preparing a conceptual schema may be effectively defining how one would like reality to become, and not necessarily how it exists at the time the conceptual schema is prepared. The difference between these two is the difference between representational modelling and creative modelling.

The ANSI/X3/SPARC DBMS Study Group was formally discharged in 1977.

Its efforts had done more to stimulate research in the field of data base management than to advance the cause of standardisation.

In May 1974, the top committee on data processing standards of the International Standardization Organization, ISO/TC 97, assigned responsibility for data base management to its sub-committee, SC 5, responsible for Programming Languages. It further instructed SC 5 to establish a study group to recommend the actions required.

This ISO Study Group on DBMS was duly launched and met four times between June 1975 and November 1977, when it took the opportunity of the fact that its parent committee SC 5 was meeting during the same month, to seek formal status as an ISO Working Group with a more clearly defined scope of work. The group became ISO/TC 97/SC 5/WG 3 on DBMS and its scope was as follows:

(i)   define the concepts for conceptual schema languages;
(ii) define or monitor definition of conceptual schema languages;
(iii) develop a methodology for assessing proposals for conceptual schema languages;
(iv) assess candidate proposals for conceptual schema languages;
(v)   define concepts for conceptual level end user facilities;
(vi) define conceptual level end user facility.

Since November 1977, this group has been meeting regularly. There were three meetings during 1978, and two during 1979, for example. Progress towards the first item in this list has been extremely slow, due largely to the kind of research-orientated influences which plagued the work of the ANSI/X3/SPARC DBMS Study Group. In a sense, one could perhaps assert that the ISO Study Group carried on where the ANSI group left off. Certainly, the two groups are to be compared with respect to their minimal short-term positive impact on DBMS standardisation work.

The idea of conceptual schema emerges from all this committee work as some kind of holy grail. There is no intention here of questioning the potential value of such a facility if sufficient agreement could be reached in a working group for its twenty members to go out and promote the specifications. Nevertheless, it is not clear that the revolutionary zeal of the proponents of some of the approaches to a conceptual schema can ever have an impact on the field of data base standardisation.

9.6 EXISTING STANDARDISATION ACTIVITY

At the time of writing, three ANSI standards committees are actively engaged in refining the proposals emanating from the Codasyl organisation into ANSI standards. These three committees are:

X3H2   Data Description Language
X3J3   Fortran Data Base Facility
X3J4   Cobol Data Base Facility.

In addition, a further group, the ANSI/X3/SPARC Data Base Systems Study Group (DBS–SG), has the responsibility for monitoring and co-ordinating the work of these three standardising committees. These three committees are expected to complete their work by mid-1980 with a view to the standards being formally approved by mid-1981.

In a very real sense, these three proposed standards form the first members of a family of standards. The need for careful co-ordination and definition of compatible interfaces between these three is far greater than between any pair of programming language standards. The role of the above mentioned DBS–SG is clearly critical in this matter.

It is perhaps useful to analyse the facilities to be provided in the X3H2 Schema DDL *vis à vis* the much sought-after conceptual schema discussed in the previous section. The Schema DDL is fairly clearly associated with the Codasyl approach to data base management. Certainly, the recent transfer of the more physically oriented factors out of the Schema DDL into the Data Storage Definition Language has left the former fairly uncluttered. Nevertheless, there are some protagonists among the research fraternity of the view that grouping data items together into record types represents a physically oriented data definition factor. They assert that such factors have no place in a conceptual schema, one argument being that one might wish to change the grouping, and application programs which take advantage of this grouping would then have to be modified.

Another reason why the Schema DDL is felt not to be a candidate for the much sought after conceptual schema is that the conceptual schema should provide further facilities for the information systems designer. An important example of such facilities is the following. The concept of validating data prior to storage is well known. It is usually achieved either by special validating programs (edit runs) or else by incorporating the validation rules in the updating programs. In this way, the semantics of the data (or what the data mean) are often rather obscure. A very important aspect of an ideal conceptual schema would be the provision of facilities for specifying such validation criteria.

9.7 IMPACT OF A DATA DICTIONARY SYSTEM

There has been widespread recognition during the past decade of the importance of building and maintaining a data dictionary. It is useful to think of a data dictionary as a facility for storing data about data. The application of such a facility is not restricted to a situation where the application data are being handled with a DBMS. However, in a DBMS-oriented environment, there is usually much more data about data to take into account.

Interestingly enough, a data dictionary application is usually so complex that the easiest way to build the dictionary is as a data base using a DBMS. There are several data dictionary packages available commercially which are certainly not built using a DBMS, but each major DBMS now available on the market offers a data dictionary system as an optional extra.

The most significant development work on data dictionaries is that undertaken by the British Computer Society Data Dictionary Systems Working Party (DDSWP). This group started work in about 1974 and released its first report in mid-1976 [12]. The group is still very active and is currently developing detailed specifications for a data dictionary system.

Unlike the other U.K. based development group DBAWG, the DDSWP does not have formal links with the Codasyl organisation. The reason for this is a technical one. The group feels that the kind of data dictionary system which it is proposing should be seen as independent of the Codasyl approach, in the sense that it should be equally usable with any DBMS including, of course, one built according to the Codasyl proposals or in compliance with the emerging ANSI standards. Whether the DDSWP's view will be accepted by the data processing community is a delicate question.

A DBMS-independent data dictionary system is an attractive idea; so for that matter is the idea of the conceptual schema discussed in the previous section. An observer would be excused for wondering about the difference between these two. As one of the few who has been involved to some extent with both ISO/TC 97/SC 5/WG 3 and DDSWP, the differences I observe are more involved with concept and scope, but nevertheless there is potentially a great deal of overlap. What is confusing is that there are clearly defined software products in widespread use which are classed as data dictionary systems. People tend to give meaning to the term by referring to these products. An excellent insight into the capabilities of systems is to be found in the texts by Lefkovits [13] and later by Lomax [14]. The term 'conceptual schema' is more used among researchers, each of whom needless to say has his own definition.

Shall we ever see a standard data dictionary system? The first step in this direction is currently being taken by ANSI following the initiative of their above-mentioned DBS-SG. ANSI is creating a new committee to develop a standard so-called Information Resource Dictionary System. The term 'information resource dictionary' is deliberately broader than 'data dictionary' and this is intended to emphasise the role of such a system as a repository for more than 'data about data'.

9.8 IMPACT OF RELATIONAL DATA BASE THEORY

No discussion of the future directions of data base management would be complete without some reference to Codd's relational theory [15]. Many researchers seem to think that the DBMS of the eighties will be based on this approach.

The programming language fraternity has seen this all before. In the early sixties it was widely asserted that Algol was superior to Fortran. A few years later along came PL/I and similar assertions were again heard.

The main problem with relational theory, as I contended in a paper in 1974 [16] and at greater length in a review of the relational approach in [5], is that the terminology used to express the theory obscures fundamentally sound ideas.

Nevertheless, relational theory has had its impact on the way in which relationships can be handled when defining a data base using a Codasyl-compliant system [7]. The term 'structural constraint' has been introduced to refer to this capability.

The next aspect of relational theory which will have impact is the multi-record-at-a-time DML. It should be explained here that the DML to be provided in the ANSI standard Cobol and Fortran data base facilities has essentially a single-record-at-a-time logic. In other words, each DML statement included in a Cobol or Fortran program to retrieve a record from a data base produces *one* record only. Many feel that this is a serious shortcoming. However, in practice a facility which retrieves an unpredefinable number of records (say twenty thousand) can create more problems than it solves.

The single-record-at-a-time logic is tied in to the current hardware technology with primary and secondary storage. The DML statement moves the records (one at a time) from secondary to primary. One needs working space in primary storage to accommodate these records. Hence, the fundamental problem in the multi-record-at-a-time logic is that of managing the working storage.

Predictably, considerable progress will be made during the eighties on these problems. However, the community of data processing users will not accept evolution any more than they did in the mid sixties when IBM (no less) proposed dropping Cobol and replacing it with PL/I. Instead, multi-record-at-a-time DML statements based on Codd's relational theory will need to be added to the single-record-at-a-time ones now included in the emerging ANSI standard.

9.9 CONCLUDING REMARKS

It should be clear from the foregoing discussion that standardisation in the area of data base management has far to go. Although standardisation in programming languages should settle down somewhat during the eighties, the most significant perturbation to the otherwise tranquil picture will be the infusion of data base facilities into the programming languages.

Data base management can never be divorced from programming languages. Although individuals tend to claim a special interest in one or the other but not both, the two fields are inexorably interwoven.

9.10 REFERENCES

[1] Bachman, C. W. and Williams, S. B. (1964), A general purpose programming system for random access memories, *Proc. Fall J. Comput. Conf.*, **26**, 411-422.

[2] Codasyl Cobol Committee (1968), Cobol extensions to handle data bases, April 1968 newsletter of ACM special interest group in business data processing.

[3] Codasyl (1969), Data base task group October 1969 report.

[4] Codasyl (1971) Data base task group April 1971 report, (ACM, New York; BCS, London; LAG, Amsterdam).

[5] Olle, T. W. (1978), The Codasyl approach to data base management, Wiley (ISBN 0-471-99579-7).

[6] Bachman, C. W. (1969), Data structure diagrams, *Data Base*, 1, No. 2.

[7] Codasyl (1978), Data Description Language Journal of Development, January 1978.

[8] Data Base Administration Working Group (1975), June 1975 report, BCS.

[9] ANSI (1975), Interim report of ANSI/X3/SPARC study group on data base management systems, *ACM/Sigmod Newsletter fdt*, 7, 2.

[10] Tsichritzis, D. and Klug, D., eds. (1977), The ANSI/X3/SPARC DBMS framework: report of the study group on data base management systems, AFIPS Press.

[11] Sibley, E. H. (1973), Data base management systems — user requirements, in Data Base Management Systems (ed. D. A. Jardine), North Holland/ American Elsevier.

[12] BCS Data Dictionary Systems Working Party (1977), *Data Base*, 9, No. 2 (also available from BCS).

[13] Lefkovits, H. C. (1977), Data dictionary systems, NCC.

[14] Lomax, J. D. (1977), Data dictionary systems, NCC.

[15] Codd, E. F. (1970), A relational model of data for large shared data banks, *Commun. ACM.*, 13, 377-387.

[16] Olle, T. W. (1974), Current and future trends in data base management systems, Proc. IFIP-74 Congress, 998-1006, North-Holland.

CHAPTER 10

Graphics

by David L. Fisher

The next related area to be discussed is graphics. One of those who took a leading part in establishing the international standardisation work on graphics is David L. Fisher, Director of the Computer Laboratory at the University of Leicester in the U.K., who in this chapter explains the motivation for the standardisation work, and its current state.

10.1 HISTORICAL NOTE

Computers tend to produce lots of numbers, and these in turn imply lots of paper output. The trend is ever upwards. Yet for many scientific (and some commercial) applications numbers alone are not enough. One number often has little meaning unless measured against a neighbour. Graphs offer an excellent visual method of making such comparative assessments, and being visual these assessments can be made at extremely high speed. Indeed many scientific applications are not really completed until results are presented in a form that is more appropriate, concise and digestible than pages of printed figures.

Such problems existed long before computers were invented, and so elementary graphical methods are long established and well understood, but it was the advent of computers coupled with their ability to produce vast quantities of numbers at very high speed that really made the development of automatic graph-plotting devices a necessity.

Such devices have been available commercially almost as long as computers (mid-fifties) and to a considerable extent their development has reflected that of computers themselves. At first graphical devices were electro-mechanical and designed to ape the existing manual methods, and one firm, Calcomp, came to acquire an extraordinarily large share of this market.

It was not long, however, before improved technology found better and more interesting ways of presenting graphical information. Cathode-ray tubes (CRT) were an early development. At first they were used as storage devices or part of elementary operator consoles. Towards the end of the fifties they started to appear in the role of on-line graphical devices. Shortly thereafter cameras were set in front of them, the composite devices were installed off-line and micro-film recorders were created.

Such developments were fairly simple extensions of traditional graphical techniques. Most of the computing fraternity only really became aware of more advanced interactive graphical techniques when Dr. Ivan Sutherland and his Sketchpad [1] project burst upon the scene in the early sixties.

Early interactive graphics systems proved very expensive and normally claimed a substantial and dedicated local processor, but the eventual availability of cheap computer power in enormous quantities has made many different developments possible.

Graphics terminals themselves are becoming increasingly 'intelligent', and respectable interactive graphics facilities can now be attached to almost any mainframe without imposing any disproportionate adverse effects on the rest of any competing terminal system. Given a dedicated mainframe coupled to a suitable graphics device, extraordinarily sophisticated graphics can be undertaken such as the manipulation of high precision diagrams or the presentation of solid shaded objects as colour movies (for example, the rotation of complicated castings or the simulation of a pilot's view on the approach to touchdown).

10.2 SOME HARDWARE CONSIDERATIONS

Early CRTs were modest modifications of the then current television technology. The storage tubes, refresh displays and micro-film recorders that followed were sophisticated and often very expensive extensions of cathode-ray technology in which an electron beam was deflected from one point on a screen to a second, thereby drawing a line (a straight one being the desired effect) on the surface of the screen.

Tektronix can claim with some justification that their introduction of cheap storage tube terminals helped to cut the cost of interactive graphics, but now the wheel.has gone full circle, and graphics displays are returning to television technology. The result is a raster display that fills spots in sequence across the screen exactly in the manner of any domestic television set. Such displays can be both cheap and versatile.

Conventional electro-mechanical plotters are also becoming extremely cheap, and they now have high-speed rivals based on photo-copier technology. Colour at all levels of graphics is becoming commonplace.

But the real point is that there are now many possibilities opening up before the average user. A remarkable level of versatility on a wide variety of devices using many sophisticated and varied techniques is already available for very modest sums of money. The use of computer graphics is poised to explode. Unfortunately confusion will follow and will be graphics' most serious inhibitor unless some useful and effective standards can be established soon.

Unfortunately the situation is very complicated. Consider magnetic tape for example. It is relatively easy to define a format for $\frac{1}{2}''$ 9-track tape phase-encoded at 1600 b.p.i. (say), and that prescribes what information goes on tape and also, roughly, where it goes, sufficient anyway to get it read by a tape unit operating to the prescribed standard.

Graphics is not so blessed. There is no agreement, for example, over the aspect ratio for a display screen — not even agreement on a set of acceptable aspect ratios. The resolution offered by a display (in effect the number of points on the screen that can be referenced) or a plotter is determined largely by the price.

Under these circumstances it is not possible to supply information that will make a mark or draw a line in the same place or in the same way on different graphical devices. There is, as yet, no such concept as the 'same place' or the 'same way'. It is impossible, therefore, to determine when two pictures drawn on different devices are in fact the same. Furthermore there is the added complication that two 'identical' pictures drawn on the same device may have been drawn by quite different methods, and so, despite the fact that the results look the same on one occasion, other occasions will almost certainly exist when the two methods cannot produce the same picture.

Each device is likely to have its own unique protocol for dialogue with the controlling medium, whether this be a computer or some off-line device. This is a common situation in computing but yet another unwelcome layer of problems in graphics.

10.3 SOFTWARE

It has already been established that the user of computer graphics is, in some sense, 'spoilt for choice'. The application of standards can limit the choice available, cut out some of the worst excesses and thereby usefully reduce the confusion, but before defining a new standard in virgin territory such as graphics it is necessary to establish what is normal practice.

Some success has been achieved by graphics software packages. These have usually created an interface consisting of calls to subroutines, in a Fortran library, that provide facilities aimed at a specific environment.

The Ghost [2] system produced by the Culham Laboratory (UKAEA) in 1965 was one of the first 'general-purpose' packages. It was aimed at the typical research scientist extracting conventional two-dimensional graphical output from computer programs. It was designed to reflect the individual and natural actions required to plot graphs manually, such as selecting the paper, setting up the area of the paper to be used, defining the scales, drawing the axes, annotating the axes, plotting the curve etc. It insulated the user from most of the vagaries of the graphical equipment and soon developed device-independent facilities as far as the user was concerned. It is still widely used and still growing in popularity, but it has never really been energetically marketed and so Ghost has missed a wonderful opportunity to achieve a position of national dominance.

A somewhat later entry, but one actively marketed by CAD Centre, Cambridge is Gino–F [3]. It is similar to Ghost in many respects. It is a highly portable package of Fortran subroutines offering a valuable degree of device-independence. It has a more obvious modular structure than Ghost, it contains three-dimensional facilities and it was designed to support a useful level of interactive graphics. It is therefore capable of a wider range of graphics applications although it was aimed originally at engineers, and it is now the U.K.'s most successful and widely used graphics package and it is flourishing.

Other countries have produced similar packages, almost all built upon Fortran for portability reasons. GPGS [4] is a particularly well respected example and this is now a *de facto* national standard in Norway.

The U.S.A. has several such packages, of which DISSPLA [5] is one of the best known. The U.S.A. is also responsible for the Calcomp [6] routines, which are unusual in that they do not fit any normal pattern. Nonetheless they are by far the most widely used set of graphical routines. The early origins of these routines pre-date Ghost. They form a loosely coupled set of routines, having evolved with time rather than conforming to any planned structure, function or strategy. They are intended to support one manufacturer's hardware. It just so happens that the hardware in question is that most regularly available, so much so that users and other manufacturers have found it useful at times to adapt the software to other hardware as well. Thus in a rather limited sense they have become a form of industry standard for graph-plotters and their existence is both interesting and informative, but their lack of a coherent structure disqualifies further serious consideration.

10.4 THE FORMATIVE STAGES

The success of packages such as Gino–F, GPGS and DISSPLA has served to precondition all thoughts on standards for computer graphics, in that a similar user interface has been virtually the sole target for all the work undertaken to date.

A few dedicated individuals have been trying to set up standards for graphics software for some time now, but the whole issue was really set alight by a proposal from the BCS that Gino–F should be considered as an international standard for graphics software. As it happened it was soon shown that any such package could not itself be considered as a standard, but that it would be considered as an implementation of a specification that might be considered as a standard.

IFIP/WG 5.2 (graphics) was the first committee to respond to the U.K. initiative with a meeting at Seillac in France in May 1976. This meeting appeared to separate the logic of graphics and the modelling dependent upon the graphics, but its main contribution was that it fired imaginations, especially those of the Americans attending.

Under the aegis of ACM SIGGRAPH they had already set up the Graphics Standards Planning Committee (GSPC) and this they now divided into four groups:

1. State-of-the-Art;
2. Core System Definition;
3. Core System Interface;
4. Methodology.

Group 1 reported in ACM Computer Graphics [7] in June 1978, but Group 2 was the most active, and after several iterations involving experts world-wide, its work culminated in a report in an issue of Computer Graphics dated 'Fall 1977', often referred to as the CORE Report [8]. This was an attempt to define a substantial interface between the graphics user (pitched at programmer level) and some supporting graphics software system, with the idea of providing a standard that was sufficient, extensible, flexible, portable and to a large extent device-independent.

Such is the way of the world however, that there can be no international standard unless there is an appropriate committee to approve it.

Once again the U.K. took the initiative and inaugurated an ISO working group, labelled TC97/SC5/WG2, in London in February 1977. Its first self-appointed task was to put the Gino–F initiative in its true perspective. It met a second time in Toronto in August 1977, by which time it was obvious that its continued existence was dependent on formal procedures for the establishment of national representatives to the group and the proper conduct of its business.

Accordingly the BSI set up a working group labelled DPS/13:WG/5 under committee DPS/13 (Programming Languages) thereby reflecting the roles and relationships within ISO of TC97/SC5/WG2 and TC97/SC5. The Germans (DIN) were already similarly organised as were the Dutch (NNI). The Americans set up a group under the heading ANSI X-3 SPARC/CGPL.

TC97/SC5/WG2 was taken on board as an official permanent ISO working group at the meeting of TC97/SC5 at The Hague in November 1977, and it is now the official ISO body on all matters concerning graphics. It met in this full capacity for the first time in Bologna in September 1978.

10.5 THE SPARRING BEGINS

By the time of the Bologna meeting it was evident that the Americans had been working to produce a number of implementations of the CORE Report, and these had revealed a number of loopholes, inconsistencies and shortcomings in the specification of the CORE. Meanwhile the Germans had developed their own Core [9] to a simpler and more compact specification.

Other proposals were also threatening, and it was clear that the ISO working group would have to try to draw the separate proposals together to give one consistent composite proposal at best or a small number of compatible solutions at worst. To this end they created a small Editorial Board co-chaired by 'neutral' Dutch and U.K. chairmen. The rest of the Board consists of representatives from national standards organisations with a proposal already in the pipeline, that is initially ANSI and DIN. It first met in February 1979 and produced a number of recommendations [10], amendments and corrections for both the American and the German proposals.

The Germans accepted the suggestions and incorporated almost all of them without question, but after a promising start the Americans faltered.

By the time of the meeting of TC 97/SC 5/WG 2 held in Budapest in October 1979, both proposals had undergone a further round of development. The CORE, now known as GSPC79, had, in the opinion of many, become bloated and no longer relevant to today's needs. On the other hand, the German proposal (GKS) was subjected to a detailed examination, and several useful changes were made.

DIN put GKS (level 5.2) before TC 97/SC 5 at its meeting in Turin in November 1979, and this level of GKS has been put to TC 97 for approval, to be processed as a draft ISO standard.

Unfortunately there is still no knowing what the eventual outcome will be. GKS will become a DIN standard no matter what happens to it within ISO. The Americans have suffered some setbacks but the CORE still looks set to become an ANSI standard and will probably go before ISO as well. Two ISO standards could result, both pitched at about the same level (that is, similar user interface), but not necessarily compatible. Whether implementations of either standard will be superior to existing packages will not be proven for some years yet.

10.6 OTHER ACTIVITIES

Meanwhile the U.K. group, DPS/13:WG/5, is trying with very limited resources to direct energies to other related topics.

A standard is of cosmetic value only, if it cannot be enforced, and it cannot be enforced unless implementations of the standard can be checked and certified against the standard. This implies that the standard must be constructed so as to allow checks to be undertaken, and organisations have to be available to undertake the tests. Both are substantial problems.

The U.K. group has been looking at ways of formally describing logical interfaces where a useful level of certification can take place. If it is not possible to prove actual pictures to be alike, for example, it may be possible by finding an interface further away from the display and nearer the software to check that the information crossing that interface conforms to a specification extracted from a standard, and such a level of certification, although not ideal, would nonetheless represent a valuable step forward.

Some members of the group have also set up a library of general-purpose graphical subroutines attached as a chapter to the NAG project [11]. This library is intended to be highly transportable, and in order to achieve this objective it has been necessary to create a software graphics interface of fundamental Fortran subroutines lying between the local graphics system and the portable library subroutines. This interface has proved to be a useful test vehicle, in that the interface has been designed with both the ANSI and DIN proposals in mind, and special measures are being taken to certify the package at a number of different levels.

10.7 SUMMARY

These are interesting times. The rate of change of hardware is stimulating and the pace of the development of standards is interesting and much is threatening. This chapter could be grossly out-of-date before it reaches print, but nonetheless it is unlikely that any international standard covering graphics software will have much direct impact on computing for some years yet. The world is not like that, is it?

10.8 REFERENCES

[1] Sutherland, I. E. (1963), Sketchpad: a man-machine graphical communi-cation system, SJCC, Spartan Books.

[2] Calderbank, V. J. and Prior, W. A. J. (1978), Ghost graphical output system: user manual, CLM-R177, Culham Laboratory, U.K.

[3] CAD Centre (1975), Gino-F user manual, Cambridge.

[4] Universities of Delft and Nijmegen, GPGS users' manual and GPGS users' tutorial.

[5] Integrated Software Systems Corporation, DISSPLA manuals, San Diego.

[6] Calcomp (1976), Programming Calcomp electromechanical plotters.

[7] Ewald, R. H. et al. (1978), Final report of the GSPC state-of-the-art sub-committee. Siggraph-ACM Comput. Graph., 12, Nos. 1-2.

[8] Status report of the GSPC (1977), Siggraph-ACM Comput. Graph., 11, No. 3.

[9] DIN (1979), Graphical kernel system (GKS): Proposal of standard, DIN 00 66 252.

[10] ten Hagen, P. J. W. and Hopgood, F. R. A. (1979), Towards compatible graphic standards, Mathematisch Centrum, Amsterdam.

[11] Ford, B. and Sayers, D. K. (1976), Developing a single numerical algor-ithms library for different machine ranges, Trans. Math. Softw., 2, 115-131.

CHAPTER 11

Operating system command languages

by Ingemar Dahlstrand

As most programmers know, in order to solve a problem using a computer one needs to know not only a programming language in which to write the program, but a command language for the particular computer, or at least commands necessary to compile and run the program. Such command languages vary from computer to computer and even differ for different operating systems for the same computer. The need for some standardisation has often been expressed. In this chapter Ingemar Dahlstrand, Director of the Lund University Computing Centre in Sweden and a member of the programming language working group of the Swedish standards body Standardiseringskommissionen i Sverige, describes the problems involved in standardising command languages, and the progress to date.

11.1 INTRODUCTION

We now come to a kind of language that as yet has no standard – command language.

Command languages are relative newcomers in data processing. In the early days there were no command languages. What had to be done to run a program, like starting it and mounting tapes, was done by pressing buttons or by instructing operators – orally or in writing. In the early sixties, the first steps were taken to run a batch of jobs without manual intervention between each job. Instructions had to be replaced by 'control cards' – and command languages, also called job control languages or JCL, were born.

With the advent of multiprocessing computers, command languages grew rapidly and developed new functions like reserving resources and calling for priority. Out of this headlong and largely unplanned growth emerged a group of languages that hid their underlying similarity of purpose and functions under a bewildering variety of difficult syntax and semantics.

What they have in common is the following: the basic entity of the command language is the batch job (normally divided into job steps) or the interactive session; data are organised in files, that can be saved from job to job; activities in the job are initiated by commands that can compile and execute a program and perform different operations on files; program text and data can be included in the job besides the commands. On the other hand there are great dissimilarities between the languages, functionally as well as syntactically: the attributes that can be given to files, like record lengths and block lengths, vary a great deal; the means of organising program files into libraries, and the intermediate stages of compilation, are different. Most manufacturers' command languages have an undeveloped syntax and are difficult to learn and to use. A few manufacturers (Burroughs, ICL) have however developed good, high level command languages.

11.2 EARLY EFFORTS AND THE FROSTAVALLEN CONFERENCE

By 1970 command languages had grown to be a major headache at many computer installations and different groups — American, Dutch and British — started to work on:

(i) inventories of existing command languages and their functions;
(ii) proposals for future machine-independent command languages;
(iii) compilation from machine-independent command languages to existing command languages.

An early proposal for a machine-independent command language was SJCL, developed by Code, Inc. on order from the U.S. Department of Defense in 1970-71. It was a rich language, already containing most of the facilities needed in a general command language. Unfortunately, this project was discontinued without any implementation attempt.

The first machine-independent language actually to be implemented seems to have been Unique at Nottingham University (I. A. Newman *et al.*). It was intended to provide both simple and sophisticated users with a high level interface to the university's ICL 1906A with the alternative of having the Unique statements compiled instead for a CDC 7600 or an IBM 360/67. Emphasis was placed on a powerful default-setting mechanism, use of task-related high level commands and, where possible, support for both batch and interactive use. By 1974 the system was already running 4000 jobs a week, catering for 80% to 90% of all users at the centre.

Other early projects at this time were GCL at UKAEA Culham Laboratories (Dakin) and ABLE at Bristol University (Parsons). A good overview of these early standardisation developments — and their continuation up to 1977 — is given by Mason in the IFIP/WG 2.7 Bulletin (No. 1, p. 24).

An IFIP Conference in Lund/Frostavallen in 1974 [1] brought together, for the first time, a majority of the groups working on command languages. One outcome of the conference was the establishment of a working group on command languages, IFIP/WG 2.7 (Chairman F. Hertweck). The working group issues a bulletin [2] at three to four month intervals, recommended for all who want to keep up with the field, and recently organised a new working conference in Berchtesgaden [11].

Another outcome of the Lund conference was a general agreement on the fundamental aspects of command language standardisation:

(i) it would be possible to define and implement a standard command language;

(ii) a command language was needed as a separate language. Before and during the conference there was a considerable body of opinion that command languages were unnecessary, that it would be better to extend the programming languages to take care of the extra facilities needed. In the end the issue was toned down as being premature until we know more about command languages;

(iii) no existing command language was proposed as standard, this being in marked contrast to the situation in programming languages;

(iv) a general command language ought to have the form of a high-level language, including variables and conditional statements.

11.3 SPECIAL ASPECTS OF COMMAND LANGUAGE STANDARDISATION

This might be as good a place as any to make some philosophical reflections about command languages before going on with the process of their standardisation.

A command language differs from a programming language in a very important respect. A programming language — be it high-level or low-level, technical-scientific or administrative-commercial — is usually concerned with one question alone: how to produce the wanted results from input data. The language may be more suitable for one purpose or another, it may be wordy or concise, but in the main it is concerned with one thing only — the algorithm of the data processing task at hand.

Now a command language is not like that. It has its algorithmic content too, but it is not only concerned with *what* to do — the transformation of input data into results — but also with *when* to do it (priority, resources, scheduling), *whether* to do it (access rights), *how* to do it cheaply (choice of physical storage, blocking), and *whom* to charge for it. It is concerned with storage having a lifetime beyond the current job, and it has to adapt the job to an environment.

It is obvious that portability must take on a different meaning in this context. Where a programming language can — and should — be 100 per cent portable, the very goal must be set differently for a command language.

Let us look at one example: the scheduling requirements of a job. The priority of a job is likely to vary from one run to another. It depends on circumstances like the day of the month, the degree of hurry, how the machine is loaded and so on. It is not likely that the priority you need today has any relationship to what another user of your job needs another day, running on another installation. So you are not really interested in transporting the scheduling information unchanged. What is important is that the way of giving scheduling information be the same as far as possible at both installations, saving you the trouble of having to learn new ways.

Another example is the accounting information. You will probably get a new account number when you move to a new place, and very likely the rates will be different, perhaps the resources that are charged for too. Again, your interest is not that the accounting information should be portable unchanged, but that you should be able to use the same type of information.

A third example is that you may want to change, rather than retain, the volume numbers of your tapes when moving to a new place.

All this goes to illustrate a main point of command language standardisation: only the algorithmic information can, and should, be portable. For the rest of the information, the first purpose must be to separate it from the algorithmic information as best we can, and then make sure that the same modes of expression are valid over a wide range of machines.

11.4 THE CCL PROPOSAL

One of the first developments within the IFIP/WG 2.7 framework was in 1976 when a group at Denmark's Technical University, Lyngby, (Gram *et al.*) presented preliminary specifications for a Common Command Language CCL [3]. It was test implemented on the IBM 370/165 of NEUCC (North European Computing Centre).

A number of important concepts were united in CCL:

(i) the principle of a high level command language containing variables, simple expressions, assignment statements and conditional and iterative statements. There was the block structure concept and the idea of letting the execution of a block produce a status variable that could control the continued execution;

(ii) the idea of connecting the names of external files with a hierarchy of users. This provided a means of ensuring that each file had a unique full name and created a system of automatic protection. Files belonging to a user or his sub-users were accessible to him for reading and writing; those belonging to users at nodes encountered on the way to the system manager at the root of the hierarchy were accessible for reading only; other files were inaccessible unless explicitly made public;

(iii) the problem of 'connecting' command language files to internal files within programs was settled by regarding it as a case of parameter passing. The program execution is, in effect, a procedure call with the command language file as the actual, and the internal file as the formal, parameter.

The language contained many facilities for file creation and handling, and for compiling, linking and executing programs with a minimum of paper work. About the only important concept missing was the procedure concept. Some of these facilities are hinted at in the example which follows (comments in right-hand column):

```
CCLDEMO: JOB (FREE)                          (the run's name and account)
BEGIN PROJECT := NN;
        EXTERNAL TRANS := FILE ON DISK;  (a file is created on disk)
STEP1: RUN FILE := MY.ABS.PROG1,         (execution of an absolute program)
        F_1   := TRANS,                   (the program's file No. 1 and
        F_5   := *;                       file No. 5 are assigned; the
--                                         latter takes data, delimited
<data>                                     by -- and ++, directly from
++                                         the job stream)
STEP2: BEGIN CPU := 300;                  (step 2 is given 300 secs CPU time)
    FORTRAN IN := MY.SOURCE.PROG2;        (compilation)
    RUN OBJLIB  := MY.OBJLIB,             (linking with a private library)
        F_5      := TRANS,
        F_0      := FILE ON TAPE('4711'),  (call for tapes No. 4711
        F_1      := FILE ON TAPE('4712');  and 4712)
    END STEP2,
    IF STEP2 < WARNING THEN               (if step 2 went right, the
    REMOVE TRANS                           transaction file is deleted)
END JOB;
```

CCL marked an important step, by being the first such language to be implemented on machines and to be proposed — however modestly — as a possible standard. It now has a Univac 1100 implementation besides the IBM 370/165 one, and has some official support from the Swedish Board of Technical Development for further implementation.

11.5 THE ANSI AND BCS COMMITTEES

There are two other official committees in the command language field. ANSI has set up one called X3H1 (Chairman L. Frampton), which has recently issued a Users' Requirements Document proposal [4]. The other one is the British Computer Society's Working Party on Job Control Language, started in 1974 (Chairman I. A. Newman) which regularly updates a Journal of Development [5]. From this I should like to quote some ideas.

The classification of users has several times been a topic for discussion in command language committees. The one proposed by the BCS JOD seems very satisfactory:

(i)   application packages that do not require explicit file handling;
(ii) application packages that do require explicit file handling;
(iii) program development and debugging for own use;
(iv) tailoring systems for other people's use;
(v)   developing system programs and interfaces for a user community, and tailoring for machine and system efficiency.

Another problem topic has been the treatment of compilation. The problem here is that compilers usually work in different stages. Nowadays most compilers produce an intermediate code (relocatable code or object code) that is then mapped or linked into absolute code, which is then loaded and executed. Old-time compilers went directly to absolute code, and this happens in some load-and-go compilers today, even to the point that the absolute code cannot be saved for later runs. These processes are difficult to describe in a portable manner.

The BCS JOD settles the question by postulating that from the user's point of view the compilation is a language check and preparation for a run. The possibility (if it indeed exists) of saving intermediate code is a time-saving feature, an optimisation, to be separated conceptually from the rest of the process. Incidentally, there is a very interesting discussion of message levels during compilation including a call for a message level where not only source code errors, but also non-standard language features used, should be signalled.

A third interesting discussion concerns the default problem. Heavy use of defaulting – which everybody agrees is necessary – carries with it definite difficulties for portability since much information will not be explicit. Widening this discussion, the BCS JOD proposes a general User Environment Tailor that will not only specify defaults but also modify syntax, specify logon-logoff, expand filenames, modify responses and so on. A processor converts the user program into Standard Command Language, written in a standard syntax and with all defaults filled in, and this in turn into local command language. This seems to settle not only the default problem but some related problems, like library handling, as well.

11.6 NETWORKS AND COMMAND LANGUAGES – THE KIWINET PROJECT

One of the really difficult questions connected with command languages has long been their relation to networks. Connecting computers of different manufacture into networks has been going on for some ten years. The primary purpose of a network is to make available to a wide range of users the databases or programs or special computing power present in the different component computers of the network. To be more precise, the purpose is to make these resources *easily* available; the user should be able to connect to different computers from the same terminal with a simple protocol. But without a common control language you still have to be aware of which computer you are using and use its command language and local programming language dialects. An obvious example of this philosophy is the Arpanet. Some groups started to discuss the possibility of a common network command language; we may mention the Cyclades Network (France), the Ein Cost 11 (Switzerland), the NPL–NCC (United Kingdom) and Kiwinet (New Zealand). I will go deeper into this last project because it has led to a complete and fairly well documented command language proposal.

The Kiwinet project was started as a university project in 1975 but the interested parties now include other computer centres with a wide range of computers. The project committee contacted C. Unger of the Dortmund University group and H. Sayani, then chairman of the ANSI/X3 command language sub-committee, and also investigated the best manufacturer-supplied command languages, the Burroughs WFL and ICL SCL, as candidates. Eventually it was decided to build a new command language around some of the SCL concepts as a start [6, 7].

A network command language can have at least four different purposes, as D. Rayner once pointed out (Bulletin No. 1, p. 17):

(i)   to provide a network standard command language;
(ii) to provide uniform access to files as if the network had a single filing system;
(iii) to provide an interface for users who want to view the network as a single computer facility;
(iv) to enable users to run different parts of the same job on different computers and pass data between them, possibly with some degree of synchronised parallelism.

Kiwinet intends to provide (i) and (iv) but not (ii) and (iii), that is, the user has to be well aware that there are different nodes in the network and he can route his job and data between these, using an AT clause and a SITE attribute.

The Kiwinet project defines three languages: a command language NCL, a response language NRL, and a network access language NAL (the latter need not concern us here, however).

The NCL is interesting not only because it covers the network aspect but also because it is a very comprehensive language. It recognises variables of the modes integer, real, boolean and string, and events, files, peripherals and environments. Most of these modes can be compounded into arrays, sets or queues. The treatment of peripherals, files and environments seems definitive; the list of peripheral attributes has 24 entries, file attributes 46 entries, and environment attributes 20 entries. The file attributes cover the logical and physical blocking of the file, its history, owner, access rights, use mode, labelling, etc. This does not mean that every user will have to deal with these properties of all his files; but they will be available when and if needed.

The NCL is complemented with many system macros to handle files and environments, compile and execute, logon-logoff and so on. The definition of a macro or code procedure allows for use of both keywords and defaults (signalled in the declaration by () and :=, respectively). Imagine the following declaration has been made:

```
MACRO WHATSIT = (INTEGER (COPIES)   C
                ,REF FILE (INPUT)    INF  := FILEA
                ,REF FILE (OUTPUT) OUTP := FILEB
                ,STRING (TEXT)       T
                ,REF INT             R    := X );
```

Here are some examples of calls using positional parameters, keyword parameters or a mix of both. The meaning is explained in terms of the complete positional parameter call.

Call: WHATSIT (5, MYFILE, , "STOP");
Meaning: WHATSIT (5, MYFILE, FILEB, "STOP", X);

Call: WHATSIT (INPUT := MYFILE, TEXT := "GO", COPIES := 3);
Meaning: WHATSIT (3, MYFILE, FILEB, "GO", X);

Call: WHATSIT (5, TEXT := "STOP", INT1);
Meaning: WHATSIT (5, FILEA, FILEB, "STOP", INT1);

A new, ground-breaking attempt in this project is the definition of a response language with the purpose of giving at least a minimum range of error types to be explicitly handled and a minimum requirement for error message formats.

11.7 UNIX SYSTEMS

Let us now turn to another interesting command language, this time in the United States, namely the Unix system at Bell Laboratories.

The Unix system seems to be one of those things that just happened. In the words of the reference [8]: 'Although the basic UNIX system was literally developed in an attic by two people in a year, and has been available only as an unsupported package, the benefits it provides are so compelling that currently there are nearly 1000 UNIX systems scattered around the world'. That makes it easily the most successful so far of all machine-independent command languages.

The file system of Unix has a fairly conventional hierarchic structure, but it has a couple of important user concepts too:

(i) directories are files. That means the handling of a directory, for example, listing it or searching it, is done by ordinary user programs;

(ii) a file is just a sequence of bytes. This is so revolutionary that it is best to point out the attributes a file does *not* have:

    — there are no tracks or cylinders or other physical device characteristics;

    — there are no physical or logical records or associated counts — the only bytes are the ones put there by the user;

    — no fixed/variable length distinction, no visible blocking or buffering;

    — no preallocation of file space — the file is always exactly as big as you made it;

    — no access methods — the bytes are accessible in any order, and all files are identical in form.

Peripherals are also files in this system, organised in a special directory for convenience. This means, for example, that the same program (written in the C programming language) that can be used to copy files also becomes a spooling program.

When a user logs into the Unix system a command interpreter called the Shell accepts commands from the terminal and interprets them as requests to run programs. Any program file that is executed in Unix has two files opened for it automatically, an input and an output file that are connected to the user's active terminal. These may be redirected before execution:

    program <in >out

instructs the Shell to arrange that 'program' take its input from 'in' and place its output on 'out'; 'program' itself is unaware of the change.

It is part of the Unix philosophy to run simple programs in sequence to produce interesting results. As an example, suppose we have to find out how many times user 'joe' is at present logged in. It can be done be running three programs:

who >userlist	'who' produces a list of everybody logged in on 'userlist'.
grep joe <userlist >joelist	'grep' searches 'userlist' for occurrences of the pattern 'joe' and stores them in 'joelist'.
wc <joelist	'wc' counts the length of 'joelist' = the number of logins requested!

This seems compact enough, but can be written in one line as follows:

    who | grep joe | wc

The | has the effect that the output of its left-hand side is used as input to its right-hand side. This technique, called 'pipe-lining' for easily understandable reasons, does away with the intermediate files 'userlist' and 'joelist'. But not only that. It also sweeps away the concept of the job-step, which was really only a hold-over from primitive command languages, and in effect introduces the file manipulation expression.

11.8 NICOLA'S ABSTRACT MACHINE CONCEPT

How do we reconcile file concepts as different as those of Unix and Kiwinet? Are we forced to choose between them, or can they be accommodated in one future system?

Part of the answer lies in the user classification mentioned in the discussion of the BCS JOD. The simple file concept of Unix belongs to the amateur user, while the complete possibilities for file definition belong to the more sophisticated system tailors.

The way to bridge the gap is through the concept of abstract machines, studied and elaborated by the Dortmund Group (C. Unger *et al.*) that is defining Nicola [9], working closely with the Kiwinet people. The start of serious research into this topic is a very welcome development. Many problems all over the language field are basically problems of faulty or inconsistent abstraction.

The group notes that most users do not need a very detailed knowledge of the computer system. A user is better served by an abstract model of the system, an 'abstract machine' (AM). This machine abstracts from the 'real' machine and therefore hides some details in order to offer a simple application-oriented interface to the user. There will be various levels of these AMs according to the levels of the users, and there will be different kinds of abstractions according to different kinds of users (scientific, administrative, etc.). We need therefore to define a basic abstract machine (BAM) from which all other AMs may be derived, step by step.

An AM is a named collection of the following items:

(i) a user-oriented description of the syntax and semantics of the command language and the response language;
(ii) a set of modes available to the user;
(iii) a default environment of the user.

The mechanism for definition of a new AM from an existing one must be included in the command language. One of the things necessary is to define the response handling. Responses in the lower (= less abstract) AM may no longer be meaningful at a higher level of abstraction. Therefore the UE ('undesired event') giving rise to the response will have to be reformulated so that it is meaningful to the new user. All this has to be done explicitly when defining the new AM.

It will be most interesting to see the effect of the implementation of these ideas by the Kiwinet and Nicola groups and to see them in use.

11.9 FUTURE PROSPECTS

Having covered so many committees and projects in a short while, how do we summarise the prospects for a common command language in the near future?

We may soon find out. In May 1979 the Codasyl command language committee published its Journal of Development [10], containing a draft proposal for a common operating systems command language, COSCL. This is in itself a major event, considering the impact that Codasyl's earlier work (Cobol, DBMS languages) have had on the computing world. COSCL, like most of the languages discussed above, is a high-level language with a well-developed file concept, control structures and a procedure facility. Several features in it, among them the definition and handling of parameters, are of considerable interest also for other programming languages. Otherwise, the committee has mainly tried to use existing and tested ideas, this being part of the design criteria. If the COSCL proposal can touch off a joint effort of the committees working in the field, we shall have a good common language available in a fairly short time.

11.10 REFERENCES

[1] Unger, C., ed. (1975), Command languages, Proc. IFIP working conference on command languages, North Holland.

[2] Hertweck, F. ed., IFIP TC 2 WG 2.7 Bulletin.

[3] Madsen, J. (1977), CCL – a high level command language: design and implementation, ID-754, Dept. of Computer Sciences, Tech. Univ. of Denmark, Lyngby.

[4] ANSI (1979), OSCRL user requirements (Rev. 2 of 1979-01-22), Subcommittee X3H1.

[5] BCS, Working party on job control language, Journal of Development/77/119.

[6] Hopper, K., James, N. S., and Jenkins, P. C. (1977), KIWINET system control and access, Report No. 34 – preliminary language specifications, Massey University Computer Centre, New Zealand.

[7] Hopper, K., James, N. S., and Jenkins, P. C. (1978), Report No. 35 – technical progress report.

[8] Kernighan, B. W. and Mashey, J. R. (1979), The UNIX^{TM} programming environment, *Softw. Pract. Exper.*, 9, 1-15.

[9] Kugler, H. J. *et al.* (1979), Project NICOLA: progress report No. 3, University of Dortmund.

[10] Codasyl (1979), COSCL Journal of Development.

[11] Beech, D., ed., (1980) Command language directions, Proc. 2nd IFIP working conference on command languages, North Holland.

CHAPTER 12

Metalanguages
by Roger S. Scowen

One thing that strikes the reader of programming language standards is that, although many make use of a metalanguage to define the language concerned, each metalanguage is different. This has naturally led to suggestions that the metalanguage used in standards should itself be standardised, and indeed work has begun on this. The author of this chapter, which gives the position in March 1980, is Roger S. Scowen of the National Physical Laboratory in the U.K. and a member of BSI: DPS/13.

12.1 INTRODUCTION

A metalanguage is a 'language or system of symbols used to discuss another language or symbolic system' says Chambers Twentieth Century Dictionary. Not quite right — a metalanguage might be used to discuss itself — but near enough.

Fraser Duncan has said that English is our ultimate metalanguage. English has indeed often been used, see for example Fig. 12.1 from the Book of Common Prayer where it is an admirable choice for defining the form of Church services. It is clear, and easily understood by those who need it.

Nevertheless English has serious disadvantages: it is easy to be ambiguous without realising it and English can be difficult to analyse rigorously. Alice [1, 2] has many problems with English in her journeys in Wonderland and through the Looking-Glass, see Figs. 12.2-12.8.

English has also been used for defining programming languages, but here the disadvantages far outweigh the benefits. Rigour is all important and a formal definition is required where possible. 'That pestilent fellow, the critical reader' [3] is essential in this context. The syntax of a programming language is almost always defined using a metalanguage — in fact a syntactic metalanguage. Typically the syntax consists of a number of rules; each one names part of the language (called a non-terminal symbol of the language) and then defines all its possible forms. A terminal symbol of the language is an atom that cannot be split into smaller components of the language.

N. WILT thou have this Man to thy wedded husband, to live together after God's ordinance in the holy estate of Matrimony? Wilt thou obey him, and serve him, love, honour, and keep him in sickness and in health; and, forsaking all other, keep thee only unto him, so long as ye both shall live?

The Woman shall answer,

I will.

Then shall the Minister say,

Who giveth this Woman to be married to this man?

Then shall they give their troth to each other in this manner.

The Minister, receiving the Woman at her father's or friend's hands, shall cause the Man with his right hand to take the Woman by her right hand, and to say after him as followeth.

I *N.* take thee *N.* to my wedded wife, to have and to hold from this day forward, for better for worse, for richer for poorer, in sickness and in health, to love and to cherish, till death us do part, according to God's holy ordinance, and thereto I plight thee my troth.

Then shall they loose their hands; and the Woman, with her right hand taking the Man by his right hand, shall likewise say after the Minister,

I *N.* take thee *N.* to my wedded husband, to have and to hold from this day forward, for better for worse, for richer for poorer, in sickness and in health, to love, cherish, and to obey, till death us do part, according to God's holy ordinance; and thereto I give thee my troth.

Fig. 12.1 – English used as a metalanguage in the Book of Common Prayer. Text in Roman type is words actually spoken during the marriage service. The italic 'N.' is replaced by a Christian name of the bride or groom. All other italic text gives instructions and indicates the appropriate replacement for each 'N.'. The formal ambiguity does not matter in practice.

"I don't know what you mean by 'glory,' " Alice said.

Humpty Dumpty smiled contemptuously. "Of course you don't – till I tell you. I meant there's a nice knock-down argument for you!"

"But 'glory' doesn't mean 'a nice knock-down argument,' " Alice objected.

"When *I* use a word," Humpty Dumpty said in rather a scornful tone, "it means just what I choose it to mean – neither more nor less."

Fig. 12.2 – How to discover the meaning of a word.

Impenetrability! That's what *I* say!"

"Would you tell me, please," said Alice, "what that means?"

"Now you talk like a reasonable child," said Humpty Dumpty, looking very much pleased. "I meant by 'impenetrability' that we've had enough of that subject, and it would be just as well if you'd mention what you mean to do next, as I suppose you don't intend to stop here all the rest of your life."

"That's a great deal to make one word mean," Alice said in a thoughtful tone.

"When I make a word do a lot of work like that," said Humpty Dumpty, "I always pay it extra."

"Oh!" said Alice. She was too much puzzled to make any other remark.

Fig. 12.3 – A word might have a very complicated meaning.

"... How old did you say you were?"

Alice made a short calculation, and said, "Seven years and six months."

"Wrong!" Humpty Dumpty exclaimed triumphantly. "You never said a word like it."

"I thought you meant 'How old *are* you?'" Alice explained.

"If I'd meant that, I'd have said it," said Humpty Dumpty.

Fig. 12.4 – The conventional and literal meanings might differ.

"Can you do Addition?" the White Queen asked. "What's one and one and one and one and one and one and one and one and one and one?"

"I don't know," said Alice. "I lost count."

"She can't do Addition," the Red Queen interrupted.

Fig. 12.5 – Sentences in simple language are not always easy to understand.

"... The name of the song is called 'Haddocks' Eyes.'"

"Oh, that's the name of the song, is it?" Alice said, trying to feel interested.

"No, you don't understand," the Knight said, looking a little vexed. "That's what the name is *called*. The name really *is* 'The Aged Aged Man.'"

"Then I ought to have said, 'That's what the *song* is called'?" Alice corrected herself.

"No, you oughtn't: that's another thing. The *song* is called 'Ways and Means': but that's only what it's *called*, you know!"

"Well, what *is* the song, then?" said Alice, who was by this time completely bewildered.

"I was coming to that," the Knight said. "The song really *is* 'A-sitting On a Gate': and the tune's my own invention."

Fig. 12.6 – An object is not the same as its name.

... every now and then the oars got fast in it, and would hardly come out again.

"Feather! Feather!" the Sheep cried again, taking more needles. "You'll be catching a crab directly."

"A dear little crab!" thought Alice. "I should like that."

"Didn't you hear me say 'Feather'?" the Sheep cried angrily, taking up quite a bunch of needles.

"Indeed I did," said Alice: "you've said it very often – and very loud. Please, where *are* the crabs?"

"In the water, of course!" said the Sheep, sticking some of the needles into her hair, as her hands were full. "Feather, I say!"

"*Why* do you say 'Feather' so often?" Alice asked at last, rather vexed, "I'm not a bird!"

"You are," said the Sheep: "you're a little goose."

Fig. 12.7 – Words often have more than one meaning.

"I quite agree with you," said the Duchess: "and the moral of that is – 'Be what you would seem to be' – or if you'd like it put more simply – 'Never imagine yourself not to be otherwise than what it might appear to others that what you were or might have been was not otherwise than what you had been would have appeared to them to be otherwise.'"

"I think I should understand that better," Alice said very politely, "if I had it written down: but I'm afraid I can't quite follow it as you say it."

"That's nothing to what I could say if I chose," the Duchess replied, in a pleased tone.

Fig. 12.8 – English can be difficult to analyse and understand.

This formal definition has three distinct uses:

(i) it names the various syntactic parts (that is, non-terminal symbols) of the language;

(ii) it shows which sequences of symbols are valid sentences of the language;

(iii) it shows the syntactic structure of any sentence of the language.

Thus a syntactic metalanguage is an essential weapon in the armoury of every computer scientist. Yet although the concepts are well known, everyone tends to use a slightly different notation. As a result syntactic metalanguages are still barely understood by many programmers, and the general public is almost completely unaware of the possibility of the unambiguous notation for defining syntaxes.

12.2 ALGOL 60

The popularity of syntactic metalanguages in computer science started when Peter Naur edited the Algol 60 report [4] in 1960. This was not the first time a syntax had been formally defined but it certainly opened computer scientists' eyes to the value of a formal definition. The rigour and clarity were so overwhelming that the Algol 60 report set new standards for the definition of programming languages. The syntax was described using a notation known as BNF, standing originally for Backus Normal Form, and later for Backus Naur Form.

BNF was inadequate to express simply some elements of Algol 60, for example, comments and strings. Here Peter Naur completed the definition in English rather than write long rules which would have been less clear, that is:

The sequence of basic symbols

; **comment** ⟨ any sequence not containing ; ⟩ ;

is equivalent to

;

rather than something like

⟨semicolon symbol⟩ ::= ; | ; **comment** ⟨comment symbols⟩ ;
⟨comment symbols⟩ ::= ⟨single comment symbol⟩
    | ⟨single comment symbol⟩ ⟨comment symbols⟩
⟨single comment symbol⟩ ::= ⟨letter⟩ | ⟨digit⟩ | ⟨logical value⟩
    | ⟨operator⟩ | ⟨bracket⟩ | ⟨declarator⟩ | ⟨specificator⟩
    | , | . | $_{10}$ | : | := | ⊔ | **step** | **until** | **while** | **comment**

and then replacing an actual semicolon by ⟨semicolon symbol⟩ in all other relevant definitions.

Repetition was expressed as a recursive definition and some people found this confusing when first meeting the Algol report.

A new feature was to give a clear English name for each non-terminal symbol.

In earlier uses of BNF, the rules had been made shorter by abbreviating names, for example, 'ulbl' for 'upper-lower-bound-list'.

12.3 COBOL

Cobol was initially developed at the same time as Algol 60. The format of each statement was defined using another notation:

[ ]   Square brackets enclose an optional item.

{ }   Braces enclose items from which a choice must be made. The alternatives are listed vertically.

...   Ellipses indicate optional repetition of the preceding item.

This notation had less impact on computer scientists, probably because so few were concerned with Cobol and the problems of data processing.

12.4 FORTRAN

The syntax of Fortran, an earlier language, has always been defined using English rather than a formal notation, even in the ANSI standards, see Figs. 12.9 and 12.10.

Subscripts.

GENERAL FORM	EXAMPLES

Let v represent any fixed point variable and c (or c′) any unsigned fixed point constant. Then a subscript is an expression of one of the forms: v
    c
    v+c or v−c
    c * v
    c * v+c′ or c * v−c′
	I
	3
	MU+2
	MU−2
	5 * J
	5 * J+2
	5 * J−2

The symbol * denotes multiplication. The variable v must not itself be subscripted.

Fig. 12.9 — An extract from the first Fortran Manual (reprinted in reference [5]).

7.1.1.2   LOGICAL ASSIGNMENT STATEMENT

A logical assignment statement is of the form

$$v = e$$

where v is a logical variable name or a logical array element name and e is a logical expression.

Fig. 12.10 — From the ISO Fortran Standard [16]. Is this definition ambiguous? An earlier paragraph defines the logical operators such that .AND. binds more strongly than .OR. If this is true for the conjunctions 'and' and 'or', the definition is wrong.

However, there is a metalanguage used within Fortran itself — the FORMAT statement used to define the structure of data and results. Few people have considered this as a metalanguage even though it is rigorous and it is also much more compact than anything possible with BNF.

The latest standard for Fortran [7] has used a 'railway-track' notation to describe the syntax. This is almost self-explanatory — any smooth continuous route (no turning back is allowed) represents a valid string of symbols. It appears in an appendix to the standard as a helpful tool for understanding the new standard. The notation is not formally defined so it is not perhaps surprising that there are some anomalies in its use — see Fig. 12.11.

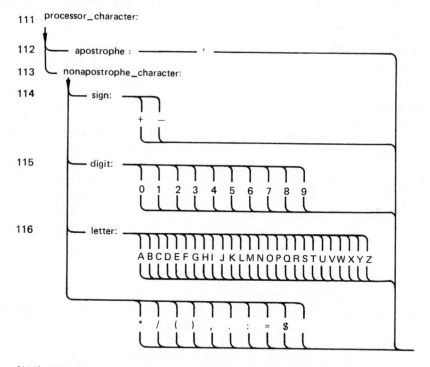

(111) A blank is a processor character. The set of processor characters may include additional characters recognised by the processor.

Fig. 12.11 — Part of an appendix to Fortran 77 [7]. It is obvious but not formally stated that the sequence of 12 characters

apostrophe:'

is not a processor-character. It is not quite so clear that blank is the processor-character defined after $, but that line-feed is not.

12.5 ALGOL 68

The designers of Algol 68 [8] attempted to extend the power and generality of an algorithmic language, removing both the limitations and the arbitrary features of Algol 60. At the same time they tried to define the whole language and BNF was extended to become 'van Wijngaarden' grammar. While formally successful, the notation and report were too complicated for most people to understand and Algol 68 must so far be judged as a glorious failure. There are now several relatively simple introductions to Algol 68 — both the language and the meta-language used to define it — see for example reference [9].

12.6 THE PROPOSED BRITISH STANDARD METALANGUAGE

Many other syntactic metalanguages have been used, often varying slightly, but with good reason, from one of the notations decribed above.

This chaos continued for many years. Then, in 1977, Niklaus Wirth published an article [10] asking why there are so many notations and no standard. His solution was paradoxically to invent another. This provoked little public response but Ian Pyle wrote to BSI suggesting some action. As a result an earlier working party was revived to see what should be done.

The working party set itself four objectives:

   (i) to consider whether a standard metalanguage was needed, and if so:

  (ii) to define the required properties of a standard metalanguage;

 (iii) to define what a standard should not do;

 (iv) to define the syntactic concepts which must be expressed and to decide a suitable notation for each concept.

These objectives are considered in more detail below.

12.7 IS A STANDARD METALANGUAGE REQUIRED?

This was certainly the most difficult question confronting the working party. Even hindsight — that normally infallible prophet — might be unable to answer. A standard metalanguage that is generally adopted and becomes a familiar notation would show the answer to be 'Yes'. But if the standard metalanguage is ignored, who is to know whether no standard was required after all or whether the working party's suggested one was unsuitable?

In fact the working party never did answer this question; it was almost entirely a matter of personal opinion. However, they did identify various problems caused by the lack of a standard:

   (i) many different notations — it is rare for two different programming languages to use the same metalanguage. Thus human readers are handicapped by having to learn a new metalanguage before getting to grips with the new language itself.

(ii) concepts not widely understood — the lack of a standard notation prevents the idea of a rigorous unambiguous definition from being as widely adopted as it deserves;

(iii) imperfect notations — because a metalanguage must be defined for every programming language, it is almost inevitable that sometimes the metalanguage contains defects. For example, neither metalanguage used in the draft British standards for Coral 66 and RTL/2 could be typed easily and there were some unfortunate errors;

(iv) special purpose notations — when a metalanguage is defined for a particular programming language, it is natural to make it as simple as possible. This can frequently be done by taking advantage of special features in the language to be defined — however, the metalanguage is then unsuitable for other programming languages;

(v) few general syntax processors — the multiplicity of syntactic metalanguages has limited the availability of computer programs to analyse and process syntaxes, for example, to list a syntax neatly, to make an index of the symbols used in the syntax, or to produce a syntax-checker for programs written in the language.

In practice, experienced readers have little difficulty in picking up and learning a new notation, but even so the differences obscure mutual understanding and hinder communication. A standard metalanguage would enable more people to crystallise vague ideas into an unambiguous definition. It would also be useful because other people needing to provide definitions would no longer need to reinvent similar concepts.

Instead of fruitless arguments whether or not a standard metalanguage was required or desirable, the working group set to work to define a metalanguage and leave posterity to decide.

12.8 THE REQUIRED PROPERTIES OF A STANDARD SYNTACTIC METALANGUAGE

Objectives are specified more easily than they are achieved. The working party had no great difficulty agreeing the required properties, but later had much more difficulty in satisfying all the constraints. They decided that the standard should be:

(i) concise — so that languages can be defined briefly and thus be more easily understood;

(ii) precise — so that the rules are unambiguous;

(iii) formal — so that the rules can be parsed or otherwise processed by a computer when required;

(iv) natural — so that the notation and format are relatively simple to learn and understand, even for those who are not themselves language designers. The meaning of a symbol should not be surprising. It should also be possible to define the syntax of a language in a way that helps to indicate the meaning of the constructions;

(v) general — so that the notation is suitable for many purposes including the description of many different languages;

(vi) simple in its character set — the notation should avoid, as far as is practicable, using characters which are not generally available on standard keyboards (both typewriters and computer terminals) so that the rules can be typed, and be processed by computer programs;

(vii) self describing — the notation should be able to describe itself;

(viii) linear — a syntax should be expressed as a single stream of characters read from left to right — this simplifies printing a syntax. Computer processing of a syntax is also simpler.

It was also agreed, fairly painlessly, that it was more important to define a simple standard quickly rather than to attempt to define a notation sufficient for every requirement. So the working party noted that:

(i) the language being defined must, like the metalanguage itself, be linear, that is, the symbols in a sentence of the language can be placed in a line reading from one end to the other. For example knitting patterns and cooking recipes are linear languages, but electric circuit diagrams are not,

(ii) the notation would not be suitable for defining a two-level grammar, such as that used in Algol 68.

12.9 THE METALANGUAGE

The working party started defining the syntactic metalanguage by listing the concepts that should be expressible with the new notation. Only then did they go on to decide the method for denoting each concept. This was by no means easy, not least because everyone preferred the notation he was familiar with. However, agreement was finally, if reluctantly, reached on all issues except a notation for comments.

It was natural to define a notation suitable for use with the full ISO character set. However, many of these characters cannot be printed on ordinary typewriters and computer terminals. So it was necessary to recognise that alternative representations would be required for many metasymbols.

It is confusing if a character can have more than one meaning in a language so the working party tried to avoid using a character with two different meanings. This proved more difficult when the metalanguage is represented with a limited character set. Fig. 12.12 summarises the various ways of denoting the metasymbols.

Metasymbol	ISO character	Alternative representation (if any)
Comment delimiter	!	*
Defining symbol	=	
Definition separator	/	
Terminator symbol	;	.
Grouping brackets	( )	
Brackets round optional symbols	[ ]	(/ /)
Brackets round a sequence	{ }	(: :)
Exception symbol	–	–
Escape delimiter	?	+

Fig. 12.12 – Metasymbols proposed for a standard metalanguage and alternative representations.

The working party took as a starting point Wirth's proposal [10] which was based on BNF and contains many common extensions:

(i) terminal symbols of the language are quoted so that any character, including one used in the metalanguage, can be defined as a terminal symbol of the language being defined;

(ii) a meta-identifier (the name of a non-terminal symbol in the language) is written as a single word so that:

    (a) it need not be quoted, and

    (b) no explicit concatenation symbol is required;

(iii) [and] indicate optional symbols;

(iv) { and } indicate repetition;

(v) each rule has an explicit final character so that there is never any ambiguity over where a rule ends.

The main differences in the draft standard syntactic metalanguage are further features which experience has shown are often required when providing a formal definition:

(i) defining an explicit number of items. Fortran contains a rule that a label field contains exactly five characters. An identifier in PL/I or Cobol has up to 32 characters. Rules such as these can be expressed only with difficulty in Backus Naur Form. In practice, such definitions are often left incomplete and the rules qualified informally in English;

(ii) defining something by specifying the few exceptional cases. An Algol **end**-comment ends immediately preceding the next **end**, **else** or semi-colon. A rule like this cannot be expressed concisely or clearly in Backus Naur Form and is also usually specified informally in English;

(iii) including comments. Programming languages and other structures with a complicated syntax will need many rules to define them. The syntax will be clearer if explanations and cross-references can be provided. Accordingly the draft standard metalanguage contains a comment facility so that ordinary text can be added to a syntax for the benefit of a human reader without affecting the formal meaning of the syntax;

(iv) providing a symbol to introduce an escape sequence. A user may wish to extend the syntactic metalanguage for special purposes. An escape sequence is defined so that extensions are made consistently;

(v) using brackets to group items together. It is an obvious convenience to use round brackets in their ordinary mathematical sense;

(vi) allowing a hyphen in meta-identifiers. A long meta-identifier is easier to read if it can contain hyphens to separate the words which form it.

12.10 THE COMMENT NOTATION

The working party failed to agree on a notation for comments. Some favoured end-of-line comments, others wanted each comment to be terminated by an explicit character. The advantages of each notation can be summarised:

(i) Comments starting with ! and ending at the end of each line:

(a) it is always easy to see where a comment ends;

(b) rules and comments can easily be turned into comments, for example, to express alternative possible rules or define a subset;

(c) a missing ! character causes an error only in the current rule rather than a cascade of errors.

(ii) Comments starting and ending with !

(a) any space can be changed to new-line without affecting the meaning of the syntax;

(b) those who do not understand the metalanguage (such as typists and printers) will be able to copy rules and get them right;

(c) comments can be placed anywhere, and are not restricted to ends of lines, which (among other things) makes cross-referencing much easier.

12.11 EXAMPLES SHOWING THE DISADVANTAGES WITH THE TWO NOTATIONS

With end-of-line comments typists and printers may introduce errors in a syntax by breaking a line of a comment and not repeating the comment-delimiter character of an end-of-line comment. Experience has shown that this error occurs frequently in published Fortran programs.

In following these examples, it should be noted that an exclamation mark within apostrophes cannot start a comment (being considered different from a 'nude' exclamation mark) but, in the second proposal, can finish one because an apostrophe has no meaning within a comment.

(i) End-of-line comments — a legal comment

comment = '!' {character _ new-line} new-line / gap-character
! The working party failed to agree on a notation for
! comments.
;

(ii) End-of-line comments — an illegal comment

comment = '!' {character _ new-line} new-line / gap-character
! The working party failed to agree on a notation for
comments.
;

When comments start and end with a comment-delimiter character it is not possible to write an arbitrary set of rules and comments as comments. This makes it difficult to express a family of related languages simultaneously. For example this difficulty could occur in the definition of the syntactic metalanguage itself.

(i) Explicit characters — an illegal comment

comment = '!' {character _ '!' } '!' / gap-character
! The working party were unable to agree on a
notation for comments, some members preferred:
comment = '!' {character _ new-line} new-line
/ gap-character;
! ;

(ii) Explicit characters — a legal comment

comment = '!' {character _ '!' } '!' / gap-character
! The working party were unable to agree on a
notation for comments, some members preferred:
comment = comment-delimiter-character
{character _ new-line} new-line
/ gap-character; ! ;

12.12 THE DRAFT SYNTACTIC METALANGUAGE

Naturally the syntactic metalanguage should be able to define itself. In the example below, the symbols letter, decimal digit, character, new-line and gap-character are not defined. The position of comments is stated in a comment but not formally defined. An end-of-line comment notation has been assumed.

```
syntax = syntax-rule {syntax-rule};
syntax-rule
    = meta-identifier '=' (definitions-list / escape-sequence) ';'
    ! A syntax-rule defines the sequences of symbols denoted by a
    !   meta-identifier

    ;
definitions-list = single-definition {'/' single-definition}
    ! / separates alternative single-definitions

    ;
single-definition = {term};
term = factor ['_' factor]
    ! A term denotes any sequence of symbols defined by the first
    !   factor that does not start with a sequence of symbols
    !   denoted by the second factor

    ;
factor = [integer] primary
    ! The integer denotes the number of repetitions of the primary

    ;
primary = optional-sequence / repeated-sequence
    / '(' definitions-list ')' / meta-identifier / terminal;
optional-sequence = '[' definitions-list ']'
    ! The brackets [ and ] enclose symbols which are optional

    ;
repeated-sequence = '{' definitions-list '}'
    ! The brackets {and} enclose symbols which may be
    !   repeated any number of times

    ;
terminal = " ' " {character _ " ' " } " ' " / ' " ' {character _ ' " ' } ' " '
    ! A terminal symbol denotes the characters between the quote
    !   symbols ' ' or " "

    ;
meta-identifier = letter {['-'] (letter / decimal-digit)}
    ! A meta-identifier is the name of a syntactic element of the
    !   language being defined

    ;
integer = decimal-digit {decimal-digit};
escape-sequence = '?' {character _ ';'}
    ! The meaning of an escape-sequence is not defined in the
    !   standard metalanguage.
```

```
;
comment = '!'{character _ new-line} new-line / gap-character
! A comment is allowed anywhere except in the middle of
!   an integer, escape-sequence, meta-identifier or terminal.
!   A comment is necessary after a meta-identifier when it is
!   immediately followed by an integer or another
!   meta-identifier.
!
! A gap-character is a space, new-line, tabulation, etc.
!
! The working party were unable to agree on the form of a
!   comment, some members preferred:
!     comment = '!'{character _ '!' }'!' / gap-character;
!
! The last two rules would then be written:
!       escape-sequence = '?' {character _ ';'}
!         ! An escape sequence is used for denoting symbols
!            that cannot otherwise be expressed. !;
!       comment = '!' {character _ '!'}'!' / gap-character
!         ! A comment is allowed anywhere except in the middle
!            of an integer, escape-sequence, meta-identifier
!            or terminal. A comment is necessary after a
!            meta-identifier when it is immediately followed
!            by an integer or another meta-identifier. !;
;
```

A draft proposal on the above lines was circulated for comment by BSI, dated 1st November 1979 [11]. At the time of writing the comments are in, but have yet to receive detailed scrutiny. It seems clear however that some revisions will be necessary, and this chapter should be read only as an indication of work in progress, not as describing a finished product.

12.13 EXAMPLES

Computer languages are often similar in many ways, but the same concept will have different names in different languages. There may be other subtle differences. An if (or conditional) statement is one such feature that is almost universal.

These examples show how the syntax of this construction is defined in six different languages, repeating each in the draft metalanguage.

12.13.1 Ada

5.4 If Statements

An if statement effects the choice of a sequence of statements based on the truth value of one or more conditions. The expressions appearing in conditions must be of the predefined type BOOLEAN.

    if_statement ::=
      if condition **then**
        sequence_of_statements
      {**elsif** condition **then**
        sequence_of_statements}
      [**else**
        sequence_of_statements]
      end if;

---

    if-statement = 'if' condition 'then'
      sequence-of-statements
    {'elsif' condition 'then'
      sequence-of-statements}
    ['else'
      sequence-of-statements]
    'end' 'if' ';';

12.13.2 BCPL

5.8 Test Commands

Syntactic form: **test E then C or C**

---

    test-command = 'TEST' expression 'THEN' command
      'OR' command;

12.13.3 Cobol 74

5.13 THE IF STATEMENT

5.13.1 Function

The IF statement causes causes a condition (see page II-41, Conditional Expressions) to be evaluated. The subsequent action of the object program depends on whether the value of the condition is true or false.

5.13.2 General Format

$$\underline{\text{IF}} \text{ condition;} \begin{Bmatrix} \text{statement-1} \\ \underline{\text{NEXT SENTENCE}} \end{Bmatrix} \begin{Bmatrix} ; \underline{\text{ELSE}} \text{ statement-2} \\ ; \underline{\text{ELSE}}\ \underline{\text{NEXT SENTENCE}} \end{Bmatrix}$$

5.13.3 Syntax Rules

(1) Statement-1 and statement-2 represent either an imperative statement or a conditional statement, and either may be followed by a conditional statement.

(2) The ELSE NEXT SENTENCE phrase may be omitted if it immediately precedes the terminal period of the sentence.

```
if-statement = 'IF' condition [';']
     statement-or-next-sentence [';']
     'ELSE' statement-or-next-sentence;
statement-or-next-sentence = imperative-statement
    / conditional statement
    / 'NEXT' 'SENTENCE';
    ! The phrase 'ELSE NEXT SENTENCE' may be omitted
    ! if it immediately precedes the terminal
    ! period of the sentence.
```

12.13.4 Coral 66

```
Conditionalstatement = IF Condition THEN Consequence      7.9
                       IF Condition THEN Consequence
                       ELSE Alternative
```

```
conditional-statement = 'IF' condition 'THEN' consequence
    ['ELSE' alternative] ;                          ! 7.9
```

12.13.5 Fortran 77

> 11.5 Logical IF Statement
>
> The form of a logical IF statement is:
>
>   IF (e) st
>
> where: e is a logical expression
>
> > st is any executable statement except a DO, block IF,
> > ELSE IF, ELSE, END IF, END, or another logical IF
> > statement

logical-if-statement = 'IF' '(' logical-expression ')'
(executable-statement _ (do-statement
   / block-if-statement / else-if-statement
   / else-statement / end-if-statement
   / end-statement / logical-if-statement));

12.13.6 RTL/2

> ifst ::= IF condition THEN sequence [ELSEIF condition
> THEN sequence] ... [ELSE sequence] END

if-st = 'IF' condition 'THEN' sequence
   {'ELSEIF' condition 'THEN' sequence}
   ['ELSE' sequence] 'END';

12.14 REFERENCES

[1] Carroll, L. (1865), Alice's adventures in Wonderland, Macmillan.
[2] Carroll, L. (1871), Through the looking-glass and what Alice found there, Macmillan.
[3] Fowler, H. W. (1965), A dictionary of modern English usage, 2nd edition, Oxford.
[4] Naur, P. *et al.* (1960), Report on the algorithmic language Algol 60, *Commun. ACM.*, **3**, 299–314; *Numer. Math.*, **2**, 106–136.
[5] Backus, J. W. (1979), The early history of Fortran I, II and III, *Ann. Hist. Comput.*, **1**, 21–37.

[6]   ASA (1964), A programming language for information processing on automatic data processing systems. *Commun. ACM.*, 7, 591-625.

[7]   ANSI (1978), ANSI X3.9-1978: Programming Language Fortran.

[8]   van Wijngaarden, A., *et al.* (1976), Revised report on the algorithmic language Algol 68, Springer Verlag; (1975), *Acta Inf.*, 5, 1-236; (1977), *SIGPLAN Not.*, 12, No. 5, 1-70.

[9]   McGettrick, A. D. (1978), An introduction to the formal definition of Algol 68, *Annu. Rev. Autom. Program.*, 9, 1-84.

[10] Wirth, N. (1977), What can we do about the unnecessary diversity of notation for syntactic definitions? *Commun. ACM.*, 20, 822.

[11] Ichbiah, J. D., *et al.* (1979), Preliminary Ada reference manual, *SIGPLAN Not.*, 14, No. 6, Part A.

[12] Richards, M. (1969), The BCPL reference manual: technical memorandum 69/1, University Math. Lab., Cambridge.

[13] ANSI (1974) ANSI X3.23-1974: Programming Language Cobol.

[14] Inter-Establishment Committee on Computer Applications (1970), Official definition of Coral 66, HMSO.

[15] Barnes, J. G. P. (1976), RTL/2 design and philosophy, Heyden.

[16] ISO (1972), ISO/R 1539-1972: Programming Language Fortran.

CHAPTER 13

Flowcharts and decision tables
by Dr. Roger G. Johnson

Programming languages are a means of describing algorithms and solutions to problems. Another means is the flowchart, an important feature of program documentation and used by many programmers as an aid to program design. Decision tables are another means of representing diagrammatically aspects of a problem which has to be programmed. Their standardisation is discussed in this chapter by Dr. Roger G. Johnson of the School of Mathematics, Statistics and Computing at Thames Polytechnic in the U.K.

13.1 INTRODUCTION

The need for good documentation of both manual and computer systems has long been recognised. Two of the most common components of the documentation of any system are flowcharts and decision tables.

The flow chart seeks to show the flow of information through a system. This could be data through a program or pieces of paper through an office. In showing a movement the flowchart is essentially procedural, it shows a sequence of events.

The decision table, however, seeks to specify the possible courses of action at some point in a system. It is, therefore, non-procedural. It is possible to include decision tables in flowcharts and to define programs, entirely or in part, by decision table. Because of its tabular format it is possible to embed decision tables in programs in place of complex code and then to use a preprocessor to convert them to source code.

It is useful to see the two techniques as complementary rather than as alternatives.

13.2 FLOWCHARTS

The most widely used technique for designing and documenting computer applications is flowcharting. The origins of flowcharting go back before computers when they were used to record the movement of information around manual systems. A number of different sets of symbols have emerged from different sources.

The three types of symbols which are used are:

(i) Horizontal Form Flow Chart (HFFC) symbols, Fig. 13.1;
(ii) American Society of Mechanical Engineers (ASME) symbols, Fig. 13.2;
(iii) computer-based symbols.

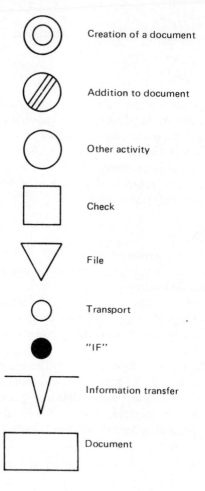

Creation of a document

Addition to document

Other activity

Check

File

Transport

"IF"

Information transfer

Document

Fig. 13.1 — HFFC symbols.

While all three are used to represent computer systems, the third type is by far the most commonly used. It exists in a variety of forms. There is the internationally accepted ISO standard [10] shown in Fig. 13.3. The symbols used in the ANSI standard are equivalent to the ISO symbols [1]. Those used in the ECMA standard, shown in Fig. 13.4, are slightly different. However, the concepts that may be represented are essentially the same.

A flowcharting standard was produced by the BSI in 1966 and was revised in 1973 [3]. This standard is again very similar to the ISO standard.

The NCC produced a set of standard symbols, shown in Fig. 13.5, which allowed the same concepts to be represented as the ISO standard, but used fewer symbols [15]. This was achieved, for example, by distinguishing between types of storage device by using 'striping' rather than differently shaped symbols. This idea had already been used in other standards for adding references to boxes by using a stripe across the top of a box, but now a second stripe across the bottom specified the device, as shown in Fig. 13.6.

In addition to the symbols, most standards include conventions on the use of symbols. These cover topics such as the normal direction of flow from box to

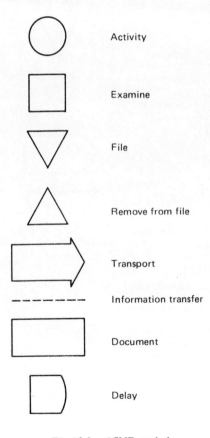

Fig. 13.2 – ASME symbols.

box, cross-referencing and the use of offpage connectors. While there are some differences, the conventions are very similar.

The choice between the different systems is essentially a matter of preference. However, the NCC standard with only one symbol for files seems closer to the spirit of program-data-independence which has been increasingly accepted in the past few years. Also the use of one symbol to represent data passing between computer and non-computer parts of the system avoids the necessity of inventing new symbols as new peripheral devices are invented.

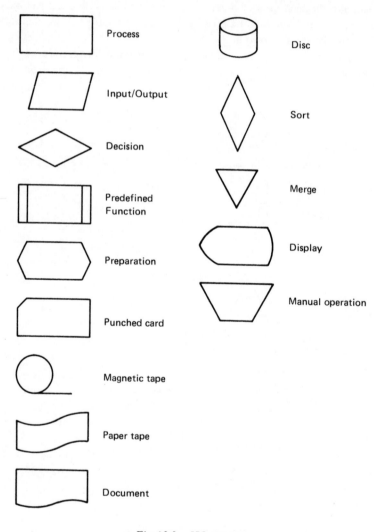

Fig. 13.3 – ISO symbols.

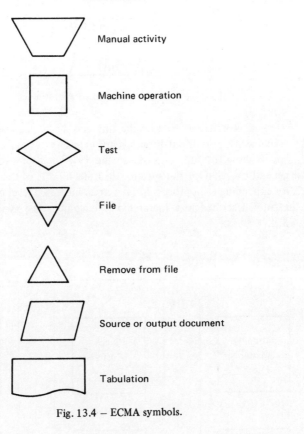

Manual activity

Machine operation

Test

File

Remove from file

Source or output document

Tabulation

Fig. 13.4 – ECMA symbols.

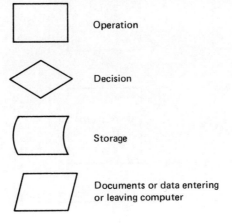

Operation

Decision

Storage

Documents or data entering
or leaving computer

Fig. 13.5 – NCC symbols.

Fig. 13.6 — NCC symbol with striping.

A radical alternative to flowcharting has been proposed by IBM, called HIPO (Hierarchy plus Input-Process-Output). The system uses a hierarchy of diagrams to show the functions of a system [9]. The topmost diagram shows the most general overview of the system. Each diagram is of the type shown in Fig. 13.7. By expanding each process in turn to an increased level of detail the system can be fully described in a hierarchy of diagrams. The symbols are shown in Fig. 13.8.

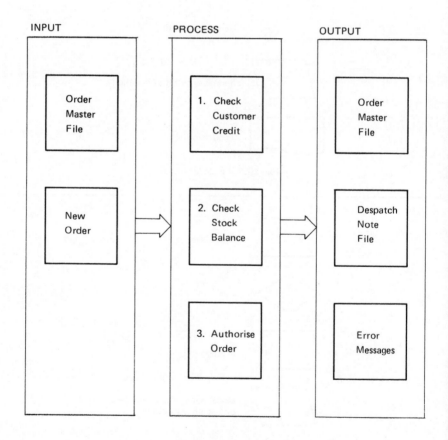

Fig. 13.7 — HIPO diagram.

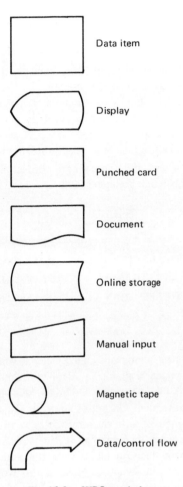

Data item

Display

Punched card

Document

Online storage

Manual input

Magnetic tape

Data/control flow

Fig. 13.8 – HIPO symbols.

The effectiveness of this new approach is difficult to judge. The ability to specify increasing levels of detail in a systematic manner seems a welcome facility which is not readily available with flowcharts. However, a judgement on the general approach of this new technique must await greater user experience than is now available.

13.3 DECISION TABLES

The earliest development work on decision tables began in 1957 at General Electric with a research programme called the 'Integrated Systems Project'. The object was to study the possible role of the computer in the whole manufacturing process in a factory, from the arrival of an order to the despatch of the finished goods. The project revealed that the methods then in use, flowcharts and narrative, were inadequate to express the complex logic of the system being examined.

Other existing forms of notation were considered as alternatives and the truth table was adapted to describe the problem.

The 'decision structure tables' developed by GE were unusual in the light of subsequent work, since their rules ran horizontally as shown in Fig. 13.9 which comes from a GE paper [20].

Fig. 13.9 shows how the rules were read horizontally, the first row being:

'IF animal AND 4 legs AND nose length not less than 3ft AND neck length less than 3ft THEN name is elephant'.

ANIMAL	LEGS	NOSE LENGTH	NECK LENGTH	NAME
YES	4	NOT LESS THAN 3ft	LESS THAN 3ft	ELEPHANT
YES	4	LESS THAN 3ft	NOT LESS THAN 3ft	GIRAFFE
YES	–	NOT LESS THAN 3ft	NOT LESS THAN 3ft	FREAK

Fig. 13.9 – An early type of decision table.

The project produced a language called Gecom, which contained a mixture of the features later made available in Algol and Cobol and a decision table language, Tabsol (TABular Systems Oriented Language) which became an integral part of the subsequent Gecom-II compiler. This has been the only real attempt to design a language with decision tables as an integral part of it. This early work has been reported in a number of papers [6, 8, 16, 20].

Other early users of decision tables were the Sutherland Company, Hunt Foods and North American Aviation. Most of this work was concerned with documentation aids, however, rather than the writing of programs.

During the period between 1959 and 1963, most of the better known early processors were designed, including the Rand Corporation's Fortab, Insurance Company of North America's Loboc as well as GE's Tabsol.

In 1959, the Systems Group of Codasyl began studying the idea of a machine-independent systems oriented language. After two years' work the committee's report described a decision table language, called Detab-X (DEcision Tables – eXperimental) which constituted an extension to Cobol 61. Useful introductions are references [17, 18].

Nothing came of the Detab-X proposals, except for the general acceptance of the standard decision table format which is shown in Figure 13.10.

The rules, which can be evaluated in any sequence, are read vertically. For example, rule 3 is: 'IF age greater than 60 AND age less than 65 AND sex is male THEN group 2'.

	1	2	3	4	5
Age < 18	Y	N	–	–	–
Age > 60	–	N	Y	–	Y
Age > 65	–	–	N	Y	–
Sex = 'Male'	–	–	Y	Y	N
Group	1	2	2	3	3

Fig. 13.10 – A typical decision table.

The facilities offered by Detab-X were basically the writing of decision tables in the procedure division of Cobol programs to specify logic and the writing of the data division in a tabular format using a facility for abbreviating data names.

In many situations it is important that rules are specified for all possible transactions. Consequently tests were developed for checking whether any rules had been forgotten. A table whose rules cover all possible combinations is said to be 'complete'.

It is often equally important that a table should specify only one rule for any possible set of conditions. A table which specifies more than one rule for some set of conditions is said to be 'ambiguous'.

The checking for completeness and non-ambiguity rapidly becomes complex as the table size increases. Consequently at least one computer assisted system is now available [12].

After this considerable period of activity, very little happened until 1965 when the best known of the early preprocessors became available. The preprocessor was written by a group from the Los Angeles Chapter of the ACM and accepted limited entry decision tables embedded in Cobol programs and generated equivalent Cobol source code. To ensure that this preprocessor became widely available, it was written in a restricted subset of Cobol and was written up in a paper [5]. For a number of years after 1965 most commercial preprocessors were based directly on Detab-65. This tended to restrict the use of decision tables, since it was an experimental design, with a number of serious shortcomings and was intended to stimulate further development which has taken place only in the last few years. The absence in Detab-65 of facilities for handling extended entry tables is the reason many preprocessors of the early 1970s did not support such tables. Better preprocessors are now commercially available, and this may explain some of the recent revival of interest in the use of decision tables.

In 1969, King pointed out the importance of the relationships between conditions in decision tables [13].

In the table in Fig. 13.11 there are four rules. However, it is clear that rule 4 can never be satisfied. For the two conditions to be simultaneously false is logically impossible. It could, therefore, be omitted from the table without affecting the table's ability to have a rule for every possible condition; that is to say, the table would remain complete. Removal of impossible rules simplifies the table and makes its translation to computer program quicker.

| Age > 18 | Y | Y | N | N |
| Age < 65 | Y | N | Y | N |

Fig. 13.11.

This work is also very important in the conversion of decision tables to flowcharts and, thus, to source code. Considering Fig. 13.11, the most obvious flowchart to be drawn is:

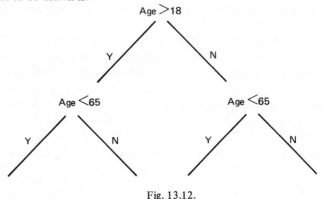

Fig. 13.12.

However, if we know that the two conditions cannot simultaneously be false then we can convert the table instead to:

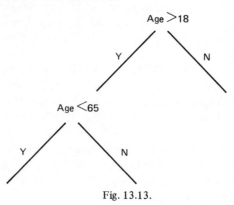

Fig. 13.13.

This will save a redundant test whenever the value of age is not greater than 18.

It is apparent that a number of different flowcharts can be produced from one decision table. Fig. 13.14 shows an alternative form to that in Fig. 13.13.

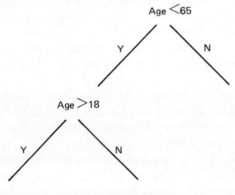

Fig. 13.14.

The ability of the decision table to represent a processing operation in a non-procedural manner has been exploited to create optimal code with respect to average run time [2, 19]. Suggestions have also been made for improving program logic by converting operations into a series of decision tables and then converting back to optimised source code [7].

In 1977 the BSI published a set of recommendations for 'Decision tables used in data processing' [4]. Despite its title, the standards discuss the use of decision tables only for documentation and do not consider their use for programming. They were criticised in the press when they were published for failing adequately to define their interpretation of a table, and for failing to take account of recent developments in decision table practice. The standard contains a rather unorthodox suggestion concerning compound conditions. While reasonably discouraging the use of negated condition entries, for example:

Age not over 10 years,

the recommendations then propose the much more confusing use of compound conditions in a stub, for example:

Age over 10 and under 21 years.

The meaning of this condition is clear for a 'Y' but if the condition entry is 'N' then the test is for Age less than 11 years or Age greater than 20 years. Whilst a single condition of this sort can be understood in a table, a series of these conditions can quickly obscure the meaning of a table. Most authorities warn against the use of such compound conditions.

The method suggested in the BSI standard for constructing a table is to write down all possible combinations of conditions. In practice, tables of five conditions are common, which can yield 32 rules if they are limited entry rows and more if any are extended entry rows. Considerable effort is required to allocate actions to each rule and the task is prone to error. Furthermore simplifying such a table is also a lengthy task. Other approaches to the construction of tables exist which avoid many of the difficulties just described. However, their complexity places them beyond the scope of this chapter. Discussions of the construction and interpretation of decision tables are contained in references [11] and [14].

Despite its obvious shortcomings, the BSI recommendations are an attempt to provide a standard for the use of tables. It is to be hoped that a revised version will be more useful. In particular, a recommendation on the precise interpretation of a decision table would be welcome. Attention is also needed in the standardisation of the format of tables for input to preprocessors. This would be particularly welcome for Cobol and PL/I. In the longer term it would be beneficial if the compilers for programming languages were extended to accept decision tables, to provide more efficient run-time code than currently obtained by the use of preprocessors.

13.4 REFERENCES

[1] ANSI (1970), ANSI X3.5-1970: Flowchart symbols and their usage in information processing.

[2] Bayes, A. J. (1973), A dynamic algorithm to optimize decision table code. *Aust. Comput. J.*, 5, 77-79.

[3] BSI (1973), BS 4058: Data processing flow chart symbols, rules and conventions.

[4] BSI (1977), BS 5487: Decision tables used in data processing.

[5] Callahan, M. D. and Chapman, A. E. (1967), Description of basic algorithm in Detab-65 preprocessor, *Commun. ACM.*, 10, 441-446.

[6] Cantrell, H. N., King, J., and King, F. E. H. (1961), Logic-structure tables, *Commun. ACM.*, 4, 272-275.

[7] Cavouras, J. C. (1974), On the conversion of programs to decision tables: method and objectives, *Commun. ACM.*, 17, 456-462.

[8] Codasyl Systems Group (1962), Proc. decision table symposium (20/21 Sept. 1962), ACM.

[9] IBM (1976), HIPO – a design and documentation technique, IBM GC-1851-1.

[10] ISO (1971), ISO/R 1038: Flowchart symbols for information processing.

[11] Johnson, R. G. (1974), Logical relations between conditions in decision tables, Ph.D. thesis, University of London.

[12] Johnson, R. G. and King, P. J. H. (1978), Computer-assisted decision checking system, *Comput. Bull., Series 2*, No. 15, 22–24.

[13] King, P. J. H. (1969), The interpretation of limited entry decision table format and relationships among conditions, *Comput. J.*, 12, 320–326.

[14] Metzner, J. R. and Barnes, B, H. (1977), Decision table language and systems, Academic Press.

[15] NCC (1973), Systems documentation manual.

[16] Nickerson, R. C. (1961), An engineering application of logic-structure tables, *Commun. ACM.*, 4, 516–520.

[17] Pollock, S. L. (1962), Detab-X: an improved business-oriented language, Rand memorandum RM-3273-PR.

[18] Pollock, S. L. (1963), Analysis of decision rules in decision tables, Rand memorandum RM-3669-PR.

[19] Reinwald, L. T., and Soland, R. M. (1966), Conversion of limited-entry decision tables to optimal computer programs, *J. ACM.*, 13, 339–358 and 14, 742-756.

[20] Schmidt, D. T. and Kavanagh, T. F. (1964), Using decision structure tables, *Datamation*, 10, No. 2, 42–52 and 10, No. 3, 48–54.

CHAPTER 14

Other potential programming language standards

by Brian L. Meek

Chapters 2–13 have dealt with those languages for which international standards, or drafts intended to lead to international standards, currently exist; topics related to programming languages on which drafts exist which are the subject of international standardisation activity; and topics of general applicability to programming languages which seem to warrant chapters of their own even though standardisation work at an international level is limited or non-existent. This chapter rounds off this survey by summarising briefly the main further languages and related topics which are potentially the subject of international standard-isation. Some of these are already the subject of national standardisation, others are not, while two have been chosen for international standardisation, but work had not, at the beginning of 1980, progressed sufficiently to warrant treatment in a separate earlier chapter. Real-time languages are not included, since Chapter 8 covered that entire area, including the potential candidates.

The author is Brian L. Meek, Director of the Computer Unit at Queen Elizabeth College, University of London, U.K. and member of BSI: DPS/13; except for the section on APL, which was contributed by Peter Cyriax of APL-Plus Ltd., U.K.

14.1 INTRODUCTION

The list of potential candidate languages for standardisation is capable of almost indefinite extension, and the choice of where to draw the line is largely arbitrary. The choice here is based on those which, to my knowledge, qualify under at least one of the headings of: having achieved widespread use, preferably in more than one country; having stood the test of time; having been implemented on several machine ranges; having been adopted somewhere as an official or unofficial standard; or having, in my judgement, potential in at least two of these. Most have been talked about informally in standardisation circles, as being languages to which attention might have to be paid in future. However, absence of a language from this list does not necessarily mean that it is regarded as unworthy of consideration. In particular, suggestions about the possibility of standardising assembly languages have been raised and it would certainly be of major importance if it could be achieved. However, the problem is so complex because of the great variety of machine codes and architectures that it has not been included in this discussion. Something will be said at the end of the chapter about how anyone who feels that standardisation would be beneficial to a particular language should go about the task of promoting its claims, and getting it accepted onto the programme of work of one of the standards bodies.

14.2 ALGOL 68

Algol 68 was designed by working group WG 2.1 of IFIP, who are the official sponsors of the language. The defining document is the Revised Report [1] published in 1974 as a revision of the original report published in 1968. The language has been implemented on various ranges of large mainframe computers (with the variations typical of implementations of any language), and in subset form on some minicomputers. The subset, which is officially recognised by IFIP/WG 2.1, is a pure subset so there are no standardisation problems there. Any standardisation would inevitably be based on the Revised Report in the light of interpretations and rulings since made by WG 2.1, which continues to support the language. The only major difficulty is that one of the most widely used versions, Algol 68-R [2], differs considerably from the Revised Report, mainly though not wholly because it appeared well before that Report, being based on the original report, though with a good many variations, some of which were incorporated into the Revised Report. However, this version was written for a now-obsolescent machine range, the ICL 1900 series, so this may be a problem which will diminish with time apart from the desire of ICL users to preserve their investment in Algol 68-R programs.

Despite all this, the main problems may be procedural rather than technical. There is the point that the Revised Report is not of the form normally acceptable to standards bodies; nevertheless ISO rules do not seem to preclude referencing a document which is not itself an official standard and in any case IFIP is a liaison member of the responsible ISO committee, TC 97/SC 5. A possibility is for a P-member of SC 5 to produce a standard, referencing the Revised Report for the definition of the syntax and semantics, but otherwise being of the form expected of official standards, dealing with questions of conformance and other requirements of an implementation.

A second and possibly more important point is that WG 2.1 have stated that they regard the Revised Report as the definitive final form of the language. This is somewhat at variance with the standards bodies' normal procedure of inviting public comment which, at least in principle, could result in alterations. There is the possibility that IFIP would be unwilling to continue to support the language (in the sense of answering queries about interpretation) if the language definition were to change as the result of the standardisation process; or alternatively might be unwilling to subject Algol 68 to a standardisation procedure which might result in such changes.

The biggest problem, however, might well prove to be the caution, amounting almost to suspicion, with which IFIP and ISO might approach the question of standardising Algol 68, as a result of the chequered history of the attempts to standardise Algol 60 — already described in Chapter 4. Certainly some members of IFIP/WG 2.1 think that a standardisation exercise would have no benefits. The formal position at present is that the ISO/TC 97/SC 5 meeting in Turin in November 1979, when setting up its Algol experts group, gave the group the task of investigating the possibility of standardising Algol 68. Whether Algol 68 becomes formally standardised, or remains informally standardised on the basis of the Revised Report, probably depends almost wholly upon the findings of this group, and the reception its eventual report will receive within SC 5.

14.3 APL

Dr. Kenneth Iverson of Harvard University invented APL in 1957. He wanted to provide a notation that people could use to describe algorithms. It had to be concise and unambiguous — essentially an extended and revised version of mathematical notation.

Iverson joined the IBM Research Centre at Yorktown Heights, where he continued to use and develop his notation; and in 1962 published his book — 'A Programming Language' [3] (hence APL) — to describe it. A small group of people under his supervision wrote an APL interpreter for the IBM 360 in 1966. This is the system described in 'APL 360' [4], which provides a formal definition of APL, and is still widely used even though it is now out of date.

By 1969 APL had escaped from Yorktown Heights into the real world of computing and IBM made it 'a product'. Despite this, the emergence of APL as a major computer language was due primarily to two time-sharing companies — IPSA and STSC. Both offered only APL services using enhanced versions of APL 360. Co-operation between these two companies, Dr. Iverson, and a small community of implementors, has helped to keep APL remarkably well standardised. However, its increasing popularity now represents a danger. It is available on all major computer systems, plus several minis and micros. The informal method of maintaining consistency no longer works.

APL is different from other programming languages, in ways which affect the nature of an APL standard:

(i) APL has simple syntax, but powerful semantics;
(ii) APL is not a language running within a host operating system — it is a complete system in itself;
(iii) the APL notation employs a special character set.

The simple syntax is welcome: the semantics are those laid down by Iverson, and susceptible to rigorous definition because of their basis in mathematics. Despite this, recent implementations on small machines have important restrictions and errors. The generality of the notation also gives rise to uncertainty in some extreme cases.

When APL was implemented on a computer certain extensions were necessary. A user needs to create, edit, save, and retrieve APL programs; to access files (APL now has its own private filing system); to talk to other processes; to trap and detect errors; to interrogate the environment ... APL contains all these facilities, but they are not part of the original notation. Worse, these facilities are often influenced by the host operating system and machine architectures; and the number of people involved in implementing APL is growing. Significant differences are beginning to arise, and they affect portability of applications and of users.

The APL character set is different from all others, and has more than 128 characters. The extra ones are formed by overstriking characters from the 'primary' APL character set, which causes some trouble with 'God-like' operating systems which think that backspace is a delete key. The 'primary' APL character set itself is overlaid onto the ISO character set according to an agreed mapping. So an APL terminal can be merely an ordinary terminal with a different print wheel. Some people use APL without an APL terminal. These few unfortunates use a system of mnemonics to represent the APL characters, but this is different on each implementation that supports it.

In summary, APL is possibly the most portable DP system in general use. This is due partly to Iverson's original concept, partly to the way APL has developed into a complete system, and partly to responsible behaviour on the part of a few individuals – but the increasing popularity of APL, and the diversity of machines on which it is available, is threatening this situation. More and more systems mean more and more differences. An international standard is urgently needed, and the initiatives towards actually achieving it began in France. With the support of the French government agency, the Bureau d'Orientation de la Normalisation en Informatique (BNI), the French standards body, AFNOR, put forward a proposal to produce an official standard. This was accepted by letter ballot of ISO/TC 97, and at the meeting of TC 97/SC 5 in Turin in November 1979 the project was effectively launched, with AFNOR expecting to produce a first working draft for circulation to the international standards community early in 1980. The intention was to hold an international meeting of an experts group later in that year, immediately before the APL Congress 80 meeting to be held in Leiden. At the expected rate of progress of international standards, a national AFNOR standard can be expected in 1981 or early 1982, followed by an effectively identical international ISO standard in 1983.

14.4 LISP

The list processing language Lisp was based on a paper on the machine computation of recursive functions published by Professor John McCarthy of MIT in 1960 [5]. Its value as a tool for research into artificial intelligence, and as an implementation language for software systems such as interpreters, has meant that it has been implemented on a variety of machine ranges, principally though not wholly for the use of computer scientists, machine intelligence researchers, and so on. Though all implementations are derived from McCarthy's definition and its subsequent first implementation at MIT [6], there have been the usual variations which have created problems of transferability and communication for the users of the language. This has led to suggestions from time to time that a standard version of Lisp would be desirable.

It is not hard to see why, despite the age of the language, no action has been taken on standardising Lisp. The users, though widespread, are relatively few in number and almost all are academic researchers. Implementations have been developed in research environments rather than by computer manufacturers and software houses. The investment in Lisp systems and programs, though important and valuable to those who have made them, is negligible in commercial terms compared with the major standard languages like Fortran and Cobol, or even APL. All these reasons mean that Lisp would be regarded by any standards body as, at best, a low priority, and quite possibly as not warranting official standardisation at all.

It may seem from this that it is hardly worth the effort for Lisp users to put together a case for standardisation. Only those users themselves can judge that. If enough of them think that doing the work needed to produce a standard is better than living with the lack of a standard, a 'do-it-yourself' approach of the kind described at the end of this chapter might produce something useful, even after so many years, and even if the resulting 'standard' is never recognised by an offical standards body.

14.5 MUMPS

The language Mumps – whose name, though contrived, is neater than some of the acronyms used for programming languages – differs from the others discussed in this chapter in that a standard does exist for it. The name is derived from 'Massachusetts General Hospital Utility MultiProgramming System', and the language was developed in the second half of the 1960s specifically for the needs of a medical community. As the word 'system' implies, it is more than just a language – a Mumps implementation contains a built-in operating system and command language, as well as the programming language itself, which is interactive.

As Mumps spread outside its original home, implementations on different machine ranges produced variants on the original specification, in the manner of all programming languages. As a result a Mumps Development Committee came together and produced a Mumps Language Standard [7]. Shortly afterwards this was accepted as an official ANSI standard [8].

This history perhaps indicates how a programming language can be developed on effectively a 'do-it-yourself' basis, and even accepted by an official standards body. As such it may serve as a model for other cases discussed in this chapter, such as Lisp and Snobol.

At present, Mumps remains a national standard only, and has not to date been put forward to ISO as a TC 97/SC 5 work item. This is why it appears in this chapter, rather than earlier in Part 1. Mumps is used quite widely in medical institutions in other countries, but to date it seems that the American national standard is sufficient for the needs of its users. Time will tell whether this will remain the case; the specialist nature of the user base suggests that it may.

14.6 SIMULA 67

As its name implies, Simula 67 dates from 1967; it was developed at the Norwegian Computing Centre in Oslo [9]. It is an 'impure superset' of the Algol 60 of the Revised Report (see Chapter 4); impure in the sense that a few of the features of Algol 60 are left out or altered.

Simula, though really a general-purpose language, has special features designed to aid the description and simulation of active processes, the most notable being its concept of **class**. Since Simula has dropped the 'own variable' feature of Algol 60, and includes input and output in its definition, the major items (with hardware representation) which have caused variations in the implementation of Algol 60, standardisation should (in principle) be fairly straightforward. On the other hand, despite the elegance and power of the language and its implementation on several different machine ranges, its use has remained limited, principally to applications needing its special features. At its meeting in Turin in November 1979, ISO/TC 97/SC 5 gave its newly-formed Algol experts group the task of investigating and reporting on the feasibility of producing a standard for Simula, in addition to its similar task for Algol 68 mentioned earlier in this chapter.

14.7 SNOBOL

Snobol was developed at the Bell Telephone Laboratories in the early 1960s as a language for non-numeric computations – primarily handling of character strings, though it can also be used for such applications as list processing and the later versions were also provided with numeric facilities capable of coping with most kinds of scientific calculation. Of the later versions, Snobol 3 was the first to be implemented on a significant number of different machine ranges. This was followed by Snobol 4 [10] and this is the version now usually meant when 'Snobol' is mentioned. Snobol 4 is widely implemented, both under that name and under variants, the best known probably being Spitbol.

Though there are differences between implementations, Snobol has a good reputation for compatibility when transferring programs from one version to another. Standardisation of the language would thus, presumably, be a fairly straightforward task, though inevitably somewhat time-consuming.

What stands in the way of standardising Snobol is, rather, the same as for Lisp — the fact that the use of the language, though widely scattered, is low in volume and confined mainly to academic research environments. With its distinctive and powerful pattern-matching facilities, Snobol has had the greatest impact in text analysis applications, though it has been used in a variety of contexts for applications requiring sophisticated means of manipulating character strings. The nature of the language does bring it within the scope of the ANSI/ISO text processing project discussed in the next section, but unless it is chosen as the base language for the text manipulation part of that project, the user base for Snobol is likely to remain primarily academic, despite its extra-academic origins.

Thus, as with Lisp, it seems doubtful that any official standards body would consider the use of Snobol substantial enough to warrant the effort and cost of producing a standard. On the other hand, there is a demand; for example, Allen Tucker in his book on programming languages [11] says in his concluding discussion of the future of programming languages that 'it is appalling that Algol and Snobol have not yet been standardised.'

As with Lisp, the answer may be 'do-it-yourself' within the Snobol user community.

14.8 TEXT PROCESSING

The growth of direct, interactive keyboard entry of programs and data to computer systems, and the subsequent development of word processing, could be expected to lead naturally to proliferation of text editing and formatting utilities and the requirement for some kind of standardisation.

As far as the formal standards bodies are concerned this began, not surprisingly, in the United States, and the establishment in 1978 of a project on text processing with a responsible ANSI committee, X3J6. In the latter part of 1979 this had progressed sufficiently for the project to be submitted as an international project to ISO. Though it overlaps various areas within data processing standards (and indeed outside) the project was allocated to ISO/ TC97/SC5 when approved by letter ballot, though with the requirement to maintain liaison with other ISO committees. At the November 1979 meeting in Turin of SC5, ANSI were asked to nominate a convenor for an international group of experts to work with ANSI/X3J6 on this project. Subsequently the first meeting of this group was scheduled for March 1980. The aim is to produce, within a single standard, associated languages for the description and the manipulation of text. In the absence of a single defining document on which existing editors, formatters, and other more elaborate text processing systems (up to and including computer typesetting) are based, it seems unlikely at the time of writing that a standard in anything like final form will appear for some years.

14.9 DISCUSSION

This chapter has discussed languages already in the process of entering, or on the fringe of, the standards arena, and some which are in some sense 'established' and on which a need for standardisation has been voiced. What do the supporters of these languages — or any others — need to do in order to persuade the standards bodies to produce official standards?

The first essential is to be prepared to do the work. Many of those engaged in standards activity are there because of their particular interest in one language, who will not want to get involved in another, and all are likely to be heavily engaged in existing commitments. If there is not at least a nucleus readily available of a working party to do the technical work of producing drafts, the most that can be hoped for is an expression of sympathy.

The second essential is that the need for a standard must be shown — variations between implementions, problems caused by lack of portability, etc. These should be backed up by documentary evidence.

The third essential is that the expected benefits of standardisation must clearly be shown to exceed the costs if producing it. Investment in programs, costs incurred by lack of standardisation, likely future levels of use — all should be quantified if possible, or at least provided with credible order-of-magnitude estimates or lower limits. Standards cost a lot to produce, and standards bodies will be unwilling to provide the resources to issue drafts for comment, go through all the other procedures described in Chapter 1, and eventually publish the standard, unless identifiable benefits are going to result. At the very least, they will wish to know how many copies of the standard are likely to be sold.

The fourth point, perhaps not essential but certainly very important, is that a substantial body of users of the language (and hence of the proposed standard) is identifiable. This has several advantages. One is that the proposal should be seen to represent a requirement not just of one individual or group, but a significant and (if possible) representative group of users. It is useful, and it saves time, to get the support of such an identifiable body of users first, before going to the standards organisations. Second, such a body may be seen as a source of expertise from which the technical working group or sub-committee can be formed — the need for which has already been noted as the first essential. Third, this body of users forms a ready-made public interested in the language, from whom comments on the various drafts can be solicited (rather than having to rely solely on more general appeals for comment, mostly to people who will happen not to be interested).

With all these conditions satisfied, there is at least a reasonable chance (though still subject to the amount of other activity which the committees concerned have to cope with) that the project will be approved. The less well the conditions are satisfied, the more doubtful will be the committees that the effort is worthwhile.

In given cases, it will not be possible to satisfy all of these conditions. For example, the present evidence suggests that neither Lisp nor Snobol has the degree of investment and number of users likely to convince a standards body of the need to add that language to the work programme. In some cases of that kind, a body of users of the language could still 'go it alone' and produce a standard for itself. In the case of the two languages cited, however, there do not seem even to be identifiable, representative user groups (as exist with Pascal and APL) who might be capable of doing that – and who would satisfy the fourth condition above.

There remains in that case the final possibility, of individuals or groups producing a draft standard on a 'do-it-yourself' basis, following the 'rules of the game' as far as their resources permit, and seeking to publish it for comment using regular channels such as the technical journals. This of course has its limitations. It could not be used for anything as bulky as the Cobol or PL/I standards, unless a book publisher would take it; and a journal editor would certainly be reluctant to publish a revised version in full, a year or two later. (Publication of replies to comments, and a list of amendments to the draft 'standard' should, however, be acceptable to most journals. It should be noted that one rule of the game is that the official standards bodies do not, for obvious reasons, like the word 'standard' to be attached to documents other than their own.)

To stand any chance of success, a 'standard' produced in this way would need to be drafted with the same care and regard to precision as an official standard, and follow the same format (using the most recent ones as a guide). It might be wise to obtain advance assurance from the journal's editor that this format would be acceptable and to negotiate arrangements for subsequent comment and revision. If possible, the advice of someone experienced in drafting official standards should be obtained, either directly or as part of the journal's refereeing procedure. The journal chosen should be one likely to be read by many of the potential users of the 'standard', but its publication should be accompanied if possible by appeals for comments through letters to other journals, and so on, and presentations at meetings, seminars and conferences.

This may seem tedious, and to require a lot of dedication, but if done thoroughly should ensure that the resulting 'standard' gains a level of acceptance approaching that of official standards. (Though, as has been seen with existing official standards, that may not prove to be sufficient to achieve the aim desired while producing it.) There is even an outside chance – not one, however, on which many hopes should be pinned – that the 'standard' might subsequently be adopted by an official standards organisation and given its seal of approval.

Whatever is or is not done, there is no point in waiting for a standards body to take an initiative. It is people who make standards, by co-operating to agree on them, and it is people who make standards work, by having the self-discipline to observe them once produced. The standards organisations can encourage and aid this process, and provide a framework; but they are not sufficient in themselves to guarantee that needed standards are produced, nor in the last analysis are they essential for it. Ultimately, it is the users of a language who produce a standard for it — or ensure by their action or inaction that there is no standard.

14.10 REFERENCES

[1] van Wijngaarden, A. *et al.* (1976), Revised report on the algorithmic language Algol 68, Springer Verlag, (1975), *Acta Inf.*, 5, 1-236; (1977), *SIGPLAN Not.*, 12, No. 5, 1-70.

[2] Woodward, P. M. and Bond, S. G. (1974), Algol 68-R users' guide, 2nd edition, HMSO.

[3] Iverson, K. (1962), A programming language, Wiley.

[4] Falkoff, A. and Iverson, K. (1968), The APL 360 terminal system, in Klerer, M. and Reinfelds, J., eds., Interactive systems for experimental applied mathematics, Academic Press.

[5] McCarthy, J. (1960), Recursive functions of symbolic expressions and their computation by machine, *Commun. ACM.*, 3, 184-195.

[6] McCarthy, J. *et al.* (1962), Lisp 1.5 programmer's manual, MIT Press.

[7] O'Neill, J. T., ed. (1976), Mumps language standard, NBS handbook 118.

[8] ANSI (1977), ANSI/X11.1-1977: Programming Language Mumps.

[9] Dahl, O. J., Myhrhaug, B., and Nygaard, K. (1971), Simula 67 common base language, Norwegian Computing Centre S-22.

[10] Griswold, R. E., Poage, J. P., and Polonsky, I. P. (1971), The Snobol 4 programming language, 2nd edition, Prentice-Hall.

[11] Tucker, A. B. (1977), Programming Languages, McGraw-Hill.

Part 2. The Issues

Participants:
A. M. Addyman, University of Manchester, U.K.
W. S. Brainerd, Los Alamos Scientific Laboratory, University of California, U.S.A.
G. M. Bull, Hatfield Polytechnic, U.K.
I. Dahlstrand, University of Lund, Sweden
D. L. Fisher, University of Leicester, U.K.
I. D. Hill, Clinical Research Centre, Harrow, U.K.
B. L. Meek, Queen Elizabeth College, University of London, U.K.
N. J. F. Neve, Ministry of Defence, U.K.
A. H. J. Sale, University of Tasmania, Australia
R. S. Scowen, National Physical Laboratory, Teddington, U.K.
J. M. Sykes, Imperial Chemical Industries Ltd., Wilmslow, U.K.
J. M. Triance, University of Manchester Institute of Science and Technology U.K.

MEEK: Perhaps I should begin by explaining that this discussion is not taking place in 'real-time'. It is, rather, an imaginative realisation of a discussion which might have taken place had we all been together in the same place at the same time, with the leisure to talk over the issues surrounding the question of standardisation of programming languages – and the time to consider our words carefully before they are uttered! I'd better make it clear that the imagination concerned is my imagination, since I have edited this part of the book, but is confined – I hope – to the way in which we might have expressed ourselves in informal conversation, and has not extended to 'putting words in people's mouths' in the sense of attributing opinions which they do not hold. All the views expressed have been sent in as written comments – I have simply edited them, with the aid of the participants, into conversational form. This may seem a curious device, but standardisation has the reputation of being a dry-as-dust subject – taken up by dry-as-dust people, perhaps! – and it has been done deliberately to make the end result more readable. I hope it won't sound too artificial, though I suspect it may turn out to be more structured and logical than most informal discussions are in practice. In fact, to make the structure more believable I have cast myself in the role of a rather informal chairman. It would have meant too much self-sacrifice to confine myself only to that role, and not to offer opinions of my own, but I've done my best to see that my own views – which I have published elsewhere [1] – don't dominate.

One thing I must do before we start is welcome two participants who are not among the contributors to Part 1 – Arthur Sale and Mike Sykes. Arthur Sale is Professor of Information Science at the University of Tasmania and has been closely involved with standardisation of Pascal. Mike Sykes is from ICI's Central Management Services department, was for several years Chairman of BSI: DPS/13, and has been particularly concerned with standardisation of database management systems.

THE PURPOSE OF STANDARDISATION

Let's begin by considering the purpose of standardisation. I suppose that in some ways it is fairly obvious, but could we have a go at defining what the purpose of standardising programming languages is – and, maybe, what it isn't?

FISHER: I think it can be summed up in one word: communication. Communication at all levels – between organisation and organisation, programmer and programmer, program and program – and between levels – programmer and organisation, programmer and program, and so on. Communication in the full sense of the word, with the aim of helping to achieve portability, to help in education, and to reduce or control unnecessary duplication.

DAHLSTRAND: The key purpose must be portability. Suppose we got to the point where you could expect your program to run anywhere as a matter of course – that would have a tremendous impact on data processing.

HILL: Portability is not the only thing. Even if there were only one model of computer in the world, so that portability was trivial, questions of responsibility would still make standardisation necessary. If a program fails to work correctly, it can be checked against the appropriate standard. If it is incorrect by the standard, that is the programmer's fault and it must be rewritten. If it is correct, however, a fault by the compiler-writer is indicated. In either case the action to be taken is clear because the responsibility is clear.

ADDYMAN: Strictly speaking, all that is needed in that case is a language definition. Although a standard for a programming language is often little more than a language definition, there is a growing demand for it to contain more. A standard could for example, specify the performance criteria, error diagnostics etc. Another distinction I should like to make between a language and a standard is to use the word 'standard' only to refer to a document produced by a recognised standards-producing body, such as BSI, ECMA and ANSI. Given this definition of the term 'standard', we should ask why such an organisation produces standards for anything. In most cases we find the answer is safety or economics. In our field it is usually economics.

BULL: I know we are talking primarily about standards produced by standards bodies, but I don't think we should underestimate the benefit of standards such as the U.K. Ministry of Defence standard for Coral 66, or even company standards. Although it can be argued that the greatest benefit derives from an international standard, most of the discussion and comments will, I'm sure, apply to all forms of standards.

SYKES: I believe it is worthwhile distinguishing between two kinds of purpose for a standard. In the first kind we are looking for sameness for its own sake. In many such cases, quality is hardly a consideration — as for example the side of the road on which we drive, the arrangement of instruments in an aircraft, the frequency of the electrical supply. In other cases the uniformity issue dominates — screw threads, plugs and sockets, etc. Notice that the question is usually one of fit. The second kind of purpose is to guarantee a property which the user would have difficulty in assessing for himself. Although sometimes this will guarantee uniformity, usually it is a minimum which is specified. One gets uniformity (within limits) in sizes of eggs, fruit etc. but more often one gets a minimum of some property which is not conveniently measured. Electrical or mechanical safety is the best example, but there are others — the corrosion-inhibiting power of ethylene glycol for motor car cooling systems, the percentage of duds in ammunition, for example. So the motivations for standards are: fit, to make communication possible; safety, to reduce the risk of injury to human (or other) beings; protection, from poor quality; and cost saving and the reduction of inconvenience. Most of the benefits of programming language standardisation fall into the last category. But, although Tony Addyman said that the usual motivation behind standards in our field was economics, the cost reduction is hard to estimate and long-term, so the motivation is therefore weak.

MEEK: So we have portability (or communication, or fit); responsibility; economics, and possibly safety and performance (in which I include protection from poor quality). I want to say something later about the last two. As for responsibility, David Hill said that it made standards necessary even if there were only one kind of computer, and I suppose economics would do the same. Nevertheless, there is more than one model of computer in the world and portability isn't trivial, so I'd like to stick to that for the moment.

DAHLSTRAND: Tony Addyman and Mike Sykes just raised the question of cost. When I started to work on portability, I was asked to make an estimate of the costs attributable to lack of portability of computer programs. It was quite easy to show that the costs simply of rewriting programs and retraining programmers were amounting to several millions of dollars a year in Sweden alone. But there is more to portability than just the costs. Portability is vital to creating an information network, just as a standard gauge was vital to creating a railway network or a standard voltage to creating an electrical network. Railway networks transformed industry and commerce in a way that single railways could never have done. How much reloading between railway wagons of different gauges was actually done in — say 1850? — we don't know, and I suggest we don't really care, because the immediate cost saving, though an important effect of standardisation, was not the most important effect. When we have portability, we shall see a whole new dimension of machine sharing, people sharing and program sharing. We shall probably want to design better programs than now, because a program's usefulness will no longer be bounded in space and time to a single installation.

HILL: The railway gauge analogy is an interesting one in making clear that, in standardisation work, it is not always possible to make choices on strict grounds of technical merit. Arguments made in favour of the broad gauge (that greater speed, comfort and safety were attainable) were almost completely irrelevant compared with the economic facts that change one way was financially possible, and that change the other way was not. This was partly because of the inherent cost difference (to narrow a gauge means only rebuilding trains and track; to widen a gauge means reconstructing every cutting, embankment, bridge, tunnel and station too), but mainly because there was in existence so much more of the narrower gauge. Those of us who argue that Fortran and Cobol are lacking in technical merit appear likely to founder on the same rock.

SCOWEN: Portability, with standards as currently defined, is impossible to achieve. The Fortran standards define only the action to be taken by a conforming program when run by a conforming implementation. Yet there is no way of determining whether an arbitrary program does conform to the standard; for an example of some of the difficulties, look at the NCC's Manual on standard (1966) Fortran [2]. In any case it is a mistake to talk of a program conforming to the standard; it may conform with some data but not other data, for example

```
    REAL  X(10)
    READ(5,100)  I
    X(I) = 3.14
    WRITE(6,110)  X(I)
    STOP
100 FORMAT(I10)
110 FORMAT(1X, F12.5)
    END
```

This program is not a conforming program if an integer value cannot be read from stream 5, nor if the value is outside the range 1 to 10. Genuine portability will be possible only when standard programming languages are specified 'down to the last bit', as in CAP's Micro-Cobol. I can see no other way of solving the problems of, for example, floating point arithmetic, different collating sequences, the different values for the maximum size of an integer, and so on. M. A. Malcolm [3] has written standard Fortran programs whose aim is not to run identically on different standard Fortran compilers, but to discover some of the properties of the floating point system; thus they give results which depend on the computer architecture, differing from one machine to another.

MEEK: I think we all know that portability depends on many more things than programming languages. My belief is that the long-term answer must be to standardise in some other areas too. And I do not think that language standards should be based on the defeatist attitude that total portability is unachievable and therefore why bother to try. Incidentally, I thought your Fortran example unfair; the implementation can at least understand what is required of it, even if it is unable to execute it. Your definition of conformance is surely far too rigid.

SCOWEN: It's not my definition, it's ANSI's!

SALE: May I point out that we are in danger of talking as though portability is the most important aim of standardisation? It isn't, of course; there is no single point which so dominates as to be the most important aim. Any doubters need only observe our own performances – we compromise in many different ways in standardising a programming language. If portability were the primary aim, then we should not have evolutionary standards like Fortran 77 and the varieties of Cobol; we should codify and freeze such languages. To be a bit provocative, I would say that, as I see it, portability is regarded as a highly important aim by users of a language, but standards committees rate other attributes more highly, as judged by their performances in the past. Nevertheless, before we leave portability could we try to pin down what exactly we mean by it? Some of the comments which have been made do not square with my concept of portability.

DAHLSTRAND: I think we can all agree on a basic definition of portability – you would like to be able to move a program unchanged and get the same results. But it then depends on what you mean by 'the same results'. If the task is to compute 10/3 to four decimal places then both 3.33331 and 3.33334 are correct and hence 'the same result' in this context.

SCOWEN: This shows that the calculation to be programmed is not defined. I would therefore claim that it cannot be programmed.

HILL: And anyway, once you decide that 'the same' can mean 'approximately the same' you run into trouble by losing one of the most fundamental laws of mathematics, namely that '$a = b$ and $b = c$' implies '$a = c$'. If machine A gives approximately the same answers as machine B and B approximately the same as C, it does not follow that A, B and C are all compatible.

DAHLSTRAND: It might not be a bad thing to get slightly different results from different runs, even on the same machine — it would remind us about rounding errors and the like. But, to get back to the purposes of standardisation, I agree with Arthur Sale that portability of programs is only one of them. For instance, in industrial real-time control portability of programs is only a secondary consideration; the important thing is what we might call portability of people, a common language and a shared set of concepts to start working from. A third important purpose is the setting of quality standards (where we have not yet got very far), minimum levels of things like generality, consistency, naturalness in languages. We would not be very happy with a standard which did allow programs to be transported, but made them unreasonably hard to write.

BULL: I agree wholly with Ingemar Dahlstrand that portability must include moveability of programmers and their skills and the commonality of programmer education, which are just as important as the transferability of programs. It is factors such as those which help to make standardisation economically worthwhile.

SCOWEN: I was going to make the point about portability of programmers too. The costs of computing are much greater than that of programming — they include systems analysis and design, production of a validation suite, documentation, maintenance and development, and so on. In my view the value of portability just of programs is overrated.

MEEK: Several different points have come up in the last few minutes — that portability means more than just transferability of programs, and, following Arthur Sale, that portability itself is only one factor. Perhaps we should look at some of those other factors now. Even while we have been discussing portability, the point has come up that mere transferability is not enough — an element of predictability about what happens when you transfer a program is also needed. Or, to put it another way, what is wanted is not just compatibility, but some measure of safety as well. When Tony Addyman and Mike Sykes mentioned safety and performance and protection against poor quality earlier, I said that I wanted to make some remarks about them, and this seems a good point to do so, especially since Ingemar Dahlstrand mentioned quality standards just now. If I buy a piece of electrical equipment which says that it is to some British Standard specification, I expect that standard to guarantee to me not merely that the equipment will perform the desired function when plugged in and switched on, but will not blow up or otherwise do damage, and also perform its function at a reasonable minimum level of efficiency. At present I cannot write a standard conforming program or, more important, buy a standard conforming compiler with anything like that sort of assurance. Surely the purpose of standardisation should include such aims? But there doesn't seem to have been any attempt even to think about such aspects. Am I being unfair?

BULL: I think you are being a little unfair. One of the significant advances in language standardisation is taking place with Basic. The standard for Basic not only specifies the syntax and semantics but also specifies the exceptional conditions which can occur during the execution of a conforming program. In order to conform to the standard an implementation must process the exceptions in the way specified. Moreover, there is, as part of the standard, a definition of language features which allow the user to handle the exceptions by program. In this way the behaviour of the program is completely defined.

ADDYMAN: The draft proposed Pascal standard is following the example of Basic in this respect, to a limited extent. It specifies the exception conditions, but leaves a degree of flexibility (perhaps too much for Gordon Bull) in the way in which they must be dealt with.

SYKES: Where I think Brian Meek was being unfair was in asking for a measure of efficiency, because efficiency, as we all well know, is almost impossible to measure. Besides this, there are often tradeoffs between translation time and execution time — sorting programs are notorious for this — which cannot fairly be dictated. In any case the user can surely do some tests before he buys. Safety standards — for example that no implementation should ignore overflow — are much more important. On what Gordon Bull and Tony Addyman were saying, may I point out that in 1964 PL/I had ON conditions for most execution time exceptions, including overflow, end of file, subscript out of range, and others? The PL/I standard is dated 1976. I do not see how Gordon can claim that what is being done in Basic is a 'significant advance'.

MEEK: Before anyone else jumps on me, I'll concede that I was overstating the case a bit, in saying that no attempt at all had been made to think about these issues. But I don't think the Basic standard, or the proposal for Pascal, or even the PL/I standard go anything like far enough. Incidentally, I think the difference between PL/I and Basic is that ON conditions were part of the language in PL/I and had to be tackled, whereas Basic has pioneered specification of exception handling in a language whose definition does not address such matters. As for efficiency, I never suggested that it would necessarily be easy to define or measure, merely that it is something that should be looked at. I still don't think my basic principle has really yet been given serious consideration, let alone gained acceptance.

ADDYMAN: You are quite right. However, we must be careful not to over-specify our requirements — over-specification can prevent the introduction of new techniques in the construction of compilers. There are many examples one could quote. Over-specification may also give an economic advantage to one vendor or class of vendors. Examples of this would be the detailed specification of the arithmetic to be performed on 'real' numbers or the choice of a particular character set as the values of the character type of a language.

SALE: To make this aim of certifiable quality achievable is going to need a substantial change of attitude in the software industry. However, I'd say that the task of achieving this change of attitude, at this time, is properly the job of validation packages and not yet of standards. First we must evolve measuring techniques, then we can enforce them. The exception conditions of Basic and the error conditions of Pascal are simply one issue in a much bigger problem.

NEVE: May I take up Brian Meek's point about not being able to buy a compiler with any form of assurance that it will perform at a reasonable level of efficiency? Clearly what constitutes a minimum level of efficiency is a very subjective matter and liable to variation from case to case, but I do not think that this remark applies to Coral 66. The Ministry of Defence in the U.K. have been assessing the performance of Coral 66 compilers for some years now, in addition to merely validating them against the MoD standard.

MEEK: Yes, what I meant was that the fact that a compiler was standard-conforming, given the nature of the standards that we have, was no assurance in itself, and that it ought to be. You have yourself just indicated that your tests are in addition to the MoD definition, not part of it. However, we'll be coming to validation later, and I hope you'll tell us something about the MoD validation and assessment then. We shall also be coming to the content of standards – the sort of thing Tony Addyman was instancing just now – at a later stage. Can we stick for the moment to the principle of what standards are for?

TRIANCE: Standards should allow the purchaser of a compiler to know what he is buying. They should guarantee quality and consistency with other products bearing the same name. This guarantee should not only state the functions supported but should also cover the ease of use of the product. One thing it should not include, in my view, is a specified level of performance. (By performance I mean consumption of machine resources – time and space – at compile time and run time.) However, a standard could usefully specify a means of measuring performance, analogous to standard measures of a car's petrol consumption. As with the petrol consumption analogy, the measures will not be the precise ones required by all users, but it should be possible to devise ones which give a reasonable indication of the performance in most circumstances. It would perhaps be a sensible goal for standardisation of programming languages that implementations should be identical apart from performance (and cost) so that users could make their choice purely on the basis of performance. I should add that I don't believe this goal is achievable in the foreseeable future.

BULL: I'm not sure how one can specify 'ease of use' in a standards document — indeed, I'm not too sure what John Triance means by the term in relation to a programming language standard.

MEEK: This was in relation to my remark about wanting to buy a standard-conforming compiler with the standard being some sort of guarantee of quality — what one wants is a compiler which is easy to use. I would say that this would include quality of documentation, range of compiler options and how you can select them, and so on. Clearly this is somewhat subjective and qualitative, but I don't see that this is something which standards should not attempt to tackle, at least in the long term. However, that is somewhat in the realm of content and validation, which we'll be coming to later.

DAHLSTRAND: I would agree with your earlier statement of principle in this sense — that if I move a program, I expect it to perform the same way or to give up for a good reason, such as the program being beyond the capacity of the machine, and say so. What is not acceptable is to get completely different results without warning, as happens every day under the present state of things. Would you like an example? This is one I like to show now and then. It is very simple, it just computes the square of the number 5000000 and prints it.

```
      K = 5000000
      L = K * K
      WRITE(6,100) L
100   FORMAT(1X,I15)
      STOP
      END
```

Do you realise that if you run this on four computers of different word-lengths it may give four different results (compile time error; run time abort; wrong result without warning, right result)? Can we build a discipline of computing on so shaky foundations? I am sure we cannot; and if we, as professionals, do not put an end to this happy-go-lucky computing, one day society will.

BRAINERD: I don't see anything wrong with any of the four things happening, except of course the third, getting a wrong answer. Otherwise an implementation method as well as a language must be specified, and I think that would be a terrible thing to do. Suppose, for example, it were required to give a compile-time error if the program couldn't be run correctly. This would mean that there must BE a compiler, that is, an interpreter would be an unacceptable implementation.

HILL: One thing which we haven't really discussed is whether standards should merely try to codify what exists, or try to improve things. In nomenclature, for example, most programming languages contain constructions called 'statements', which is quite the wrong word. Even though the word has become widely accepted, should the standardisers say 'No, get your English right — these things are commands'? Perhaps more importantly, should a standard try to reform bad habits? In the proposed standard for Minimal Basic, it is recommended that on machine overflow the action should be (after giving a warning message) to set the value to the machine's maximum, and continue. The U.K. has protested that this will never be useful and that overflow should be a fatal error. We are told that the reason is that most Basic compilers behave like this at present; to which my response is that this is probably the last chance to get them to change such a dangerous habit. Dare we let it go?

SYKES: It is unfortunate that few, if any, programming languages are free of design infelicities when they are first implemented. I define a 'design infelicity' as a decision which the designer or the world at large wishes he had taken differently. Algol 60 has its gloriously general 'call by name'; Cobol has ALTER; Pascal has its rigid array bounds; PL/I has a few, though there is no unanimous view on any of them. My view would be that, since every language definition has ambiguities which clearly must be resolved, thereby invalidating some implementations, it is therefore admissible to correct design infelicities. The problem of course is, where does one stop? There is no rule; there probably can be no rule. One must weigh the impact on existing compilers and application programs against the benefit for future users of having a cleaner language.

BULL: I agree with David Hill that the handling of overflow in Basic is crazy, but the way in which this was arrived at highlights the whole data processing standards process. The computer manufacturers have a vested interest in getting across their views (which usually turn out to be their implementations) to standards committees. Taking the example quoted above, since most implementations already do supply machine maximum and continue, the manufacturers tended to join together to support this position. You might argue that it would be better to exclude manufacturers, but it must be realised that it is essential to involve them, since their support is required if the standard is to be adopted on a wide scale. Manufacturers are willing to accept standards if they believe it will help them to sell. (They are not in business for altruistic reasons.) In adopting a standard there is a cost involved in changing their existing product to meet a new standard. This cost will be minimised if the changes from current practice are minimised. As a result it will be inevitable that standardisation tends to codify. Nevertheless, it is inevitable that some improvements are made as a byproduct. One of the problems of setting out to improve a language by committee is that not everyone agrees on what an improvement is. Moreover, one should always remember the adage that committees design camels rather than horses (although, to be fair, Algol 60 was a sleek thoroughbred even though it was lame through lack of input-output).

ADDYMAN: One problem which ought to be mentioned is that caused by continual improvement. For some languages the process of 'standardisation' seems to be never-ending. It reminds me of the cry 'The King is dead. Long live the King!'

DAHLSTRAND: 'Improvement' may mean any one of several different things. If you remove a restriction from a language, perhaps because you have gained a better understanding of compiling techniques, or because the efficiency gained through the restriction is marginal, then you undoubtedly improve the language, and in a way that converges quite rapidly. An example is the way Fortran 77 permits the use of integer-valued expressions in places where Fortran 66 allowed only constants or only variables or only linear functions of those. On the other hand, consider the format statements introduced in many languages as a handy way to convert variables to strings for output (and vice versa for input). After a while you begin to wish you could convert groups of variables, and introduce a special kind of DO-loop for this purpose. Later on you wish to make the field width and number of decimals depend on the size of the number, and now you have to introduce a special kind of variable within formats. You are still not happy; maybe you now need conditional formats. This kind of improvement is indeed never-ending. If you could start from the beginning, you would do all of it more simply and better as a case of string handling.

SALE: I agree completely with Tony Addyman's views. It is an observable fact that software has an optimum life, and programming languages are no exception to this. A language may be usable when it is first defined or implemented, and the next one or two revisions improve it, until it reaches a peak. Subsequent changes are usually recognised as a degradation of coherence (though they may offer more features). The only escape from this degradation is a complete revision, from the basic design upwards, since it is usually basic design decisions which prove limiting. Ingemar Dahlstrand has just given an example of this. The process can be observed in action in Fortran, where 1966 Fortran was a considerable improvement over earlier versions, but Fortran 77 is considered by most Fortran users as a disaster of increased complexity and inconsistency. Pascal is another example; the degradation changes are hovering on the horizon.

MEEK: I think you may find that the next Fortran revision, with its core-plus-modules architecture, is the complete redesign which you are asking for.

SALE: If you'll excuse me, I'll wait until I see it. However, I'd like to make one further point on the purpose of standardisation. I would like to introduce the notion that far too many standards are multipurpose. One of the cardinal tenets of our trade is to separate responsibilities, and in standards we find a confused responsibility for all the things we have been discussing. I have tried to influence the Pascal process, for example, in such a way that we may have one standard for what the language is, another standard which describes formats for Pascal programs for interchange purposes, another which specifies what constitutes a minimum-quality Pascal system, and perhaps another which defines the validation process for such systems. That is not to say that we have yet achieved all these aims, or even any one of them, but there is an attempt to separate concerns. I would like to see a much greater appreciation of the point that there does not need to be a single standard relating to Algol 60, or APL, for example, but several standards, addressing different aspects of the use of the language concerned.

WHAT LANGUAGES SHOULD BE STANDARDISED?

MEEK: Can we now turn to the question of what languages should be standardised, and how many? Questions of that sort?

TRIANCE: There are a number of conflicting considerations. The advantages of a standard are proportional to its breadth of application, and so the ideal is to have as few languages as possible applied as widely as possible. But though individual users, large and small, are able to apply this principle, it is impossible to see how it can be applied generally. If the standards bodies were to restrict the number of language standards — say, to one language for each application area — their behaviour would seem heavy-handed to users of minority languages who would be deprived of the benefits of standardisation. On the other hand, if standards were permitted for any language for which there were sufficient demand, this would conflict with the aims of standardisation. It does not make sense to create alternative standards to satisfy every local need.

HILL: Yes. The analogy of railway gauges again seems relevant. At present we seem to be merely at the stage equivalent to 'if you want 4 feet 8½ inches do it this way; if you want 7 feet do it that way; if you want 1 metre do it this óther way' — standardising each language that comes up, but making little if any attempt to choose between them. Eventually, I think the stage of choosing has to come — others can continue to exist, but only one, or at most two, will be regarded as standard.

SCOWEN: I'd like to point out that we must remember that standards do not come free. Implementors have less choice to provide what is convenient and 'efficient', code may be bigger, and may execute more slowly. Furthermore, standards are very expensive in time and effort to produce.

ADDYMAN: Absolutely right. There is an ANSI standard for Fortran and not one for Algol 60. Is this not a reflection of the cost of producing a standard — at least in the United States? A meeting of X3J9 has been estimated to cost $1 per second, and that doesn't include preparatory work, duplicating and mailing costs, and so on.

SALE: Without agreeing with David Hill's views all the way, I do agree that we have to choose. We currently have standards for some languages whose continuing development, or indefinitely extended standardisation, is positively harmful, because of their technological backwardness. Sooner or later we are going to have to learn how to dispose of obsolete languages, and the matter is getting urgent. If, in ten years' time, Pascal is still an active issue instead of being a language maintained for the sake of existing programs, I shall be very disappointed. The problem is partly that we set up self-perpetuating committees who see their role as bound up in the languages they preside over. And working on maintenance is never seen to be as glamorous as working on design or development.

SYKES: To go back to the railways analogy for a moment, assuming you can define 'application area' appropriately I can well imagine that goods traffic and passenger traffic form different application areas. Is that any reason why one should have different railway gauges? True, one has different locomotive types for the two uses, but there is more difference between steam and electric locos than there is between goods and passenger traffic. There is no sufficient reason why the low-level syntax of all programming languages should not be the same. But could we ever agree on such a syntax? As long ago as 1966, PL/I was a blend (some would say hotch-potch) of Fortran, Cobol and Algol 60. It is a good, practical language in many ways, but it has hardly set the world on fire. Existing users are understandably reluctant to abandon what they are using — not just for emotional reasons, but for sound business reasons. They want to see tangible benefit in return for the cost of conversion. New languages succeed only where they meet a genuine need; Basic, because something had to be easier than Fortran (or Cobol) for teaching to students; Pascal for not dissimilar reasons, though it is also a better language for professional programming; APL for reasons which are obvious to anyone who has used it, but a mystery to anyone else. If Ada is successful, it will be because it fills a need for a high-level language where none has been used before (with the notable exceptions of Coral 66 and RTL/2!). Anyone who believes we should specify a new language to displace existing ones had better consider the less-than-success story of Esperanto. The analogy may not be completely fair, but it is not irrelevant.

FISHER: On the question of what should be standardised, as opposed to what should not, the overall picture in software is not very impressive at present — too many languages and not enough of anything else. In academic circles the greatest fascination in computing seems to be the manipulation of the finer, more aesthetic points of correct programming language syntax. I think this might explain the apparent correlation between the numbers of academics on standards committees, and the sorts of standards produced to date —

BULL: I must interrupt! The ANSI/X3J2 committee on Basic is dominated by manufacturers and software houses, not academics. The current composition is:

12 mainframe manufacturers
4 microcomputer manufacturers
2 equipment manufacturers
3 software houses
3 U.S. government
7 academics

If you add the 7 manufacturers on ECMA/TC 21 and the 7 industrial organisations and 2 academic institutions on EWICS/TC 2 you see that Basic, which is regarded by most people as a teaching language, is dominated by non-academics.

BRAINERD: I don't understand this comment about academics at all. Is David Fisher really trying to say that standards haven't been successful when developed by academics? It is my opinion that Fortran and Cobol have suffered with lots of craziness because the 'academic' influence has been negligible. Only since the adoption of Fortran 77 has there been any academic influence on X3J3 and I think these people have made a very significant contribution to the effort to revise the standard. Obviously, the representation should be kept balanced, with strong influence from implementors and users.

MEEK: I can't say that I have noticed standardisation being dominated by academics either, at least in the sense of academic computer scientists. (Anyway for me 'academic' is not a term of abuse!) Following what Walt Brainerd was saying about users, I think that the academics who are there, like myself, are primarily there as users. I agree that there are perhaps more academic users and fewer industrial and commercial users than there ought to be, but I agree with Gordon Bull that it seems to be computer industry interests which dominate — over all users, academic or otherwise. I should perhaps add for the benefit of those who do not know, that although David Fisher is billed as 'University of Leicester', his roots are definitely industrial and commercial rather than academic, and he is not unknown for reminding his academic colleagues of the fact! But perhaps we had better let him now continue with what he was trying to say.

FISHER: I am happy to concede that the U.S. committees do not suffer from a surfeit of academics. They have other problems. But what I was going to point out was that there have been two successive versions of standards for both Cobol and Fortran; Algol 60 has had a standard; PL/I now has one, and Basic, APL, Pascal, RTL/2 and Coral 66 are on the way. Few other software standards of any sort exist, Mumps and APT being two remarkable exceptions. Yet there are easier finite functions that could be made the subjects of standards, and very usefully too, like word processing, sort/

merge systems, file updating and file archiving. We've seen in Part 1 that work is in hand on text processing, and on command languages and graphics, which are more ambitious exercises of the same kind. You could add operating systems themselves — even more ambitious, perhaps — to the list of what could be attempted, rather than just more languages. Incidentally, whatever one may think about IBM, but for their dominance of computing and the *de facto* standards it has created, total confusion would reign today.

DAHLSTRAND: Yes and no. I agree things can get very messy when the industry leader does not set *de facto* standards — command languages are a case in point. On the other hand, a mess can be cleaned up much faster when manufacturers are more nearly equal and have to go along with committee standards — look at the slow acceptance of the ISO character set, for instance.

BRAINERD: If it is true that IBM has created *de facto* standards, why is it that there is complete dominance of 'business' data processing by Cobol, a language developed by a committee outside of IBM, and 'total confusion' in the 'scientific' language field, with widespread use of Algol and its derivatives, in spite of IBM attempts to push Fortran and then PL/I? Indeed, I would say that IBM dominance has prevented acceptance and widespread use of vastly superior languages and their standardisation, with perhaps the prime example, as Ingemar Dahlstrand has said, in the area of command languages.

DAHLSTRAND: That is not quite what I meant. The problem in command languages was that nobody even had a good proposal until recently.

SYKES: On PL/I, IBM certainly pushed it — though not hard enough in my view — but although it originated Fortran I would hardly say it pushed it. Surely Fortran had no more need to be pushed than did APL. My own view of IBM and standards is that it does not create them — at least not deliberately. Other suppliers adopt IBM's design as a standard, so that they can compete with IBM for sales, of tape or disk drives or whatever, even large processors. If IBM can be accused of anything it is of failing to publicise its interface specifications sufficiently, and of abandoning its own standards too soon, so as to keep ahead of the competition. But this is a little off the point of programming languages, and if I may go back to David Fisher's main point, he could have made it even more strongly, since his two 'exceptions' are not really exceptions at all. Mumps is unquestionably a programming language, and APT is surely also a language for programming machine tools, using a computer for cross-compilation.

MEEK: I started this off by asking what languages should be standardised and how many. David Fisher has usefully extended this to other areas, and I presume that there will be general agreement that standardisation of the kind of things he listed would be desirable, at least in principle. As we have seen in Part 1, some at least are actually or potentially within ISO/TC 97/

SC 5's remit, even though they are not programming languages as such – we know text processing, graphics and command languages are, and I'd have thought sort/merge would be, and probably file handling, though perhaps not operating systems. But it wasn't clear to me that David actually meant that some of the languages mentioned should not have been standardised, merely that priorities should lie somewhere else. Perhaps we could separate the issues of what should be standardised and what should not – including what criteria you use for judging when it is worth while; how much the standards bodies can actually cope with, given the resources of men and money available, bearing in mind Tony Addyman's example of the costs; and where the priorities lie if you have to make a choice.

DAHLSTRAND: The first priority should undoubtedly be to follow the spontaneous development of the language' that occurs through implementation and extension, and standardise on the basis of that. (This is the time to change bad habits.) What resources there are over and above this minimum should probably be put into the development of a few, but well thought out, basic language features. (This is, one hopes, where 'academics' might do some good!) I think this will be a slow process, but a rewarding one, which will give us a foundation on which to build applications software. There is really no alternative to concentrating the resources like this. If we spread them too thinly to do the work well, it will have to be done again.

BULL: It might be worth recalling some suggestions made by BSI: DPS/13 to ISO/TC 97/SC 5 on the matter of criteria, at The Hague in 1977. These were (a) that the proposed standard is needed, (b) that an acceptable body exists to prepare and maintain the standard, and (c) that an acceptable validation body exists. The need was to be established on use, and a worldwide saving of about $1,000,000 at 1977 prices (about 1 per cent of the net value of the product); the acceptable bodies to produce and validate the standard were not necessarily to be the same, but they should obviously liaise at the time of development of the standard.

MEEK: Of course, DPS/13 did not get very far with those proposals on criteria; and it ought to be recorded that we were by no means united in a commitment to the kind of usage figures you have quoted. My recollection is that we agreed to put them forward to be shot at, as examples of the kind of criteria which one might apply. I must say that my own attitude is much more pragmatic, and indeed I rather shy away from rigid formulae even if they are no more than guidelines. I'd say that if there are enough users and enough implementations on different machine ranges to create problems, then this constitutes a *prima facie* case for standardisation, and if enough people feel strongly about it, they will come forward to do the work. That seems to be rather what has happened over Pascal.

BULL: May I make one further plea? With the advent of computer networks, one of the urgent needs is to standardise operating system command languages, which Ingemar Dahlstrand has discussed in his Part 1 chapter. One has only to use networks like ARPA or EPSS to know that in order to use a facility on the network one must first learn the operating system interface for the machine on which the facility is provided. Worse still, if the same facility is provided on two machines of a different brand and we attempt to use both at various times, the confusion caused is sufficient to inhibit all but the most case-hardened computer scientist.

SYKES: I sympathise completely with Gordon Bull, but we must accept that, however desirable a standard may be, there must be substantial incentive not only to create it, but to implement it. I recently went through an infuriating period when the two cars between which I alternated differed in an incredible number of respects. Apart from the standard positions of steering wheel, pedals and gear shift, everything was opposite — fuel fillers on opposite sides, stalks on the steering column transposed, radio controls transposed, handbrake on different sides of the driver. Such differences are all the more infuriating because either arrangement would be acceptable as a standard. There is no standard because there is not enough incentive to produce one. The same is probably true of command languages, with the additional consideration that it is in every potential implementor's interest to bind his users to him by providing something a little better than the competition. He sees that as a more effective way of ensuring his future market share than spending time helping to create a standard which will make it easier for his users to take their business elsewhere. Which brings us to the question of 'users insisting on standards'. Do they? My belief is that they don't — not, at any rate, until the lack of a standard actually hurts, by which time it is often too late. If you doubt this, consider how Adabas and System 2000 manage to stay in business in competition with IDMS, the nearest thing there is on IBM 370 architecture to an industry standard DBMS.

ADDYMAN: I'd like to address the question of what to do if we have limited resources. Obviously we must choose some priorities, and I am concerned about the sudden increase in the number of programming languages which are in the standards arena or are being suggested. A reasonable approach would be to try to improve the quality of the standards for the languages which are in SC 5's programme of work, but to restrict new projects to such things as command languages, graphics and other 'language-independent' topics. One area which has not been mentioned yet is the environment in which programs written in standard languages have to exist. Since this environment is between the user and the program, it can have a serious impact upon the portability of interactive programs, which of necessity must make assumptions about their environment. For example, although many environments will support line-by-line interactions, many will not support single-character interactions.

SIDE EFFECTS OF PROGRAMMING LANGUAGE STANDARDS

MEEK: I wonder if we can now go on to the question of side effects of standard-isation, both good and bad. You hear people complaining sometimes that standardisation inhibits progress, for example. It is partly a question of when you standardise — if you do it too early, you may prematurely standardise on something less than ideal, or positively bad. On the other hand, if you leave it too late you postpone its benefits, and the actual process of standardisation is much more difficult, as we well know, in the case of Basic, for example. Ingemar Dahlstrand has used the examples of railway gauges and electrical voltages. Were they too early or too late? David Hill has shown that the railway gauge was standardised too late, and it became too expensive to change to something better. But in Britain the electrical power supply voltage is dangerously high at 230 volts, and it was choosing that standard too early which has caused this — some other countries have chosen a more sensible 110 volts. Maybe it was already too costly to change to broad gauge railways at the time the standard was agreed, but I'm not sure the same was true of power supply voltages in Britain. Could we still change it now? We managed to change our currency standard, despite the cost. Sweden managed to change from driving on the left to driving on the right. Anyway, can we talk about standards perhaps inhibiting progress, and any other side effects that we can think of?

SYKES: You ask whether standards get produced too soon or too late. My answer is, 'often both'. It is almost impossible to know what the standard should be until there is some experience, by which time there is investment in something that is going to be non-standard. Even where the standard is seen to be needed, as in communications, different standards are adopted by (or thrust upon) some parts of the user population before being agreed generally — which may dismay us, but shouldn't surprise us. Incidentally, not only are opinions divided as to whether 115 or 230 is preferable as a standard domestic supply voltage, but one or two European countries have chosen the higher figure within the last 20–30 years, presumably discounting the dangers of electrocution (and insulation degradation?) against the economies of cable costs and the fire hazards of heavier currents flowing through dirty contacts.

MEEK: Which, considering how much longer electricity has been around than programming languages, perhaps has some lessons for us. Possibly suppliers of electricity give relative weights to their costs and the safety of their users in much the same way as do suppliers of language compilers. However, can we get back to side effects of standards?

TRIANCE: Standardisation does inhibit the development of new features and languages. This inhibition acts as a form of natural selection — only those features and languages with real merit survive, or at least those with real appeal. But care has to be taken not to prohibit such developments by making standards too restrictive. A good compromise for an individual language is to require implementations to have two modes of compilation, one of which only accepts standard features, and another for the more adventurous user, which permits extensions to be used.

ADDYMAN: I can't accept this — I can see little evidence of any inhibition. Some of our standardised languages are changing too frequently, often introducing features into a language before a single implementation exists. The only inhibition that I can see is again simple economics. To change voluntarily to using a new language, or even a new compiler for the current language, one has to be convinced of the benefits which will result.

HILL: I think that there is something to be said in favour of allowing implementations to have experimental extensions, provided that the compilers concerned implement true supersets, implementing the whole standard first, which I think is what John Triance is suggesting. Far too many Fortran compilers at present fail on certain standard programs in spite of all their fancy extensions.

DAHLSTRAND: It does really happen that a bad standard prevents progress, I'm afraid. For one thing, there is a certain school of management that will use any standard as an excuse to forbid variety and experimentation. We shall never know how many promising ADP languages were suppressed by the mere existence of Cobol, for instance. Standardising one of those early command languages would have been a disaster. But a lot depends on the standard. A standard like Fortran with its permissive constructs — Holleriths, sub-routines — does not prevent anybody from expanding the language, using it for new purposes, building preprocessors and so on. And in a subtle way, standards work can actually help progress, especially in the sort of active language-creating standards work going on in Fortran and command languages. You tend to look around a lot, hunt for ideas, and apply them in new places. For instance, command languages should probably be profoundly influenced by APL. APL has a number of important concepts apart from those high-visibility features, the special keyboard and the unusual order of evaluation. One is the switching between execution mode and definition mode:

∇P	switch to definition mode to define procedure P
\<program\>	enter program, including read statements
∇	switch back to execution mode
P	execute P
\<data\>	enter data as required by read statements in P

This is a simpler scheme for running a small job than any I have seen in a command language proposal so far. Borrowing an idea in the opposite direction, I think the keywords-and-defaults procedures being proposed for standard command languages are a useful feature for any programming language.

SCOWEN: The keyword and defaults convention can prevent portability completely. Consider a programmer trying to provide a portable sequence of job commands. He does not know what default values will be used at an installation, so provides his required values for all parameters. This might make his job three to six times longer. But matters may be even worse; an installation may have deleted some parameters from the commands, and his 'portable' job will then fail.

MEEK: You've given the worst possible case. Any system with defaults has that danger, if standard defaults are not specified or means are not provided to specify what defaults you want. PL/I does provide such means with DEFAULT, Fortran 77 does it with INTRINSIC, and if you extend the principle of having defaults from declarations to procedure calls, which is what I think Ingemar Dahlstrand had in mind, the language standard would either have to specify what defaults were to be used or, more flexibly (and necessarily for user-defined procedures), provide a mechanism within the language for the purpose.

FISHER: To get back to the question of inhibiting progress, a lot does depend on the particular standard. The very word is synonymous with 'suffocation' as far as many people are concerned, but this does not have to be. Experimentation, extensions and the like can still be provided by way of pre-compilers, as Ingemar Dahlstrand says. As an alternative which some may prefer, languages and packages fully equipped with extensive macro facilities should have the ability to grow and develop within any standard. But the point is that appropriate mechanisms are available for the development of facilities, without necessarily violating existing standards. Where these more disciplined mechanisms exist, they are preferable to the normal uncontrolled methods of trying new developments out on users.

TRIANCE: I fully accept the need to permit language development along the lines mentioned by David Fisher, but we must be careful. The entire standard-isation effort can be sabotaged by the use of preprocessors. Even if a language standard is rigorously enforced, it can still be flouted on a wide scale by implementing extensions and variations by means of preprocessors. Indeed it happens now with some manufacturers preferring to implement certain features such as telecommunications in a non-standard way by means of preprocessors rather than in a standard way with a compiler. If compilers are effectively standardised, then the preprocessors will have to generate code which conforms to the standard. Thus portability can be achieved by transferring the generated code, although this code may be difficult to maintain. An alternative approach to portability is to write each preprocessor in the language it is generating, so that the preprocessor itself is portable. However, it is difficult to see how conformance rules for pre-processors could be enforced. We can probably do nothing more effective than relying on the goodwill of the software suppliers and the awareness of the users – a formula which has been a notable failure in the past.

BULL: In spite of the disadvantages cited for standards, it is interesting to note that the U.S. Department of Defense is intending to keep a very tight control on the Ada language, allowing no subsets and no supersets. There is a very good reason for this which I believe we need to apply to other languages, and which might help with some of the problems raised by David Fisher earlier about standardising other things than just languages. Ada has been designed for programming real-time applications in embedded computer systems. In such systems, programs are not on the whole portable, since each system has unique characteristics. However, it is the intention of the DoD that a wide variety of tools should be produced to assist the Ada programmer – editors which know about Ada, cross-reference listers, source language indenters, simulators, debuggers and so on. It is these tools which will be moved, rather than the applications programs, and in order to ensure their portability no variants of the language will be allowed – at least within the U.S. military.

NEVE: Yes, I think this shows that the DoD have recognised the importance of taking standardisation a stage beyond merely the language, to the support environment. Ada users will be presented with a common, easy-to-learn interface whether they are developing or maintaining Ada software, and regardless of the host computer. And communication between users and the software tools that Gordon Bull mentioned will be according to uniform protocol conventions.

SYKES: Surely one of the most useful standard languages would be one for writing compilers. If one insisted on one's compiler (for any language) being written in that, a lot of work would be saved and portability would become cheap, provided every hardware architecture had one compiler: the one for the standard software writing language. This was surely part of the thinking behind ESL.

MEEK: Which, despite what Gordon Bull was just saying, is now apparently going to be a subset of Ada! I'm sorry, that wasn't strictly relevant – do carry on!

SYKES: Well, I was going to pick up the point made by John Triance about preprocessors. While he is saying 'don't put in a preprocessor what should be in the language', I would say 'don't put in the language that which can be put in a preprocessor'. Or perhaps I should say, 'don't put into the language facilities which can already be reasonably implemented in the language'.

MEEK: Given that people will produce preprocessors – assuming that they have enough regard for the standard, or at least for portability, not simply to produce an 'extended' compiler — there is a case for putting macro or similar language-extension facilities within the language itself, so that at least everyone is using the same mechanism, and in a sense not really extending the language at all. Look at all the different preprocessors that exist to produce 'structured' Fortran.

TRIANCE: It's funny you should mention that. A working party of the British Computer Society's Cobol Specialist Group is currently engaged on designing a macro facility for Cobol. The intention is that it should be able to support all the extensions currently supported by preprocessors, and thus make pre-processors redundant. The facility is going to be presented to Codasyl as a proposed enhancement of Cobol. But returning to the side effects of standards, could I just mention a beneficial effect? This is that a standard can provide a high quality of documentation of the language, and make it generally available. Some of the best Cobol manuals, for example, are those which are based closely on the standard specification.

THE FORM OF STANDARDS

MEEK: Can we deal now with the question of the form of standards? Should they be technical specifications of a rather formal kind, using metalanguages and the like, as with PL/I, or more readable, as with Fortran?

TRIANCE: The most important attribute of a standard is precision, which can best be achieved by some form of metalanguage. However, while standards are in a transitional state, as programming language standards all are, it is also important for them to be readable by those who wish to contribute to the development of languages, those who wish to write portable programs, those who wish to write books on the language, and those who wish to write related software.

SALE: I disagree strongly. Such a confusion of purpose is precisely why programming language standards are often so bad. The purpose of a programming language standard is to define the language precisely and unambiguously. The other aims call for explanatory texts, interpretations, and case-law, not for watering down the standard itself.

MEEK: I'd state categorically that anyone who wants to write a book about a language ought to be prepared to work from its metalanguage definition.

FISHER: One unfortunate result of the rather decollated creation of software standards is that the language used to specify the standard is usually special to each individual standard. The formal, concise metalanguages can be very valuable in checking the consistency of a standard or indeed an implement-ation of a standard. Nonetheless they are rather academic in appearance, and by far the most approachable and in some ways the most successful metalanguage is that used by Cobol. Perhaps standards should be in a dual form — the body of the specification produced *à la* Cobol for the benefit of the users, supplemented by an appendix in more formal metalanguage for the benefit of implementors and those charged with the job of checking implementations.

SALE: No, the other way round! The waffle goes in the appendix!

DAHLSTRAND: 'Waffle'?

MEEK: Imprecise verbiage, in this case. In Britain we commonly talk of politicians 'waffling' — rather than saying what they actually mean.

HILL: Surely David Fisher thinks that the Cobol metalanguage is 'by far the most approachable' only because he knows it the best. The Algol 60 one seems far more approachable to me — doubtless for the same reason.

BRAINERD: There should certainly be an attempt to standardise a metalanguage. Until that happens, using a metalanguage for anything other than the syntax will result in a document that is unreadable by almost everybody, as happened with the PL/I standard. If one has to learn a different meta-language to read each programming language standard, then few will have the incentive to do so. There is also a problem with the suggestion of dual forms, one informal and one formal: which one will apply when there is a discrepancy between them (as there always will be)?

BULL: I wholly agree. Although the 'dual form' sounds attractive, it invites disaster. It is hard enough to write a clear, unambiguous error-free standard without trying to do it twice.

MEEK: Surely it would have to be the formal metalanguage definition which would be the correct one?

ADDYMAN: The formal definition may be the correct one, but will it be used? To many people the effective definition of Algol 68 is not the Revised Report, but Lindsey and van der Meulen's 'Informal Introduction' [14].

MEEK: The 'Informal Introduction' says explicitly that 'the official Report is the final arbiter in case of doubt'. And in any case, surely implementors not only can work from a formal definition, but would actually prefer to do so? As John Triance implied, you need a metalanguage to define a language precisely, in much the same way that you need a programming language to define an algorithm precisely. Anyone who doubts this should see David Hill's famous Computer Bulletin article of a few years ago [4]. On the question of the metalanguage itself, we shall have to hope that the problem will disappear when the standard metalanguage work which Roger Scowen described in his Part 1 chapter eventually bears fruit. Personally, I don't find the Algol 68 metalanguage unpalatable — and I've felt that way ever since the MR93 draft, before the 'Informal Introduction' or even Charles Lindsey's 'Algol 68 with fewer tears' [15] was available — but I agree that it has had an acceptance problem.

ADDYMAN: No! You have missed my point! With Algol 68 you have a number of simple, easy-to-understand introductory textbooks, the 'Informal Intro-duction' (which is neither informal nor introductory!), and the Revised Report. The introductory texts are, of necessity, incomplete. If a programmer has a problem when learning Algol 68 and the solution is not to be found in the textbook, he is likely to do one of three things – try it and see, ask someone else, or consult the Informal Introduction. I refuse to believe that he will consult the Revised Report. To such people the Informal Introduction is the effective definition. They leave the Revised Report to the writers of compilers and the writers of textbooks.

MEEK: I try to get my own students to use the Report, and also follow my own advice, using the Informal Introduction to provide clues if I cannot follow the Report. Some of the students actually follow this advice – though I admit they do also 'try it and see', and ask someone else, usually me. But provided writers of compilers and writers of textbooks do use the true definition rather than an informal quasidefinition, I don't much mind if people regard the quasidefinition as the effective one; they just mustn't be surprised if their 'effective' definition and the actual definition conflict occasionally. I don't think we are in much disagreement about this.

BULL: We seem to be discussing only one side of a standard, namely the specification of the syntax. That is the easy part and although I welcome the time when we adopt a standard metalanguage I look forward to the day when we know how to define the semantics unambiguously.

ADDYMAN: I agree, though I would go further. Could we be clear as to whether we intend to specify the lexical rules, the syntactic rules or the semantic rules with the metalanguage? It is difficult to see how a single metalanguage could describe both the lexical rules and the syntactic rules. Consider the definition of Pascal – an identifier is a sequence of digits and letters with no intervening spaces, etc. A program consists of a sequence of lexical tokens which may have any number of spaces, etc., between the tokens. I also have some reservations about specifying the semantics. There is a distinct probability that the metalanguage will become the master rather than the servant – the semantics chosen being those which are the easiest to specify, rather than those which make for the best programming language.

MEEK: I hadn't meant to confine metalanguages to syntactic metalanguages in the discussion, though in practice that is all we have as yet. I too look forward to the time when the work pioneered by people like Strachey and Scott bears fruit accessible to all. Roger Scowen's chapter described a standard metalanguage for syntax only, of course – I should not have given the impression that all problems of formal definition will be solved by adopting a standard way of defining only the syntax. As for Tony Addyman's last point, the use of metalanguages for defining syntax has been around for a good many years now. Is there any evidence of one having been a master rather than a servant, of syntax having been chosen which was easiest to specify rather than which made for the best language?

SALE: Yes, for Pascal's syntax was clearly influenced by its definition technique, and probably by the first implementation. Or again, Fortran's lack of a formal definition perpetuates itself in irregular constructs and overloading. But what I think Tony Addyman was trying to say was that it was possible for the semantics of a language to be influenced by the adoption of a formal description method, perhaps in an undesirable direction. The choice of semantics that are easy to describe formally may well be desirable when a language is being designed, but it could be a problem when an existing language is being standardised. An example might be defining the semantics of an Algol 60 for-statement.

ADDYMAN: Thanks, Arthur. My point was about the semantics. I have seen two published formal descriptions of Pascal in which the authors began by making certain presumptions concerning some of the unclear parts of the language definition. One suspects that such presumptions were not made to make their task even more difficult.

MEEK: The question of the form of a standard depends partly on who is meant to read it, as has already been indicated. Who are standards actually for? Are they directives for a programmer to produce a program in that language (if it is to be a standard program) or for an implementor to produce a compiler for that language?

TRIANCE: Standards should certainly be aimed at the implementors. However, going back to what I was saying just now, as long as the standards are ambiguous, or are not rigorously applied, programmers will need to refer to them to produce portable programs. The same problem arises during the transition from a previous standard to the current one, and in Cobol this transition affects some users right up to and beyond the appearance of the next standard. Even in the long term I can see no ideal solution to this problem.

FISHER: The tendency, quite properly, is for standards to wrest power from the providers (mainly computer manufacturers) and put the initiative with users of computers. On that basis the targets for software standards are the producers — the implementors, to use your term — in the very reasonable expectation that the discipline and order forced upon the producers will be to the ultimate and considerable benefit of the users of what they produce — compilers, software or whatever is the subject of the standard.

BULL: Yes, the answer must be the implementor. The user should not have to go to the standard to find out about the language; the user documentation should deal with the user's needs. Again, the Basic standard insists that a standard-conforming implementation shall document all departures from the standard. Often the user is forced to consult the standard to see what is standard and what is not, since language translators often extend the language without indicating where the standard ends and the enhancement begins. I'd like to see all standard-conforming implementations being obliged to provide a switch on the language translator such that it can be put into a mode whereby all non-standard constructs in a program would be flagged. This would enable users to use an enhanced compiler and at the same time ensure that the programs are standard-conforming.

HILL: Do you mean a compile-time switch only, or one at compile time and one at run time?

BULL: Technically both, but I would argue that if I am constrained to write standard conforming syntax, such programs would invoke a standard conforming run-time system.

SALE: I am amused to see that Gordon Bull assumes that the normal mode is the 'enhanced' mode, and the 'standards' switch needs to be set on. It would be much more sensible, given a language of reasonable power, for the standard mode to be normal, thus requiring users of dangerous features to exert a little effort. Of course, this will inhibit the use of supposed enhancements, which will not be popular with suppliers of systems who currently rely on advertising 'features' rather than quality.

SYKES: The writer of a would-be portable program is, I believe, concerned only with the syntax of the standard language. Provided his source text conforms to the standard syntax it should produce essentially the same result on any implementation embodying extensions to the standard. Hence the user of a well documented implementation has no need to examine the semantics of the standard to eliminate extension, only the syntax. Besides which, of course, a switch on the implementation is clearly highly desirable.

MEEK: It seems from this description that the answer to my question 'who are standards for?' is 'it depends on what you mean by 'for''. They are for the producers to act on, but for the benefit of the users. Does everyone agree with this? On that basis, the users need not read the standards at all, but simply sit back and enjoy the benefits, just as the user of a piece of domestic equipment does not need to read the standard governing its manufacture.

BRAINERD: I disagree strongly. Users must be able to read standards in order to know how to write standard-conforming programs. If they are not able to do that, what good is it to have standard-conforming implementations?

DAHLSTRAND: I agree with Walt Brainerd. I think a standard should be directed both to implementor and user, and I don't think these categories are all that different. The implementor certainly needs a readable standard; on the other hand the user by and by, as he extends his use of the language, needs some concise, exact wording to refer to.

HILL: I support that. The aim should be for standards that are sufficiently precise for implementors and sufficiently intelligible for users. This is a difficult requirement, as lawyers and writers of Acts of Parliament well know. In general, precision and intelligibility are enemies of each other. But

I thoroughly dislike the suggestion that we should abandon that aim, as Gordon Bull is advocating and I think John Triance also, and that interpretation must be left to less formal manuals and textbooks. Once one has experienced the glorious day of knowing a language well enough to be able to throw away the − often misleading − textbooks and rely thereafter on the standard definition to answer all questions, one does not wish to use languages whose definitions are too obscure for that to be possible.

SCOWEN: But only if the standard is precise. Intelligibility for ordinary users must not be at the expense of precision. Consider an analogy with law. Lawyers and judges use the statutes to determine the law. While they were training, they used legal textbooks to learn, among other things, how to understand and interpret the statutes. But laymen rely on a lawyer's interpretation. By analogy, I would claim that only the compiler writers need use the programming language standards directly; other programmers should use simpler books to learn the languages, and consult other experts when necessary.

MEEK: I would hate to think that the law and the legal profession constituted models of what we should be aiming to do.

DAHLSTRAND: Hear, hear!

BULL: It seems incredible to me that anyone would advocate sending users to a standard document. Have you seen the size of the Cobol standard? Surely we should be harnessing the power of the computer to tell us if a program is standard-conforming or not? What we need is two things − a validation mechanism which ensures that a given translator is standard-conforming, and, if a translator is a superset of the standard, a switch to invoke the standard-conforming mode for both syntax and semantics. In this way any question of standard conformance can be answered without the user having to learn to read a standard.

ADDYMAN: In principle I agree, but I am far from confident that we can always do so. Life becomes much more difficult if an extension takes the form of a specification of some feature of the language which is deliberately left undefined by the standard. An example of this is the order of evaluation of subexpressions. Perhaps we should prohibit any extension whose use cannot be detected at 'compile time'.

SCOWEN: Unfortunately not all extensions can be detected at compile time. Some, for example giving a meaning to out-of-range array subscripts, can be detected only at run time. Others, for example giving a meaning to an expression whose value depends on the order of the evaluation of primaries, cannot be detected at all.

FISHER: I'm inclined to support Gordon Bull. Standards are ultimately for the end users, and if they do not find it easy to assess or draw benefit from the standards, then we are wasting our time.

ADDYMAN: Recent references to the legal profession remind me of another use to which standards may be put – they can be referred to in purchasing agreements and contracts. An organisation buying some computing equipment may specify that the language implementations which are supplied conform to the appropriate standards. In an extreme case, legal action may result from a dispute, and our standards would then be examined in a court of law.

SALE: We have just heard a wide spectrum of opinion about the readership of standards. Consider some examples, which may convince you that the arguments stem from ignoring the structure in the problem. Suppose that we have a language such as Pascal that defines a for-statement, and allows for-statements to be inside for-statements, and so on indefinitely. A standard for defining the language would say just that, only more precisely. But that is not enough for all implementors. Some are tempted to limit the nesting level of for-statements to some finite number, perhaps because of a compiler technique or a machine limitation. So implementors need somewhere to turn to which defines a minimum quantity that is acceptable (perhaps 7 levels deep), and perhaps also defines what I call a 'virtual infinity' – the number so great as never to be reached in practice, and in this case perhaps 15 levels deep. The user, on the other hand, may write standard Pascal programs without knowing any of this; infinitely nested for-statements are allowable. If he wants to write in a subset which is more portable than standard Pascal, he may need to refer to another document that tells him that some poor-quality Pascal compilers only allow a nesting level up to 3, but most would permit up to 7. Now to write all this into a single standard is difficult and foolish. To take another example, that of a goto-statement which jumps into a loop. The user needs only to know that this is an error, in order to avoid it. If he is a purchaser he needs to know how the particular system being offered handles such errors, which is a matter for its own documentation. An implementor, on the other hand, needs to know his responsibilities towards such errors, and the acceptable ways of handling them..I am afraid that my views are that standards are not for idle reading by anyone, and that anyone prepared to invest the effort to create a standard ought to expect to assist in making the results accessible by a separate process if such do not already exist, such as textbooks, interpretations, and so on.

THE CONTENT OF PROGRAMMING LANGUAGE STANDARDS

MEEK: I am going to leave Arthur Sale with the last word on that topic, and in fact it leads in naturally to a discussion of what the actual content of standards should be, something I seem to have put off for as long as possible. From remarks already made it seems clear that at least some people feel that simply covering the syntax and semantics of the language is not enough.

Could we decide what else should be there? And is there anyone who does not go along with this view?

FISHER: I certainly think that the present standards have many shortcomings in this respect. Usually, they are no more than imprecise specifications of the correct syntax. What is really required now is implementation specifications detailing the appropriate action to be taken on encountering incorrect syntax or a fault during execution. Additionally such qualifications should also define the format of cross-referencing tables, compile-time and execution time facilities, the content of error messages, their severity, placement and format etc. Standards should also ensure a level of reproducibility of the arithmetic across different implementations (that is, different machine architectures). Most languages would also make useful gains if they limited some of their facilities in return for an elimination of ambiguities and a precision of specification. Generally standards for languages tend to be sloppily open-ended, thereby inviting uncontrolled and conflicting extensions.

DAHLSTRAND: Yes, but a certain open-endedness is beneficial too. It does not have to be sloppy, of course. Part of Fortran's success lies in its extensibility.

BULL: I agree with much of what David Fisher said. In the Specification of Basic published by the NCC in 1973 [5] we included explicit error messages for compile-time and run-time errors. In the event I believe it is not sensible to specify the compile-time messages since to a large extent the syntax error detection is a function of the compiling technique used rather than the language itself. I do however, believe that it would be sensible to standardise the run-time error messages. Returning to an earlier remark, so many people talk of standardising operating system command languages; I believe that it is equally important to standardise the operating system response language, otherwise only one side of the interface is dealt with. This argument can also be applied to programming languages.

ADDYMAN: The specification of error messages to be produced for syntax violations is an example of the overspecification which I talked about earlier.

SALE: It is possible to standardise run-time error messages in Basic only because its standard defines the concept of execution. This of course is one of the low-level features which Basic shares with machine instruction sets, and it is not an acceptable concept for high-level languages such as Pascal. There are no run-time errors in Pascal, simply errors, and compilers are encouraged to detect as many as possible as early as possible, to date with good results. We are back on the possible stultifying effects of too-early standardisation, and the need for deleting standards.

SYKES: I support that. The creators of the PL/I standard deserve more credit than they often get. They took an existing language definition, sadly wanting in precision, and, driven by a necessity with which few could argue, transformed it through 12 iterations into something with a reasonably simple overall structure. The syntax, though it is complex, is neither bulky nor very difficult to understand. Most of the document, and the most difficult part, is concerned with the semantics — what happens when the program is executed. The reasons why this is large and difficult are that PL/I is a large and complex language (though not much more so than most useful languages), and that semantics are difficult to specify independently of the hardware and operating system environment. And, very wisely, they did not talk about 'compile time' and 'run time'. As Walt Brainerd said earlier, the standard writer must not, even indirectly, force certain actions to be done at compile time and others at execute time. He must define what happens and, only where necessary, require that certain actions happen before others. Usually such logical precedence will be implicit. If declaration before use is not required, clearly each block of code must be scanned before any of it can be executed. Incidentally, I thought that Ingemar Dahlstrand, in his example earlier, was making his distinction into four different cases rather artificially, for this kind of reason. The user is clearly entitled to be given the correct answer or to be told why he cannot have it, but it does not matter when the message is issued, and the user should not need either to know or to care.

SCOWEN: I'd like to stress the need for standards to improve the safety of computing tools. At present the Fortran standard throws too much responsibility onto the programmer, who is usually blissfully unaware of the problems. It is as though three-pin plugs and sockets had been standardised as to shape and dimensions without specifying which pin is connected to which wire. In fact plugs and sockets are designed to prevent accidents, including infants poking toys into sockets, inserting plugs the wrong way, or overloading the circuit. By contrast, the Fortran standards are unconcerned if we set overflow, or use an array subscript which is too big. Such a program does not conform to the standard, so a conforming compiler can do whatever it likes. The National Bureau of Standards validation suite, and the U.S. Federal Computer Testing validation suite, deliberately only examine the action resulting from valid conforming programs.

MEEK: I am glad you mentioned plugs and sockets. I have a set of drawings I use when talking about standards, showing varieties of plug which might exist if standards for them were like standards for programming languages — including subsets, with two pins, extended versions with lots of pins, and so on. It does help to get across the point that our language standards fall far short of what one expects of standards in other walks of life.

TRIANCE: I'd like to support much of what has been said. Standards should be concerned with all functional aspects of the user interface, which will normally include syntax, semantics and error handling. It certainly seems ridiculous that a standard should only be concerned with the behaviour of syntactically correct programs. Incidentally, just because syntax error detection is currently a function of the compiling techniques employed I do not accept Gordon Bull's point that this should prevent standards from specifying compile time messages. It should really be the other way round – compiling techniques used should be a function of the standard – although I would agree the standard should not make the compiler writer's job unnecessarily difficult.

SYKES: May I come back? Before I agree with this line, and in particular with David Fisher's specifications, I should like to see an example of the sort of standard he has in mind. Until it can be shown to be possible to satisfy his requirements, I have to take a very sceptical view. I don't believe that you can legislate for messages complaining of bad syntax except in a very general way. In fact about all you can say is that the user must be told precisely what rule appears to have been broken, and precisely where, in terms intelligible to the user. Of course, the same text may appear to infringe different rules depending on how it is parsed, and one might therefore like to know the state of the parse tree. This is a lot to ask, and perhaps all one can do is advise the user of one of the first principles of programming that I learned over 20 years ago: if you must make mistakes, make easy ones – they are easier to find than clever ones. It seems absurd to me to ask for more, because if you do, you have to define a set of incorrect programs. If you do define them, and say what is to be done with them, you have included them in the standard; they are therefore no longer non-standard, only special cases: programs that don't do anything useful. To illustrate the run-time problem: errors usually result from trying to operate on an object for which it is not ready. Uninitialised variables and unopened files are two of the most common examples. As separate compilation makes it difficult to detect these at compile time, what checks do we wish to be applied at run time? If the check has to be in advance, the user may be unwilling to accept the cost of it; if the hardware has an interrupt mechanism for detecting (for example) invalid packed decimal fields, a post mortem must be carried out. Acceptable cost will vary from user to user and from micro-processor to mainframe. Moreover, in many cases we are arguing about minor improvements in safety in languages which are shockingly dangerous as long as they still contain EQUIVALENCE or REDEFINES. I am reminded of the Irishman's reply when asked for directions: 'If I were you I wouldn't start from here'.

BRAINERD: Yes, the idea of standardising error handling sounds all very fine, but it directly contradicts what Ingemar Dahlstrand was saying earlier, also very reasonable, about the value of permissive standards. If required error messages or actions are specified for anything, then it is impossible to permit an extension in that area. X3J3 went through this process in an attempt to specify error conditions on input-output operations in Fortran. For example, one proposed error was to read data from a field that did not contain characters appropriate for the data type being read. This, of course, prohibits any extension that allows conversion from one data type to another. What happened was that during the public comment period at least one person complained that every proposed error was an extension favoured by that person. Thus, a feature was included in the language to specify an action if an error occurs, but the set of errors is implementation dependent.

FISHER: 'At least one person'? Is objection by just one person really significant?

MEEK: I must come in here! Saying that you should not specify messages or actions for anything, on the grounds that it might inhibit extensions, is as extreme as requiring that all possible errors be detected and reported in a specific way in all circumstances, which I don't think anyone is asking for. Because errors — perhaps we should say 'non-standard constructs' if we take what Walt Brainerd has been saying to its logical conclusion, but I prefer 'errors' — can interact with one another and mask one another, I don't think it is reasonable to require more than that an error should be detected and reported in the absence of any other errors. Even then the error detected is only a symptom of the actual mistake the programmer made. Consider, in Algol 60, the trivial example:

> **Boolean** x, y; **integer** p, q, yp; ...
> ...; $x := yp := q$; ...

I expect better examples could be devised, but this will do. The multiple assignment is certainly wrong, but could have arisen from at least three different mistakes — missing semicolon after y, inserted colon after p, or x being declared as Boolean rather than integer. Now, I don't care if this is reported as any of those, or simply as a mixture of types of destination in a multiple assignment. What I want is a standard which (a) would insist on the error being detected and reported in the absence of any masking errors, and (b) would specify, for each of a wide range of common errors, the form in which the report is made, so that for the four possible interpretations I have mentioned, a standard-conforming compiler would have to say, for example,

missing semicolon after y	instead of	missing semicolon
:= is not Boolean operator	instead of	invalid operator
x should have been declared as integer	instead of	wrong variable type
mixed types on left of multiple assignment	instead of	invalid assignment

depending upon how its parsing views the error. I'm not saying my versions of the error messages couldn't be improved, but even those I regard as inadequate are a good deal better than those you find on many implementations. (By the way, I'm horrified at Mike Sykes' implication that a user should be expected to know what a parse tree is, and to be able to analyse its state.) In fact, I suspect that no parsing strategy is likely to come up with all the possible explanations of an error which will occur to a human reader of a program, which simply strengthens my argument. Surely there must be areas, however limited, where the ways in which various parsing strategies will interpret a particular isolated error are few in number and predictable, and standards for the various kinds can be laid down, without causing the implementor undue hardship? Even if only a restricted realm of errors could be covered in a standard initially, this would at least be an advance on what we have now, and there would be hope that as the design of languages and implementations thereof gradually improve, the area could be widened. What I cannot accept is the implication that this is an area which standards should never attempt to touch, in which implementors should for ever have untrammelled freedom. I'm sorry, I have rather transgressed the limits of 'chairman's privilege', but I happen to feel rather strongly about this.

DAHLSTRAND: I am for standard error handling and for extensibility without having stopped to think that this might be contradictory. Can't we have it both ways, with the aid of the famous compiler switch that chooses between strict conformance and local extensions? By the way, in command language committees there is no doubt that error messages – or, more generally, response language – have to be included in the standard.

BULL: I would like to make two points. Firstly, I don't think Walt Brainerd was talking about syntax errors but run-time exceptions (although I will agree that separation of the two is sometimes difficult). Secondly, I cannot agree with Walt that a standard cannot address this area. I'm sorry to quote Basic yet again, but it is of course the standard I am most familiar with. In Basic the rules in this area are that an implementation is said to conform to the standard if it interprets the syntax and semantics according to the standard and that it interprets errors and exceptional circumstances according to the standard. An implementation may accept programs written in an enhanced language without having to report all constructs not conforming to the standard. However, whenever a statement or other program element does nor conform to the syntactic rules, either an error has to be reported, or the statement or element concerned has to have an implementation-defined meaning which is defined in an accompanying reference manual.

ADDYMAN: It does seem that there is a range of possibilities to be considered. We could specify the 'run time' error messages and/or the 'compile time' error messages (note the quotation marks!), or omit such considerations from the standard. As Gordon Bull has indicated, at the very least a standard should identify all places in which 'run-time errors' could occur and require any implementation to detail the way such errors are treated. This gives an implementor considerable freedom but provides a potential purchaser or user with information from which the 'quality' of the implementation may be judged. This approach may also lead to competition between implementors to detect and report as many of the errors as possible.

MEEK: Ingemar Dahlstrand was saying things earlier about the questions of machine architecture, reproducibility of results, and so on, which David Fisher echoed a few minutes ago. Would you like to come back on this, Ingemar?

DAHLSTRAND: Yes. You remember I said that a program should, when transferred, give effectively the same results or give up for a good reason and explain why. I think sometimes too much is made of total transferability — people try to move a computation to a smaller machine, and seem to want standards to say that they must be able to do so. I would rather not try to do it: it is not useful. I would much rather run the program on the larger machine than transfer it to my own smaller machine. We have a sort of collective hang-up, always trying to run everything on our own machines even if they are not particularly suited to the task at hand. That is probably because we are so used to programs blowing up when we try to move them.

HILL: But very often one does wish to convert to a smaller machine, quite reasonably because one wishes to run the program on the only machine available. The program may in principle be quite suitable for small machines, but it has been written by someone in Los Angeles with more store available than is good for him. For the size of each array, he has therefore taken the largest number he knows and then doubled it for luck. Trying to work out how much each can be reduced is an infuriating task, particularly when one realises that it is all so unnecessary. Given a language where variable array bounds are allowed, people declare arrays of the actual size needed and the difficulty simply never arises. Language architecture matters just as much as machine architecture.

MEEK: Ingemar Dahlstrand gave a Fortran example which would give four different results depending on the machine — or three, for those who'd rather not distinguish between compile-time and run-time errors. I took this to indicate that he thought that Fortran is still not a portable language. If that is the case, what does it need to make it portable?

HILL: The main thing needed is that manufacturers should actually implement the standard, and that users should insist on it. Yet I fear that too many users will not do so. One even meets the attitude that insisting on standard-conforming programs is stupid, when anything that will work on the machine will do really.

DAHLSTRAND: I think that Fortran is much better than it used to be, but one or two things are still missing. One of them is overflow control or — more generally — safety measures. Another thing we need is the possibility of declaring precision because precision is part of the algorithm; look at any example in a textbook of numerical analysis.

MEEK: What about environmental enquiries, which allow you to find out the precision actually available?

DAHLSTRAND: I am sceptical about environmental enquiries as an alternative to declaring precision. They are useful in certain contexts, that is, when you have a given environment and have to get the utmost precision out of it. But remember, environmental enquiries do not do the job for you; you have to write parallel code to get the most out of the environment. There is no way this could be a normal working method for the amateur user.

BRAINERD: We seem to have got into a discussion of language features rather than the standardisation process itself. However! Environmental enquiries are inadequate because they do not permit the programmer to write a portable program in the simple obvious way. It should be possible to say 'I need 9 digits precision for these data items' and have the machine do the right thing or say that it can't. Incidentally, such a facility is now being considered for Fortran by X3J3.

ADDYMAN: This attempt to allow the user to specify the attributes of his real numbers in terms of range and precision is a significant development. If successful, it should yield for the user of reals the benefits which Pascal users have received from the use of subranges of integers.

MEEK: Subranges are a more general and in some cases more valuable facility than what I think is being suggested — precision in terms of the number of significant figures. PL/I has of course had the capacity for defining precision attributes for many years. If I may make two more minor points: knowing the available range and defining the precision required are not wholly interchangeable facilities; and, parallel code ought not to be necessary if the language is designed in the right way. I would like the chance in Algol 68 to write:

mode integer = **if** *maxint* > *100000* **then int else long int fi**

and the like.

HILL: Mention of environmental enquiries, incidentally, seems to me to rule out David Fisher's dream of complete standardisation, such that a given program would produce identical results from every machine. Unless we outlaw environmental enquiries — heaven forbid, despite what others have been saying — or make every machine identical,

print(maxint)

seems effectively to destroy the dream.

SALE: I feel you have fallen into the trap of using an inadequate definition of portability. Portability does not consist in having a program produce the *same* answer on every system, but rather the *right* answer on every system. Thus

print(maxint)

does exactly the correct thing that one expects it to. The same rule permits us to use machine arithmetic that mimics the axioms of real arithmetic and still produces correct answers.

FISHER: One of the several strengths of Fortran is the fact that within the language there is a highly portable subset that is sufficient for over 95 per cent of the programs required of the language. Early in the sixties I transported programs of many thousands of source statements all over the globe with hardly a change by confining the code within that subset. The chances are that those programs would still be transportable today despite the many corruptions to the language that have taken place since. If one really seeks portability one should code within the subset of Fortran known as PFORT (Bell Telephone Laboratories) [6]. It is a little more generous than my original subset but that small measure is probably the sum total of the improvement that Ingemar Dahlstrand alluded to. It owes little to official standards. What a pity that the official 1966 basic Fortran subset is higher than PFORT.

HILL: For those interested in this, Colin Day's book, 'Compatible Fortran' [7] is well worth looking at.

MEEK: Walt Brainerd said a short time ago that we have now started discussing language features rather than standardisation, and of course he's right. We should I think resist the temptation to go much further along this road, though I don't think it follows that since a matter is one of language features rather than standardisation as such, it shouldn't concern us. The point surely is that if languages are to be standardised, they have to provide certain features that enable the aims of standardisation to be met, and if they don't have them they must be added. We don't just need to standardise languages, the languages themselves must meet certain standards – and the language standards must reach a certain standard. That is what this discussion is about. However, I think we've given this aspect a good airing. Are there other things which standards ought to contain?

TRIANCE: I did mention earlier that a standard could well include a measure of performance, though not in my view a standard level of performance. It could also cover documentation, insofar as it relates to the adherence of an implementation to the standard – things like requiring the implementor to specify the level of implementation when the standard permits levels. And if I could mention one more thing which standards should not contain, I do not think they should cover hardware representations. That should be a problem for the implementor.

MEEK: Well, there are three more points – performance, documentation, and hardware representation – for us to look at. On the matter of performance, I almost came in when John Triance mentioned it earlier, because I don't see that the argument he advanced then, that people will buy on the basis of performance when everything else is standard, at all conflicts with a requirement that to be standard-conforming an implementation must reach a certain minimum level of performance. The real difficulty I've always seen is how you can set a measure of performance which can fairly be applied to anything from a Pet to a Cray 1, and still be meaningful. I certainly agree that a standard measure of performance is a prerequisite and I'd be happy with no more than that in the short term, but I still believe that the long term aim should be that standards specify a minimum level of efficiency.

BULL: By 'performance' we seem to be implying speed, measured in terms such as how many lines of source code are compiled per second. This seems to me to be nothing to do with standardisation. After all, how do you compare the performance of an interpreter with a compiler, or a check-out compiler with an optimiser?

ADDYMAN: I think that Brian Meek is really addressing the problem of quality. With Pascal it is the intention that a number of programs in the validation suite will address the subject of run-time performance, though initially the results produced by these programs will need to be interpreted with care. There are already a dozen or so such programs which are being used by compiler writers to measure the performance of their compilers when reporting them in journal articles and in Pascal News. These come from two main sources – Brian Wichmann and Niklaus Wirth. From Brian Wichmann the compiler writers have taken the Ackermann function test [8, 9] and the Wichmann benchmark [10]. The Wirth programs were taken from two of his papers, on the design of a Pascal compiler [11] and on what to demand from and how to assess programming languages [12]. The Wichmann benchmark is particularly interesting because it is an attempt to represent the small Algol 60 program. Despite this it is being used by computer manufacturers to compare their Fortran compiler with that of their competitors. There are other measures of quality, though – for example the size of program acceptable to the compiler, line length of the program source, run-time diagnostics, and so on. This is an area to which the Pascal group and those working on the Pascal suite will be turning their attention in the very near future.

MEEK: I am glad Tony Addyman has mentioned this, because it shows that something can be done, even now, if you are determined enough. This sort of thing *is* the concern of standards – to specify means of measurement, as John Triance said earlier, and in my view to lay down minimum performance levels, which anyone who buys a compiler which meets the standard has a right to expect. Just as with diagnostics, there is no reason why the standard should not specify different levels, to cope with the different kinds of implementation and different kinds of hardware which one might have. I am sure the way forward is through validation mechanisms, much as Tony has described for Pascal. Incidentally, in my Euro IFIP paper [1] I made the point that if you have different levels of diagnostics for debugging or optimising compilers, you really need to include performance specifications in the standard as well, otherwise a compiler with rotten diagnostics might be called 'optimising' regardless of the quality of the object code it produces.

DAHLSTRAND: Language standards (the kind that give portability) are only the first step towards performance standards. If you have portability, you can start to design test batches and compare the time and cost of running them on different systems; and then you may start to find out how many different kinds, or aspects, of performance a hardware/software system may have. Could it be good at array processing, and only fair at number crunching? Good at string handling but bad at input-output? These are the kinds of questions computer buyers all over the world would like to ask and have answered. And if I may add a remark about another of John Triance's points, hardware representation, this seems to be one problem that is slowly losing importance, because everyone is getting to use a more-or-less standard, reasonably rich character set.

MEEK: I hope you are right about that. It seems very slow to me.

ADDYMAN: The standard should specify as a minimum the representation of a program using the ISO character set without resorting to the national variants. Another problem in this area is the use of French, German (or whatever) reserved words, in place of their English equivalents. Arthur Sale has been doing some work on this, haven't you, Arthur?

SALE: Yes. It is often assumed that all programmers speak English, and an English-like version (APL excepted) is all that is needed for a programming language to be portable and useful. But this is not true in a large number of countries. It is probable that many programmers in developed countries will be able to speak English and make sense of the reserved words, and so on, but it is unlikely to be true for secretaries and programming assistants, and especially not for schoolchildren. In developing countries, the lack of native-tongue versions is a major factor in inhibiting growth, by cutting off talent from access to this profession, and by making computing an esoteric art. Standards need to address what I have begun to call 'national variants' of programming languages, with suitable tools and conditions to make two-way transporting possible. In the case of Pascal, there seems no reason why 100 per cent portability cannot be achieved across natural language barriers.

MEEK: A wonderful vision has just come into my head of the Standards Association of Australia producing a version of Pascal translated into 'Strine' —

DAHLSTRAND: What's 'Strine'?

MEEK: Sorry, that is a Commonwealth in-joke! 'Strine' is the name given to a dialect of English alleged to be spoken in Australia. If you can imagine a form of pronunciation in which the word 'Australian' is pronounced 'Strine' it gives you the general flavour. But, joking apart, it is worth remembering that English is another language which isn't standardised. We all know of instances where policy decisions at standards meetings, and even standards themselves, have had to be carefully worded so that they mean the same in American English and real English – no slur intended on Walt Brainerd and his compatriots! And even English English can cause difficulties. When I was in Leeds in the early 1960s, I was learning Algol 60 and a bit of the local dialect at roughly the same time, and found that 'while' could be used to mean 'until' – locally, that is, not in Algol 60. You can imagine the kinds of problem that might cause – and if you can't, David Hill mentions it in the same Computer Bulletin article [4] I mentioned earlier. But to return to serious matters, I think we should be grateful to Tony Addyman and Arthur Sale for bringing up this very important point. Even though none of us here are affected, we should not forget the many who are, as so many English-speakers have the habit of doing. (I don't count Ingemar Dahlstrand as one affected, since his English is better than that of most English people, even if we do catch him out occasionally!)

HILL: Arthur Sale mentioned 'reserved words' just now, but I hope he means 'language-defined words'. What he said about native-tongue versions is one of the strongest arguments for insisting that languages must make their language-defined words distinguishable from user-defined identifiers. Have you seen the horrifying list of reserved words in Cobol? Imagine that multiplied by twelve, to allow for translations into a dozen different human languages.

BULL: John Triance's third point was documentation. This is not ignored in the Minimal Basic standard, which specifies that to be standard-conforming an implementation must be accompanied by documentation that describes the action taken in regard to features referred to in the standard as 'undefined' or 'implementation-defined'. Moreover, if a program element does not conform to the syntactic rules, either an error must be reported or there must be a documented implementation-defined meaning.

ADDYMAN: Yes, it is another example of the contribution to programming language standards by the Basic people. The draft Pascal standard also places requirements on the implementor about documentation.

BRAINERD: I'd like to make one further point about the content of standards. One of the negative aspects of standardisation is the fact that it is very difficult to remove any feature from a language implementation or a language standard, once it has been put into the standard. This is why one must be particularly careful of including features that will prevent inclusion of anything that will conflict with it. (Again, error actions are a prime example.) The standardisation process must develop a way of 'retiring' language features without wrecking the tremendous economic investment in programs and programmers. One scheme is being considered by X3J3 for Fortran: it is to have a 'module' of obsolete language features. This provides a list of features that are marked as being on the way out. Programmers can then avoid those features when writing new programs or converting old ones. On the other hand, the presence of these features in the obsolete module should cause all implementations of that functionality to be done in the same way. The presumption would be that such features would remain in implementations just as long as the marketplace demands them.

TRIANCE: The ANSI Cobol committee is adopting a similar approach in its next standard. The only difference appears to be that they intend to remove all features marked as obsolete in the next revision. Thus Cobol users have about five years' warning.

SALE: May I remark that the grass-roots users would probably be happier to keep the obsolete features and dispose of the extensions, in many cases?

VALIDATION

MEEK: One question which is always coming up is that of standard conformance and validation, and we have already referred to it quite a lot. Before asking for comments I'd like to get one point clear on terminology. I gather that for some people 'validation' means simply that an implementation must have been subjected to certain tests and that the results of these tests must be made available — not that the tests need necessarily have been passed. A potential purchaser can then look at the results and decide whether any variations from the standard, or failure to meet its requirements, matter as far as he is concerned. People who use the term in that way regard a requirement to pass the validation tests as 'certification'. Personally, I use 'validation' to mean proving validity — that is, validation in the context of this discussion includes the concept of certification.

TRIANCE: Implementations should, to use 'validation' in its widest sense, be able to validate the conformance of programs. This could be a compile-time option. However, there are some features which can be checked only at run time (for example, ranges of PERFORM in Cobol). Such checks can be quite expensive, and in some cases might remove the justification for a particular feature. An example is checking that table items are in the correct sequence before doing a Cobol binary search: SEARCH ALL. As for conformance of implementations, validation suites should be available, for all languages as they are currently for Cobol, Fortran and Coral. Such suites should include incorrect programs — how else can they check rules such as 'the operands in an ADD statement must be numeric'? The problem is that these tests cannot be automated while errors are handled in a non-standard way. So we are back to extending standards to cover error handling.

FISHER: A standard is only of curiosity value if it cannot be enforced, and it is hard to see how it can be enforced if it cannot be checked. The checking is complicated, expensive and of little value if the standard is imprecise, ambiguous or open-ended. There is therefore a massive problem concerning the completeness of a standard. Thus there is an argument for refusing any standard that does not provide for the checking of implementations against that standard. This implies not only that the standard is written so that it is possible to check it, that is, that it is not ambiguous, imprecise or open-ended, but that there is an acceptable institution able and prepared to check implementations against the standard. The quality of specification of a standard that was suitable (nay useful) for Algol 60, Fortran 66 and Cobol 68 is no longer sufficient for today's requirements.

BRAINERD: I don't like David Fisher's use of the word 'enforced'. No standard can be enforced in the sense that there is an international or national agency that goes around to make sure that all Cobol compilers conform to the standard. Checking is possible, difficult and worth pursuing, and I assume that this is really what we are talking about. It would certainly be useful to know which implementations do conform to a certain standard.

SALE: Whoa! In the case of Pascal there is an agency that will try to enforce the Pascal standard. It goes under the name of Pascal News, and if you think of it as a consumer organisation you won't go far wrong. If we can set up the climate correctly, users will demand a conformance report (like a check on a used car) before buying a Pascal system, and some purchasers are already showing interest. I think the publication of validation reports, and independent user action, is going a long way to make enforcement a reality.

BULL: I think we have to be careful about our use of terms in discussing this topic. The state of the art does not allow us to determine whether a translator conforms to a standard, only to check that it passes a certain number of tests designed to give us a high degree of confidence that it does.

MEEK: There could be another kind of means of enforcement, at least in principle. If standards were tough enough, and I bought a compiler which claimed to meet a standard, I'd like to feel that I could sue the company under the Trade Descriptions Act or the Sale of Goods Act if it didn't.

BULL: In West Germany that is exactly what you can do. Contracts are made with reference to DIN standards and conformance to these standards forms the basis of the contract.

MEEK: That's fine, if the standards are tough enough. As Tony Addyman mentioned earlier, you can refer to standards in contracts in Britain as well, but in our case they are not much help, since the rules for conformance are too weak. What I want is for standards to be such that you don't need to write a whole lot of extra conditions into a contract − even supposing the supplier would accept them. What I want is to be able to buy an implementation which claims to be standard-conforming and the standard itself gives me all the safeguards I need, so that the contract created by the fact of the sale gives me all the protection I want.

ADDYMAN: With Arthur Sale, I have hopes of pressure from the users. If the users insist on having validated software the vendors (who wish to stay in business) will comply. There are a number of examples outside the computing field where consumer pressure has had an impact on the vendor's products. (Real Ale?)

MEEK: For the benefit of those outside the U.K., the 'Real Ale' campaign was a grassroots consumer-based campaign against the quality of beer marketed by the big brewing combines. In the U.S.A. perhaps Ralph Nader's campaign for greater safety in cars is another example. I've often thought we need a Ralph Nader for software.

SYKES: We all know analogies are dangerous, so please forgive me for pointing out that the Real Ale analogy is nothing to do with standards. There are no standards for the quality of beer in the U.K. (except that it must not be poisonous). This is probably just as well, since what the Real Ale campaigners were against was uninteresting uniformity, as well as insipidity. As for Ralph Nader, he would have got nowhere if he hadn't been fighting for standards to improve human safety. Since few programs involve human safety, perhaps we had better sit back and allow those concerned with air traffic control systems and the like fight our standardisation battles for us. Mind you, I would support a campaign that 'EQUIVALENCE/REDEFINES is hazardous to your health' or 'GOTO: unsafe at any speed'.

MEEK: With that appealing thought, and before anyone tries to launch a campaign fund, perhaps we can revert to the specific matter of validation suites, and ask Nicholas Neve to come in, to tell us some more about the Ministry of Defence assessment of performance of Coral 66 compilers.

NEVE: Yes, I think it should be of interest. As I said earlier, the MoD have been assessing as well as validating compilers against the standard for some years. In doing this they have built up a database of their performance against which new compilers can be judged and valid comparisons made. The configuration and performance of the machine (or machines) on which the compiler and the generated code are run are of course factors which tend to obscure the results of the compiler in isolation, and so the evaluation is really of a Coral machine rather than a compiler. This is of course precisely what the customer uses anyway. The assessment of each machine includes the measurement of compile-time performance as well as the run-time performance of the code generated. The tests examine the efficiency of the code for specific language features, for example it includes tests on array indexing, part-word referencing and floating point arithmetic. Other more subjective aspects are also covered including ease of use and the quality of the diagnostics. To assess the latter aspect a program containing many errors is compiled repeatedly, and only edited where the compiler indicates an error. The number of iterations before an error-free program is obtained gives a measure of the compiler's performance in this area. The assessment is specified in an MoD document [13] and the results are available to prospective Coral 66 users via the Royal Signals and Radar Establishment.

MEEK: What we need is a requirement to go through some such process written into standards. Any more points on conformance and validation?

SCOWEN: I'd like to see a move beyond validation, towards verification. Existing methods of validating compilers treat them as black boxes: the tester supplies a suite of programs, observes the results, and judges the compiler to have passed or failed. This method has its attractions – once the suite of test programs has been produced, any compiler can be tested or retested within a few weeks, at fairly modest cost. However, there is an important limitation in this approach: although the method may discover errors in a compiler, it can never prove the absence of errors. Real arithmetic and real functions (like square root and arctan) are two simple examples of software impossible to verify using the black box technique. There are so many possible cases that it is impossible to hope that random tests will discover anomalies, such as a case I know of where a particular value was regarded by the system as representing 'undefined', yet could be generated perfectly validly by normal computations. Further difficulty arises because of the approximate nature of real arithmetic, which we have already discussed, which means that it is difficult to be sure whether answers from a few examples means that the whole is satisfactory. A preferable approach would be to specify the properties required, and then require the implementor to prove that his product possesses them. This method would be analogous with practices in other industries. For example, consider the manufacturer of a large pressure vessel for containing bulk quantities of a liquid or gas. He is required to provide with the pressure vessel the results of X-ray and ultrasonic tests which confirm that welds are of high quality and flawless. The results of compiler validation of that kind would undoubtedly be more useful. Treating a compiler as a black box at best allows us to hope that any important error would have been discovered and that other errors will not matter too much. On the other hand, the implementor has added problems. He may need to formalise his existing methods of validating the compiler, which might require considerable extra effort. But if this is the case, the existing reliability of his product is uncertain, and probably rather low.

TRIANCE: I'd like to stress again that conformance rules imposed by a programming language standard must not be allowed to stifle development. If, for example, all extensions to the 1968 ANSI standard for Cobol had been prevented, some users would have had to delay for nearly a decade the introduction of modular programming and the use of indexed files. If the average period between standards for a language is about eight years then, if we allow two years for drafting the standard and two years for its implementation, some features in the standard will be twelve years out of date by the time they become available to the user. This is too long. I am, naturally, in favour of conformance rules, but only if they make allowance for the needs of language development.

RELATIONSHIPS BETWEEN STANDARDS

MEEK: This raises the question of the time scale of standardisation activity, which I'd like to come back to in a minute. However, for the moment could we consider the relationship between standards, both between those in the programming language area, and with others outside? I think we can take for granted that portability depends on many other matters than simply standard languages — we've already mentioned word length and machine capacity, and there are also card codes, tape formats and goodness knows what else — but has anyone any other points, besides that obvious one?

FISHER: There is a need for co-ordination, and a common approach. May I give an example? Basic was once a very simple language. Now it is tending to try to be all things to all men. In particular there are plans to incorporate graphics within the language. Meanwhile the graphics fraternity is trying to create a standard for graphics software and finding it very difficult. If Basic goes its own way it may create something worse. It will almost certainly create something different. Those working on graphics seek to create a specification that can be implemented as a package of Fortran subroutines. Many such packages already exist for graphics alone, for example, Gino-F, Ghost, Disspla, GPGS, etc. Packages exist in other areas such as NAG (numerical algorithms) and Genesys (Civil Engineering). Rather than add such capabilities to each and every language, it is far better to make it possible for each and every language to access such packages. Thus every language should support a level of modular programming (à la Fortran, if you like, for that is the way the world is designed), and so a specification of a standard interface between languages is needed as a matter of considerable urgency if language standards are to be contained within reasonable proportions.

BULL: I don't agree with this point of view. Basic has always put the user first. A good example of this is the inclusion of the MAT statements and sophisticated string handling. Both of these facilities could have been provided by subroutines, but the spirit of Basic is to provide facilities in the most natural way for the user. It is hardly surprising, therefore, to see graphical capabilities being provided through statements rather than subroutine calls. Languages such as Fortran and Algol have a history of providing facilities through subroutine and procedure calls. Basic has a history of using statements. Since Basic has a subroutine mechanism which is functionally equivalent to that of Fortran, standard graphics packages can be used by Basic users if they wish.

FISHER: I really cannot agree with Gordon Bull on this very important point of principle. Irrespective of any particular case, it can only be wrong to try to stuff every 'goodie' into a language, for then it can only become bloated and will probably condemn itself to a very slow death. If all languages

pursue this course (and the tendency is for them to do just that), there will
be an enormous amount of overlap and duplication that makes a nonsense
of the standards. Large languages, in any case, start to devolve into subsets
and this too runs counter to the interests of standards. Over the next few
years micros are going to make it even more important to have a number of
simple correlated standards rather than massive all-embracing standards.
Basic will betray itself and its users if it loses its fundamental simplicity.
Fortran 77 and the structured extensions currently being considered for the
next edition of Cobol are probably the best break the other languages have
ever had. The signs are not encouraging. There must be a more rational
and reasonable way of developing standards. Just think what might happen
if we diverted just a small part of this energy away from languages and into
other software standards.

TRIANCE: It is certainly the case, as David Fisher was saying earlier, that we
need greater standardisation for communicating between programs written
in different languages. This affects procedure calling mechanisms and
parameter passing, as well as data representation in files. It may be all right
between Basic and Fortran, but I agree with David, we urgently need a more
general standard. In fact standardisation of programming languages would
be much easier if related aspects, such as character codes, command
languages and database systems, were adequately standardised. Because the
ISO character set is not universally applied, Cobol has a mechanism for
the programmer to specify the desired character set for a file, or a collating
sequence. On the point of word length, already mentioned, this really is a
major problem for a programmer who wants to optimise the use of store —
perhaps reduction in hardware costs will remove that problem.

ADDYMAN: Graphics has been specifically mentioned, but it is only one of
several language-independent standards currently being developed. In
addition we have data bases, as John Triance has said, real-time subroutines,
open system interconnection, and so on. Unless we act soon we shall find
ourselves needing a different implementation of each of these functional
standards for each standard language. I should like to see a serious attempt
made to define a language-independent 'library call'. In any given language
this would have the syntax of a procedure or subroutine call, but it would
be used to invoke a subroutine from a library. This has fewer problems than
the more general (and more useful) mechanism suggested by John Triance.
If the standard 'library call' could be agreed on, it would be a step in the
right direction. The biggest problem to be overcome will be the internal
representation of the values passed as parameters — a real value in Fortran
may well have a different representation from a real value in Algol or Pascal
on the same computer.

FISHER: Agreed.

SYKES: My first experience of communicating between programs written in different languages was in 1964 when I wrote a Fortran subroutine to be called from a Cobol program. It wasn't difficult, and I find it sad to think that such communication even now does not seem to be generally possible. This is presumably not only because of inadequate overlap between the data types of any two languages, but also because what appears to the programmer to be the same data type may, as Tony Addyman has said, be represented differently in the two cases. Fortran arrays of two or more dimensions are different from anything else; while one implementor might provide 32-bit integers another will provide 16-bit, and so on. However, PL/I in IBM implementations has unilaterally solved the problems of communicating with Cobol, Fortran and Assembler, and a study of the facility provided will give a good idea both of the problems and of how they can be solved. A more general example of communication between a user's program and other programs, operating system functions, and so on can be found in APL. The mechanism for sharing a variable between an active APL workspace and some other (auxiliary) activity is simple and very powerful, though perhaps less sophisticated than one would like. But simplicity and power are surely what we must seek in anything we hope will be standard. What every language should have, in fact, is a general mechanism for communicating with other, asynchronous processes running under the same system or a different one, for another language or whatever it may be. Given this, the only problem remaining is how to represent the objects which cross this interface. You could start with the ISO character set and see how much further you could progress from there. Not far, I suspect, but don't let me stop anyone trying. The exisiting CALL interface within every self-respecting language is simply a degenerate case, and should be recognised as such.

STANDARDISATION PROCEDURES

MEEK: Before we sum up, has anyone any points to make about the procedures which we follow in the standardisation game? Including timescale, which I mentioned just now?

HILL: There is one point that worries me. Suppose a draft standard is circulated for comment, and out of 200 people who comment, 10 do not like feature A and say so. Of the other 190, perhaps 100 like A very much, while 90 are indifferent, but none of them comment on it because they see it in the draft and are happy for it to remain there. Since the only comments received on A are critical of it, there is a tendency to change it or even remove it, perhaps reluctantly. The 100 who like it do not even know that any such thing is contemplated until they discover what has happened in the final product. The moral seems to be that those who make comments should take care to include praise of features that they like, in addition to protests about those they do not, but this is difficult to do unless you can guess which features are endangered.

DAHLSTRAND: The ideal might be to let the circulation of a draft produce a number of proposals that are then sent out for a straw vote; or would this be too slow? As for timescale, I think a five-year cycle is too short for language standards. If a standard is submitted to a major rewrite (Fortran 77, for example) you will need the feedback that results when a major part of the user community has been exposed to implementations of the new standard, including a feeling of whether the old standard is being superseded. This means ten, rather than five, years between major rewrites. Other things, like writing common extensions into the standard, might be done in a considerably shorter timescale, perhaps in the form of additions or appendices to the standard.

BULL: I feel very strongly that in many cases the mechanism for producing standards is poor; so poor that we produce standards that are not acceptable. I have in mind just the sort of problem David Hill mentions where adverse comment is received on an item in the standard so it is removed, and all those who liked it are unhappy with the final standard. Implicit in that scenario is that there is only a single solicitation of public comment. A good example (or should I say a bad example?) of this is a certain standard which shall remain nameless. A draft was circulated for public comment. Some time later, a revised draft was circulated with a covering letter saying that this would become the standard unless anyone objected. What was missing was any indication of the changes made, any response to comments, in fact anything to help one come to a decision on the draft other than re-reading the whole document again from cover to cover. The ANSI rules of procedure would be a good starting point for standards committees. Right now, there are far too many standards committees working in what I consider to be an unprofessional manner.

SALE: Excellent point! I quite agree that most standards committees (and I have observed many in different countries) undertake their work in a very slapdash manner. The end result is usually a highly politicised structure, to the detriment of the technical excellence of the standard. The solution will be a long time coming, but I can suggest two things which should be tackled. The first is support services. A standards committee should have access to packages providing word processing, the production of indexes and concordances, change-marked copies, and so on. Even for my own commentary I find it necessary to automate some of the activities – assistance to full committees is even more imperative. Secretarial assistance to produce commentaries on drafts is also an important factor. The second important factor is the encouragement of technical sub-committees. Far too many of our full committees are composed of self-recognised experts or of appointees with a particular commitment, resulting in highly political arguments. Much of the work can be delegated to small, really expert committees of two to five people, with the filtering action remaining in the hands of the full committee as a brake in case of radical action. Recognition of the difference between a technical decision and political one might be a first step.

ADDYMAN: In all the iterations of drafts which I have seen over the last few years, I have never yet seen a document of the form which Gordon Bull suggests. Quite often one will receive a summary of the responses sent out in reply to the comments received, but sometimes these amount to little more than 'we do not agree!'. Even when such a summary is available, that is no guarantee that no other changes, however benign, have been introduced. As for the committee procedures, I can find little enthusiasm for a system in which changes are made to the language being standardised by a simple majority vote – a majority of one, sometimes. How can anything which provokes such disagreement be standard!

SYKES: It must be accepted that government by referendum is impractical. Standards must be produced by small bodies of people. There must be a mechanism for ensuring that these people are not only competent, but also representative of interested parties. There must be a review procedure, but only because of possible deficiencies in the working mechanism. Is there any legislative system, however democratic, which, having published a bill, replies individually to comment from members of the electorate? I think not. In the case of standards, the only purpose of review is to discover mistakes, rather than to take an opinion poll on unspecified issues. Only if certain value-judgements embodied in a standard are objected to by a significant number of people should the standardising body reconsider, and if it doesn't change its mind perhaps it should then explain why not.

CONCLUSIONS

MEEK: Let us now try to sum up. Are we happy, if not about the present state of programming language standards, at least about the way the work is going? Are we optimistic about the future? What more is needed?

DAHLSTRAND: Well, I for one think that the work is going well at the moment. There have been a couple of very encouraging developments recently. One is the agreement reached by ISO/TC97/SC5 at The Hague in 1977 about the way future standards work should be handled (described in Part 1) and the very open manner in which ANSI/X3J3 handled the public review of the revision of Fortran, and similar developments, all showing a very encouraging attitude. Then, there was the fact that many of the issues we have been discussing here, on predictability, definition of error indications, conformance testing, and so on, were discussed at the meeting, the result of the paper on 'Criteria and Guidelines' submitted by the U.K. delegation. It is true that SC 5 did not accept the proposals in that paper as policy; nevertheless the fact that they were advanced and discussed was a sign of a new attitude to data processing standards. A recent example of these ideas in action is that both the Kiwinet and the Codasyl command language proposals define error indications.

BULL: I agree, things are getting better. There are a number of promising avenues of work being explored. The attempt to produce a standard syntactic metalanguage by the BSI, the approach to conformance being taken by the Basic standard, the international co-operative efforts on the PL/I and Basic standards, and the work being carried out by the National Bureau of Standards in the U.S.A. to produce a comprehensive set of validation routines for Basic, are all encouraging signs.

FISHER: What we need now are people, and resources. An expert in standards, either international or national, can be defined as one who is willing and has both the time and the finance to attend the necessary meetings. Note that this definition makes no reference to technical merit. Work on standards is frequently dull and monotonous. There is little prestige and certainly no monetary reward to be had for either the individual or his employer. As a result the work of creating standards is generally undertaken by enthusiasts of doubtful technical merit. They are the employees that employers have decided can be spared and can spare the time — not the best recommendations. Hence the standards movement is dominated by academics (though I do not want to reopen that particular argument!) and minor members of major government bodies. Private industry, the creators of wealth and prosperity, are very poorly represented, apart from the computer manufacturers themselves, who have an obvious interest. Thus standards can easily acquire the image normally associated with red tape, whereas they should be regarded as a tool to constrain unfortunate excesses, ease communication problems and ultimately produce more efficient results. Prestige and people of prestige are both urgently needed within the standards movement. One way of helping with this problem would be money — some remuneration for the individual and compensation for the employer for the loss of services. The lack of the necessary financial resources also has additional and equally serious consequences, certainly in the U.K. It is relatively easy for members of the U.K. to attend meetings in the U.K. sponsored by the BSI, but most of the really important standards (for example Fortran and Cobol) are driven by committees and working groups based outside the U.K. (for example Codasyl and ANSI/X3J4 for Cobol, ANSI/X3J3 for Fortran), and the best way to help mould a new standard is to get involved at the beginning in the critical committee. This costs money that is far beyond any reasonable claims any individual can place upon his employer and is a clear case for a useful level of state aid.

HILL: I agree that finance is a real difficulty. As things stand at present, if I attend a BSI meeting in London I have to meet all my own expenses. I can attend an ISO meeting abroad only if my employer is willing to meet the cost. I am not complaining, merely stating the facts, which cannot help the standardisation cause. On the other hand so many people, in so many fields, think that they have 'a clear case for a useful level of state aid'. Can the taxpayer be expected to agree with all of them?

BULL: My work in co-ordinating the three international committees working on Basic is effectively government funded, mainly from U.K. and European Community sources. Certainly without such support it would have been impossible for me to attend four ANSI meetings in the U.S.A. and six to eight ECMA and EWICS meetings in Europe each year since 1974. More recently I have received U.K. funds to enable me to assist in the editing of the Basic standard document on the Dartmouth computer system, using the Post Office International Packet Switching Service and the Telenet system to access it. On another point which David Fisher made, my experience of the people involved in Basic standards does not wholly bear out his analysis. Of course not every single one of the 50 or so people currently involved are of equal ability, status or competence, but nevertheless one of the things that have impressed me has been the professionalism of the key people involved.

BRAINERD: I'd like to come in on this. On the question of domination by academics, which David Fisher brought up again, it has been my observation that standards efforts in the U.S.A. have not been dominated by academics, and indeed, as I was saying earlier, I think standards have suffered considerably from a lack of input from the academic community. However, you may discover that I was an academic for some years, and may wish to discount my statements accordingly! More generally, and though I can speak only from my experience on X3J3, on the basis of that experience I can support what Gordon Bull has just said, and in fact I disagree with almost everything that David Fisher said. People without excellent technical knowledge or without excellent debating skills or without a certain sense of social dynamics make very little contribution to X3J3 — people in any of those categories usually do not apply for membership, or do not remain a member long. With the people we have, the work is seldom dull. Perhaps X3J3 is not typical of standards groups, because experienced 'Fortraners' come from scientific and engineering backgrounds and tend to be well educated and reasonably logical thinkers. However, Gordon Bull mentioned the 'professionalism' of the Basic standards people, and perhaps he had similar qualities in mind and it is true there as well. If I may also comment on the financial aspect, David Fisher first said that there is no monetary reward for an employer in sending a representative to a standards committee, and then said, quite correctly, that the manufacturers have an obvious interest in the standards effort (for monetary reasons, of course). The monetary rewards both for implementors and for users is huge, as Ingemar Dahlstrand pointed out right at the beginning of this discussion. If an organisation does not send a first-rate person, then it is suffering from a severe case of misplaced priorities, for exactly the reasons that Ingemar gave.

FISHER: That's fine – in theory!

ADDYMAN: It seems to me that these comments have tended to reflect the position of advantage or disadvantage of the person speaking. In abstract, it seems unlikely that academics will dominate the development of standards because academics don't have the necessary funds at their disposal. Furthermore, there can be little economic benefit to a university of a standard for Fortran, for example. It seems to me that the group who are not adequately represented on standards committees are the users – the group who will be most affected by the standards – something which I think Brian Meek mentioned when this came up earlier. This is simply because there are very few organisations which can adequately represent the users on such committees. Even when such organisations exist, individual companies have to contribute the time of their staff, and therefore money, for the benefit of the user community, rather than just themselves.

FISHER: Agreed.

DAHLSTRAND: I think we all agree that standards people should have more resources and prestige. One concrete step is the offer by X3J3 to write a letter of support for anyone wishing to be a working member.

SYKES: I remarked earlier about the motivation for standardisation being weak, and that only very large, plus some large, user organisations will be likely to support it. We should not expect this to change. It does not mean that standards are not worth having; but, human nature being what it is, let us not expect to persuade a lot more people to get involved. I think we should rather treat it as a labour of love, and be grateful for whatever help we can get. More generally, on how things are progressing, one thing that experience in programming language standardisation has taught us is that it is difficult – I would go so far as to say, virtually impossible. Every standard we have has been less successful than was hoped, in some way or other. In the case of Fortran the standard was reasonable, but the language was deemed to need extensive improvement. In the case of Cobol, the standard was less of a standard than was hoped. A more thorough job was done on PL/I, and there still aren't that many implementations of it. Dare I suggest that we should standardise only languages, or language features, which are easy to standardise, in the hope of getting it right for once? Should we even design languages so that they are easy to standardise? Such a course would conflict with my feeling that there is little justification for adding to the number of standard languages.

MEEK: I have a feeling that some of the discussion about difficulty in raising interest and obtaining financial support is rather specific to the U.K., so I would rather that were not pursued further. But on Tony Addyman's point about user involvement, the National Computer Users Forum, a group in the U.K. consisting of users' associations of computer manufacturers, recently issued a report suggesting that such associations should get more involved in standards work. This may be a way forward, and SHARE for example has representatives on ANSI committees. But in my experience of such groups, they spend more time swapping tales about what clever tricks they can do with special features of their implementations, and demanding from the manufacturer some add-on extra which some other manufacturer has provided in his compiler, than they do demanding conformance to standards.

SALE: If I can attempt to sum up my own feeling about standardisation, I think I can say that I am fairly optimistic, more so than at any other time in the past fifteen years of my association with standards committees. There are a lot of things still needing attention, but we are gradually identifying important issues like the evils and advantages of open-endedness; we are grappling with the topic of validation; and we are learning a lot about standardising things other than primitive programming languages. I feel that we have not said enough about validation, which I personally regard as being of equivalent importance to standardisation, but it promises to add yet more fuel to the software revolution one can discern taking place. I wouldn't feel able to take time off from my research work otherwise. It is too early to say that the Pascal standard will be the last of the 'old-style' loosely worded standards, for there are several more in the production pipeline. But I perceive a transitional stage towards better-designed and better-implemented standards. Signs like these, and signs of international co-operation, lead me at least to think that the standards committees are going to have a more interesting time ahead.

BULL: One worrying situation with regard to adoption of standards is the microprocessor revolution. In the early days of microprocessors (just a few short years ago) there was a tendency to shoehorn small translators into tiny memories, with the result that the implementations did not conform to any standards. It will take some time to get rid of this legacy. Moreover, since micros are being used in such wide application areas, the standards message may get diluted. However, I think that there are a number of good signs relating to standards. Perhaps the most significant is the Commission for the European Communities' four-year Informatics Plan, included within which is a substantial sum of money to aid and promote standards. The National Computing Centre in the U.K. is devoting a considerable amount of time and effort to the promotion of standards, as is the Bureau de Normalisation d'Informatique in France. On another tack, the ECMA General Assembly recently issued a statement encouraging its technical committees to invite users to join in the standards-making process (as a result of which I am now a member of TC 21 rather than an invited observer). I believe that the computing community is slowly coming to recognise the economic advantages of standards and the need for them in purchasing. It may be some while before we see their widespread acceptance, but I believe this could be encouraged if governments were to take the lead in adopting the use of standards in government departments and specifying standards in invitations to tender.

ADDYMAN: I'd like to make a slightly different point on microprocessors to that made by Gordon Bull, and one which is a bit more optimistic. It seems possible, even likely, that the use of microprocessors in small businesses and by non-computing professionals is going to increase. To many of these people, the existence of standards, and adherence to them, needs no justification — an attitude which is far from common in the computer industry. These users will have an impact because of the views which they express of our industry — remember, you only have to say 'chip' and the media are interested — and also by their purchasing decisions. Many companies in the micro-computer business, both hardware and software, are not large corporations and may be quite sensitive to adverse user reactions. Already we have a software supplier claiming that his Basic complies with the ANSI standard (hurray!) and another one has had his Cobol compiler validated by the Federal Compiler Testing Center of the GSA — the General Services Administration.

MEEK: In Britain there is a symbol called a 'kitemark'. It is devised mainly from the letters 'BS' and the appearance of the kitemark on a product not only indicates that the product concerned meets a given British Standard, but that it has been 'validated' by the BSI testing authority as meeting the standard. In the case of pieces of domestic equipment, the validating body of course does not test each individual item; but since software, being abstract and finite, can be copied exactly, if there were such a thing as a 'kitemarked' compiler, assuming a minimal standard of honesty in the supplier that he hasn't modified the product after validation, you could be virtually certain that your copy did indeed meet the standard. At present, software standards are not adequate and the testing centres do not have the resources or expertise to validate them, but I should like to hope that we are working towards a situation such that, one day, we shall be able to buy a language compiler bearing a kitemark which would guarantee that we have bought a good quality product — accurate, safe, efficient, easy to use, all the other desirable attributes we have been talking about. What I have heard in this discussion encourages me to believe that this is not an entirely idle dream.

I am not going to attempt to summarise —

DAHLSTRAND: Would you mind if I tried to?

MEEK: Not at all, if you would like to, though you are a braver man than I am!

DAHLSTRAND: Well, it seems to me that we have reached a consensus on many of the questions we have discussed; and some rather interesting disagreements and new ideas on others.

We started out discussing the purpose of standards, and identified several besides the obvious and economically very important one of portability. Standards help us to educate people and reduce unnecessary duplication. They help us to divide responsibility between the programmer and the compiler writer. A standard may assure us of a minimum level of performance and safety, for example, require that unexpected run-time errors should be reported to the user; this already being written into the Basic and Pascal standards, and has been in PL/I for a long time. Should standardising consist only of codifying existing practice, or include improvement, even trying to break bad habits? And where does the process of improving a language end?

From here we passed on to the question of what languages to standardise. Considering the cost of standardisation and the purpose of standards, it was felt that we really ought to standardise as few languages as possible, and apply them as widely as possible. This might seem heavy-handed, but in the end we shall probably have to choose and recommend. It was pointed out that too much work had gone into standardisation of languages, as opposed to other software like word processing, sort/merge, file updating and archiving, and so on. The suspicion was voiced that this might be due to over-representation of academics in the committee, which led to a heated exchange of opinions. Another interesting question was whether the domination of one supplier, specific to our industry, helped or hindered standardisation; good arguments were advanced on both sides. Finally, it was pointed out that the growth of networks now made command language standards a necessity.

Do standards impede progress? If you standardise too early, the technical content of the standard may be weak; if you wait too long it may be hard to change established local practices. Some of us felt that standards do inhibit new features and experimentation; others pointed out that committees furthered exchange of new ideas, and even added features to their languages that had never been implemented. A case was made for more permissive languages; almost any language can develop a lot through pre-compilers and macro facilities, though these might defeat the primary purpose of standardisation. The DoD intends to keep tight control of Ada, not so much for the sake of transporting programs, as for moving people and software tools.

As for the form of a standard, a precise description is very important.

Almost everybody felt that this could be achieved through a good meta-language, at least as far as syntax is concerned. So far, we have a different metalanguage for each programming language, but the research going on will probably yield a useful common metalanguage. Everybody agreed the meta-language should be directed primarily to the implementor and supplemented with some informal description for the user (and the lawyer!), but how should the user learn to write standard conforming programs? The meta-language should, ideally, be readable for the user, but some of us thought that the user would only need to read manuals, whereas others thought the manuals should be thrown away when the user had mastered the language and the metalanguage. Anyway, defining the syntax is, comparatively speaking, the easy part; the hard part is to define the semantics strictly.

Are syntax and semantics sufficient contents of a standard? No, a number of other contents were proposed: error action and formats, cross-reference tables, compile and execution time facilities, and even type of arithmetic. The discussion came to centre on the interrelated questions of open-endedness and error action. We were told how attempts to specify error messages in Fortran had broken down, because every error turned out to be somebody's extension. There was a consensus, though, that errors should be reported unless obscured by other errors; that a high level of readability is required of error reports; that an undefined language construct should either be reported as an error, or explicitly be an allowable extension; and, last but not least, error handling is indeed within the scope of standards. In parallel to this, a program that has been moved to a new installation should either give the same results or an error message stating why it cannot function in the new environment. It was agreed that Fortran was on the verge of being portable, if precision could be controlled; and the relative merits of environmental enquiries and user-defined precision were considered. Standards could contain measures of performance and conformance — performance may be the last variable left to choose between different products, which does not preclude the specification of a minimum level of performance. Hardware representation is becoming less important to include. Finally, we touched on the necessity of being able to phase out obsolete language features, via a special section of the standard.

A standard cannot be enforced if it cannot be validated. We need facilities in compilers to validate programs; and we need validation suites to validate compilers, perhaps also institutions responsible for doing so. This also sets higher requirements for the form of a standard. Enforcement by lawsuit is getting to be possible in principle, but the main enforcement will still come through ordinary user pressure; and it should be applied. We were told how the MoD not only validates, but also assesses the performance of Coral 66 systems.

We differed on the topic of relations between standards. A first solution seems to be a standard interface, that is, a procedure call and parameter passing mechanism. Things like internal representation of data will also have to be the same in different languages on the same system. Other central standards, besides procedure interfaces, are character set and command language standards. But in many cases, new features like graphics and data base handling are added as new statements to languages. This is convenient for the user but may result in enormous overlaps.

Finally, we had a word about timescale of producing standards, and the fact that we are not really happy with the way standards are produced, nor with the final results of the process.

We really covered a lot of ground, didn't we?

MEEK: Yes, and that was an admirable piece of encapsulation. Thank you very much, Ingemar. Only two things remain for me to do. One is to thank everyone who has taken part — especially for allowing me to chop their contributions about to suit the needs of my 'imaginative reconstruction', and to cut off the discussion despite the fact that there was more that people wanted to say. The other is to express the hope that we have managed to shed some light on the issues involved in programming language standardisation, for the benefit of the readers. If we have stimulated others into developing their own ideas, or possibly even into considering taking part in standards activity themselves, it will have been worth the effort. After all, if we are united on anything, it is that standards are important and valuable things, and the more we can persuade the rather disparate and idiosyncratic computing community to have regard to them, the better it will be, in the long run, for everyone.

REFERENCES

[1] Meek, B. L. (1979), Programming language standards: the way ahead, *Proc. Euro. IFIP Congr.*, 31–38, North-Holland.
[2] NCC (1970), Standard Fortran programming manual.
[3] Malcolm, M. A. (1972), Algorithms to reveal properties of floating-point arithmetic, *Commun. ACM.*, **15**, 949–951.
[4] Hill, I. D. (1972), Wouldn't it be nice if we could write computer programs in ordinary English — or would it? *Comput. Bull.*, **16**, 306–312; *Honeywell Comput. J.*, **6**, 76–83.
[5] Bull, G. M., Garland, S. J., and Freeman, W. (1977), Specification for standard Basic, NCC.
[6] Ryder, B. G. (1974), The PFORT verifier, *Softw. Pract. Exper.*, **4**, 359–377.
[7] Day, A. C. (1978), Compatible Fortran, Cambridge University Press.
[8] Wichmann, B. A. (1976), Ackermann's function: a study in the efficiency of calling procedures, *Bit*, **16**, 103–110.

[9] Wichmann, B. A. (1977), How to call procedures, or second thoughts on Ackermann's function, *Softw. Pract. Exper.*, 7, 317-329.

[10] Curnow, H. J. and Wichmann, B. A. (1976), A synthetic benchmark, *Comput. J.*, 19, 43-49.

[11] Wirth, N. (1971), The design of a Pascal compiler, *Softw. Pract. Exper.*, 1, 309-333.

[12] Wirth, N. (1977), Programming languages: what to demand and how to assess them, in Perrott, R. H. (ed.), Software Engineering, Academic Press.

[13] Neve, N. J. F. and Webb, J. T. (1976), A set of programs to assist in the assessment of Coral 66 compilers, Tech. Note 782, Royal Radar and Signals Establishment.

[14] Lindsey, C. H. and van der Meulen, S. G. (1977), Informal Introduction to ALGOL 68, Revised Edition, North-Holland.

[15] Lindsey, C. H. (1972), ALGOL 68 with fewer tears. *Comput. J.*, 15, 176-188.

The International Organization for Standardization (ISO)

ISO consists of a member body from each participating country, that body being the one deemed to be most representative of standards activity in the country concerned. No country may have more than one representative member body. For the benefit particularly of small developing countries without suitable national standards bodies, a further class of 'Correspondent Member' also exists. Correspondent members are kept informed of standards activity but do not participate in it and do not have voting rights.

The policy-making body of ISO is the General Assembly, which consists of representatives of all the member bodies and normally meets every three years. A smaller Council, which meets once a year and consists of elected representatives who serve a three-year term of office, is responsible for organisation and administration. The council has an executive committee to run the affairs of ISO between the annual meetings, and a central secretariat responsible for the day-to-day administration. There are also advisory committees on special topics such as consumer affairs, certification etc., and, most important from our point of view, technical committees.

The technical committee responsible for 'Computers and Information Processing' is TC 97, whose secretariat is provided by the U.S.A. (that is, ANSI). TC 97 maintains liaison with various other technical committees such as TC 95 (Office machines) and with outside bodies such as ECMA, CCITT (the International Telegraph and Telephone Consultative Committee) and IEC (the International Electrochemical Commission).

Under TC 97 there are more than a dozen sub-committees. That responsible for programming languages is SC 5, whose secretariat is again provided by ANSI. SC 5 maintains liaison with other TC 97 sub-committees, such as SC 9 (Programming languages for numerical control) whose secretariat is provided by France (that is, AFNOR). The programme of work of SC 5 at present (as at 1st January 1980) is shown in Table A.1. In this table, 'WG' denotes a formal ISO working group and 'EG' one of the less formal SC 5 'experts groups' (see Chapter 1).

Table A.1.

Topic	Group	Responsible body	Chapter in this book
Algol	EG	NNI	4
APL	EG	AFNOR	14
Basic	EG	ANSI/ECMA	6
Cobol	EG	ANSI	3
DBMS	WG 3	ANSI	9
Fortran	EG	ANSI	2
Graphics	WG 2	NNI	10
Pascal	WG 4	BSI	7
PL/I	EG	ANSI	5
Real-time languages	WG 1	DIN	8
Text processing	EG	ANSI	14

REFERENCE

For further information on ISO and its relation to other bodies, with reference to data processing standards, the following is strongly recommended:

Prigge, R. D., Hill, M. F., and Walkowicz, J. L. (1978), The World of EDP Standards, 3rd edition, (Sperry Univac Corporation, ref. GS-4248).

ISO STRUCTURE

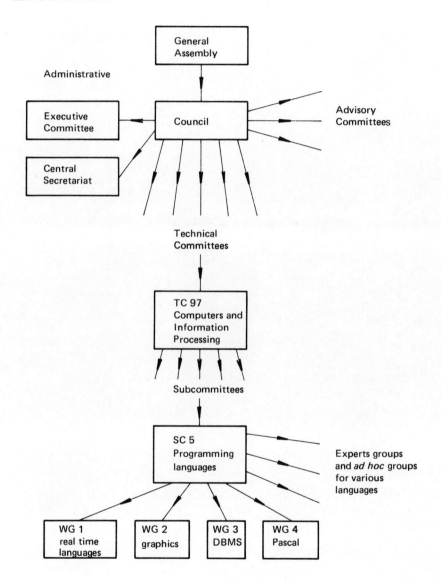

National and liaison standards bodies

Information correct, as far as could be verified, as at 1st January 1980.

AUSTRALIA

Standards body:
    Standards Association of Australia (SAA)

Equivalent to ISO/TC 97 (Computers and information processing):
    MS/20

Equivalent to ISO/TC 97/SC 5 (Programming languages):
    MS/20/5

Working groups:
    No working groups in the area of programming languages at present.

Address:
    Standards Association of Australia
    Standards House
    80 Arthur Street
    North Sydney
    NSW

AUSTRIA

Standards body:
    Österreichisches Normungsinstitut (ON)

Equivalent to ISO/TC 97 (Computers and information processing):
    FNA 001 Informatiensverebeiteng

Equivalent to ISO/TC 97/SC 5 (Programming languages):
    AG 5 Programmiersprechen

Working groups of ON/FNA 001/AG 5:

None, though some languages such as Fortran, Basic and Cobol are covered by particular individuals on AG 5.

Address:

Österreichisches Normungsinstitut
Leopoldsgasse 4
Postfach 130
A-1021 Wien 2

CANADA

Standards body:

Standards Council of Canada (SCC)

Equivalent to ISO/TC 97 (Computers and information processing):

CIPOM Canadian Standards Committee on Information Processing and Office Machines. Also covers the area of ISO/TC 95 (Office machines).

Equivalent to ISO/TC 97/SC 5 (Programming languages):

CPL Committee on Programming Languages of the Canadian Standards Association (CSA).

Working groups of CSA/CPL:

Working groups exist for Cobol, DBMS, Fortran, and PL/I.

Address:

Standards Council of Canada
350 Sparks Street
Ottawa
Ontario K1R 7S8

FRANCE

Standards body:

Association Française de Normalisation (AFNOR)

Equivalent to ISO/TC 97 (Computers and information processing):

Commission Générale de l'Informatique, de l'Automatique et des Machines de Bureau. Also covers the area of ISO/TC 95 (Office machines).

Equivalent to ISO/TC 97/SC 5 (Programming languages):

CF/TC 97/SC 5 Langages de Programmation

Working groups of AFNOR CF/TC 97/SC 5:

CE 1 Languages for the control of industrial processes
CE 2 Graphical software

CE 3 Data base management systems

There are also groups for APL, Basic, Cobol, Fortran, Pascal and PL/I, and an *ad hoc* group for control languages.

Address:

Association Française de Normalisation
Tour Europe
Cedex 7
92080 Paris La Défense

GERMANY (FEDERAL REPUBLIC)

Standards body:

Deutsches Institut für Normung (DIN)

(No information received, at time of going to press, on programming languages area.)

Address:

Deutsches Institut für Normung
Burggrafenstrasse 4-10
Postfach 1107
D-1000 Berlin 30

JAPAN

Standards body:

Japanese Industrial Standards Committee (JISC)

This is a government agency with official responsibility for standards. The Japanese Standards Association (JSA) is a non-profit-making institution which publishes and promotes the standards produced by JISC.

Equivalent to ISO/TC 97 (Computers and information processing):

The Standards Committee of the Information Processing Society of Japan (IPSJ), to which work in the ISO/TC 97 area is delegated by JISC.

Equivalent to ISO/TC 97/SC 5 (Programming languages):

Sub-committee 5 (Programming languages) of the IPSJ Standards Committee.

Working groups of IPSJ Standards Committee SC 5:

Working groups exist for Cobol, Fortran, and PL/I.

Address:

Japanese Industrial Standards Committee
Ministry of International Trade and Industry
1-3-1 Kasumigaseki, Chiyodaku
Tokyo 100

NETHERLANDS

Standards body:

Nederlands Normalisatie-instituut (NNI)

Equivalent to ISO/TC 97 (Computers and information processing):

Commissie 300 97

Equivalent to ISO/TC 97/SC 5 (Programming languages):

Subcommissie 300 97 050 (Programmeertalencommissie)

Working groups of NNI 300 97 050:

Working groups exist for Algol, Cobol, Fortran, Pascal, PL/I, OSCL (operating system command languages), and GRIS (graphical interaction standards).

Address:

Nederlands Normalisatie-instituut
Polakweg 5
P.O. Box 5810
2280 HV Rijswijk ZH

SWEDEN

Standards body:

Standardiseringskommissionen i Sverige (SIS)

Equivalent to ISO/TC 97 (Computers and information processing):

HK 30

Equivalent to ISO/TC 97/SC 5 (Programming languages):

Tk 30/5

Working groups of Tk 30/5:

30/5/1 System development
30/5/2 Checking and security
30/5/3 Data representation
30/5/4 Data format and data elements
30/5/5 Programming
30/5/6 Flow charts
30/5/7 Computer operations
30/5/8 Decision tables
30/5/9 Optical character recognition

Address:

Standardiseringskommissionen i Sverige
Tegnérgatan 11
Box 3 295
S-103 66 Stockholm

UNITED KINGDOM

Standards body:

British Standards Institution (BSI)

Equivalent to ISO/TC 97 (Computers and information processing):

DPS/- (Data processing)

Equivalent to ISO/TC 97/SC 5 (Programming languages):

DPS/13 (Programming languages)

Working groups of BSI: DPS/13:

WG 1   DBMS
WG 2   PLIP
WG 3   Cobol

ad hoc working groups on Graphics, Pascal, Fortran and Metalanguages.

Address:

British Standards Institution
2 Park Street
London W1A 2BS

UNITED STATES OF AMERICA

Standards body:

American National Standards Institute (ANSI)

Equivalent to ISO/TC 97 (Computers and information processing):

X3 (Computers and information processing)

Equivalent to ISO/TC 97/SC 5 (Programming languages):

None. The various technical committees on specific languages or areas (see below) report direct to X3. The existence should also be noted of two standing committees, SPARC (the Standards Planning and Requirements Committee) and IAC (the International Advisory Committee).

Technical Committees of X3 in the ISO/TC 97/SC 5 area:

X3H1   Operating system command and response language
X3H2   Codasyl data description language
X3J1   PL/I
X3J2   Basic
X3J3   Fortran
X3J4   Cobol
X3J6   Computer language for the processing of text
X3J7   APT
X3J8   Algol
X3J9   Pascal
X3J10 APL
X3K2   Flowcharts

Address:

American National Standards Institute
1430 Broadway
New York
N.Y. 10018

Liaison member of ISO/TC 97/SC 5:

EUROPEAN COMPUTER MANUFACTURERS ASSOCIATION (ECMA)

ECMA has a co-ordinating committee which draws up terms of reference for its technical committees and co-ordinates their work. The current technical committees in the ISO/TC 97/SC 5 area are:

TC 6   Cobol
TC 8   Fortran
TC 10 PL/I
TC 21 Basic
TC 27 Ada

In addition, the Real-Time Task Group (RTTG) is responsible for the general area of real-time languages.

Address:

European Computer Manufacturers Association
Rue du Rhône 114
CH–1204 Geneva
Switzerland

Table B.1.

	International	National										ECMA
		Australia	Austria	Canada	France	Germany	Japan	Netherlands	Sweden	U.K.	U.S.A	
Standards body	ISO	SAA	ON	SCC	AFNOR	DIN	JISC	NNI	SIS	BSI	ANSI	
Data processing	TC 97	MS/20	FNA 001	CIPOM	CGIAMB		IPSJ	300 97	Hk 30	DPS/-	X3	
Programming languages	SC 5	MS/20/5	AG5	CPL	CF/TC 97/ SC 5		SC 5	300 97 050	Tk 30/5	DPS/13		
Algol	EG							WG		†	X3J8	
APL	EG				WG					WG		
Basic	EG		†		WG					†	X3J2	TC 21
Cobol	EG		†	WG	WG		WG	WG		WG 3	X3J4	TC 6
DBMS	WG 3			WG	CE3					WG 1	X3H2	
Fortran	EG		†	WG	WG		WG	WG		WG	X3J3	TC 8
Graphics	WG 2				CE2			WG/GRIS		WG		
Pascal	WG 4				WG			WG		WG	X3J9	
PL/I	EG			WG	WG		WG	WG		†	X3J1	TC 10
Real-time languages	WG 1									WG 2		TC 27/ RTTG
Text processing	EG									†	X3J6	
OSCL								WG			X3H1	
Metalanguages										WG		
Flowcharts									30/5/6		X3K2	

† = activity but no WG.

Glossary of Abbreviations

AFNOR	Association Française de Normalisation (French standards body)
ANSI	American National Standards Institute
ASA	American Standards Association (forerunner of ANSI)
ASCII	American Standard Code for Information Interchange (usually pronounced 'Askey')
BCS	British Computer Society
BNF	Backus-Naur Form
BSI	British Standards Institution
CCITT	International Telegraph and Telephone Consultative Committee
Codasyl	Conference on Data Systems Languages
CSA	Canadian Standards Association
DBMS	Data Base Management System
DIN	Deutsches Institut für Normung (German standards body)
DoD	Department of Defense (U.S.A.)
ECMA	European Computer Manufacturers Association
EG	Experts Group (of ISO/TC 97/SC 5)
ESL	European Systems Language
IEEE	Institute of Electrical and Electronic Engineers (of the U.S.A.)
IFIP	International Federation for Information Processing
IPSJ	Information Processing Society of Japan
ISO	International Organization for Standardization
JISC	Japanese Industrial Standards Committee
JSA	Japanese Standards Association
LTPL	Long Term Procedural Language
MoD	Ministry of Defence (U.K)
NBS	National Bureau of Standards (U.S.A.)
NCC	National Computing Centre Ltd. (U.K.)
NNI	Nederlands Normalisatie-instituut (Netherlands standards body)
ON	Österreiches Normungsinstitut (Austrian standards body)
PLIP	Programming Languages for Industrial Processes

SAA   Standards Association of Australia
SC   Subcommittee (of various bodies)
SCC   Standards Council of Canada
TC   Technical Committee (of various bodies)
UNI   Ente Nazionale Italiano di Unificazione (Italian standards body)
USASI   United States of America Standards Institute (forerunner of ANSI)
WG   Working Group (of various bodies)

Index

Note: page numbers in bold face indicate complete chapters, or main sections, on the topic.